David Rakoff

The Uncollected David Rakoff

David Rakoff is the author of four *New York Times* bestsellers: the essay collections *Fraud, Don't Get Too Comfortable,* and *Half Empty,* and the novel in verse *Love, Dishonor, Marry, Die, Cherish, Perish.* A two-time recipient of the Lambda Literary Award and winner of the Thurber Prize for American Humor, he was a regular contributor to Public Radio International's *This American Life.* His writing frequently appeared in *The New York Times, Newsweek, Wired, Salon, GQ, Outside, Gourmet, Vogue,* and *Slate,* among other publications. An accomplished stage and screen actor, playwright, and screenwriter, he adapted the screenplay for and starred in Joachim Back's film *The New Tenants,* which won the 2010 Academy Award for Best Live Action Short. Rakoff died in 2012.

ALSO BY DAVID RAKOFF

FICTION

Love, Dishonor, Marry, Die, Cherish, Perish

NONFICTION

Half Empty

Don't Get Too Comfortable

Fraud

The Uncollected
David Rakoff

The Uncollected David Rakoff

*Compiled and edited
by Timothy G. Young*

With a Foreword by Paul Rudnick

Anchor Books
A Division of Penguin Random House LLC
New York

AN ANCHOR BOOKS ORIGINAL, OCTOBER 2015

Compilation copyright © 2015 by The Estate of David Rakoff
Foreword copyright © 2015 by Paul Rudnick

Grateful acknowledgment is made to the following for
permission to reprint previously published material:
Farrar, Straus and Giroux, LLC: "Letter to N.Y." from
The Complete Poems, 1927–1979 by Elizabeth Bishop,
copyright © Farrar, Straus and Giroux. Reprinted by
permission of Farrar, Straus and Giroux, LLC.
Jonathan Goldstein: Transcript of "Oh! The Places You Will Not
Go!" written by Jonathan Goldstein and David Rakoff, aired on
This American Life (PRI), Episode 470: "Show Me the Way,"
on July 27, 2012. Originally aired on *WireTap* (CBC).
Reprinted by permission of Jonathan Goldstein.
WHYY, Inc.: Interview transcripts of "David Rakoff's *Half
Empty* Worldview Is Full of Wit" and "Essayist, Mountaineer,
'Comic Saint'" aired on *Fresh Air* (NPR). Reprinted by
permission of WHYY, Inc.

The Cataloging-in-Publication Data is available from the
Library of Congress.

Anchor Books Trade Paperback ISBN: 978-0-307-94647-8
eBook ISBN: 978-0-307-94648-5

Book design by Jaclyn Whalen

www.anchorbooks.com

Printed in the United States of America
10 9 8 7 6 5 4 3 2 1

Contents

Foreword

I saw David Rakoff onstage before I ever read him. He was playing a beleaguered social worker in *One Woman Shoe*, a play by Amy and David Sedaris, which dealt with homeless and downtrodden women being required, in exchange for their welfare checks, to perform one-woman shows. Rakoff was elegant, absurd, and hilarious, as he was in all media. Many of his most delicious essays are included in this addictive volume, an ideal companion to his classically cranky collections *Fraud, Don't Get Too Comfortable*, and *Half Empty*.

David is my favorite breed of artist, because his work promises pleasure. Whenever I'd see his name, online or in a magazine or anywhere else, I'd either catapult right to his words or I'd save them for last, as an earned dessert. David was, as he put it, a "sophisticated sissy," the wayward child of Canadian therapists; he quickly and forever became a passionate New Yorker. He could be acerbic, noting the perils of nostalgic marketing by imagining an ad campaign with the tagline "Hitler wore khakis." He decried the homogenization of his adopted hometown, claiming, "They used to use Toronto as a stand-in for New York in movies, but now I think Toronto's probably too gritty and real."

David could also be ardently appreciative, whether swooning over Sinatra, early Nora Ephron, or a group of simply clad tourists, of whom he declares, "Those Mennonites are fabulous!" One of my all-time favorite Rakoff pieces is a sympathetic deconstruction of the children's book *Stuart Little*, which features a mouse given to sailor suits and professorial tweed, and carrying a cane and briefcase. This piece, which is included here, is titled "The Love That Dare Not Squeak Its Name." David remembers having the book read to him in second grade and deciding that Stuart's "courtly manners and dandy tendencies . . . made me realize that I was somewhat like Stuart and that Stuart seemed, somewhat like myself, pretty gay."

The book also includes transcripts from some of David's many appearances on NPR, which led to his enduring popularity, although in one of these interviews he describes soap opera fame as being "fame of a very specific sort. It's actually not unlike public radio fame, you know?" These transcripts are invaluable, especially when, while analyzing his acting career, David insists that he's usually offered stereotypical roles as "Jewy McHebrew" or "Fudgy McPacker."

David was often sent, as a journalist, on semi-exotic excursions, including a visit to a crafting colony where he created an "elegant egg basket that resembles nothing so much as a pair of human buttocks in rattan." He doesn't condescend to the colony, declaring instead "The week I spent there is about as close as it gets to my idea of paradise." He's never merely clever or modishly caustic, and his love for New York was unabashed: "Look Around You! Every jaunt, every stroll, every errand brings you into contact with someone not like you." David is, above all else, a class act. His work is devastating, hopeful, and yearning, and his self-awareness becomes a form of Manhattan grace.

Which brings us to the book's double crescendos: first, David's masterpiece, his novel in verse, *Love, Dishonor, Marry, Die, Cherish, Perish*. For ignorant folks like me the designation "a novel in verse" sounds like a warning from some literary Surgeon General, as in "May cause death by mind-numbing pretension." But thanks to David's giddy genius, *Love, Dishonor* . . . is an airy, profoundly charming, and irresistible epic, and it has become a beloved touchstone to countless readers.

David died only a few months after completing *Love, Dishonor* . . . , and that's how we arrive at this collection's final and heartbreaking entry: the transcript of David's last televised appearance on *This American Life*, at which time he'd already lost the use of his left arm, to the cancer that would soon kill him, at forty-seven. David was wary of being defined by his illness; he says, "I've always bridled at the term 'memoirist' because I've wanted to be known for the quality of my writing as opposed to the particulars of my biography." This does not become an issue, because David treats his disease with the same mordant, incisive flair as any other topic.

He walks onstage and mentions that "I danced a lot, all through my childhood. . . . It's an incredibly generic trait for a certain type of boy. Like a straight boy being obsessed with baseball, except it's better." He remembers once feeling that "If I just buckled down to the great work at hand . . . then my best self was just there right around the corner." He claims to be "done with all that," and done with so many things, like dancing.

And then, with ease and precision, he dances. Read this book. He's still dancing.

Paul Rudnick

The Uncollected
David Rakoff

My Sister of
Perpetual Mercy

At a Christmas party in Tokyo, I told a young Japanese man that I had a small pea-sized lump in my neck. He placed his fingertip at the side of my throat below my left ear and gently pressed and kneaded, his eyes never leaving mine. "What a fabulous accessory," I thought. It was a week later, when it had become the size of a largish grape, that I had to admit that what was growing inside of me was possibly an entrapment of a different sort. I quit my job in a Japanese publishing company, abandoned any hope of continuing a burgeoning courtship, and moved back to Canada. I was living in my parents' home again and was diagnosed with Hodgkin's lymphoma, a highly curable form of lymphatic cancer that strikes many young males. Scarcely four months after lighting out for the territories at age twenty-one, I put my life on hold: the Young Turk cut off at the knees. At the same time my sister, Ruth, older by two years, was flying home from Tel Aviv, where she was living, to take care of me.

My parents had called Ruth in Israel almost immediately after I called them from Tokyo to tell them I was coming home. She decided of her own accord to return to Canada. Her job as a cook in a restaurant in Tel Aviv was grueling and unrewarding, and she could take care of me and take a break as well. I accepted her return as a matter of course. I expected nothing less of my sister; we had always been close. As children, we had a club—the "pals" club. If one member frowned, the other one patted his or her head, immediately eradicating the frown and replacing it with a smile that magnified into a transfiguring grimace of sheer joy and ecstasy, until the now-cured pal would expire into saintlike rapture, faith in the cosmos restored, unhappiness banished. The world suddenly seemed huge to me and Ruth. We wanted to be on the same continent.

Surprisingly, my liberal-Jewish-medical-psychiatric family never discussed sex much at all; until I came out formally, my sexuality was clandestine and never inquired about, a state of affairs facilitated by my being away at college in New York. We were rather intelligent children, so we could certainly understand sex, but we were much smaller than average and grew so late that for years sex was something theoretical, something that happened to other people. I felt allied with Ruth in our refusal to stoop to something so unseemly or pedestrian as puberty. In my intellectual family, athletics, sex, the life of the Body in general were deemed less important than the life of the Mind. Ruth, I was horrified to find out, did not feel this same alliance of celibate virtue. I remember the first time I was aware that my sister was a sexual being. I was eleven and we were at a summer camp. She was thirteen and standing next to a boy; spontaneously, she leaned over to whisper in his ear. Her arms crept up around his shoulders, one hand playing with his other ear as she spoke to him conspiratorially. I thought, "What on *earth* is she doing with that awful boy?" and simultaneously, "Who does she think she is? She's too young for that gesture." I felt utterly betrayed, and exacted punishment by glaring at the boy for the rest of the summer.

What was she to do, after all? Ruth had started to grow breasts and was well on her way to becoming a bit of a raven-haired sultry Jewess, while I remained tiny and prepubescent for many years after that.

When I was fifteen, I had a brief and thwarted flirtation with a boy at the same camp—the younger brother of the corruptor of my sister's virtue, in fact. Ruth came up to me and told me she had heard I was "experimenting." There was no judgment in her voice nor, for that matter, surprise. Throughout my childhood I had never made any great effort to appear straight. The slightest examination of my character would have revealed what I already suspected to be the case. Beyond the tacit acknowledgment from her, however, we never talked about my being gay until years later, when I was away at college.

Ruth arrived at her unequivocal acceptance of my sexuality by sheer osmosis. My gradual emergence as a gay man was simultaneous with my general maturing. For so many years she had assumed and known that I was gay. Just as I, after my initial shock at age eleven, accepted her as a sexual being, a straight one, she accepted me. The shock she may have experienced at the disclosure of my desires and actions was rooted in the fact that her baby brother was growing up and having sex, not that he wanted that sex to be with boys.

I had for years been asking Ruth to casually mention to my parents that I was gay, something she absolutely refused to do in favor of my telling them myself. The night before I finally came out to my parents, I had warned her minutes before that I would do it. She waited in her room with her boyfriend. Afterward, I walked down the hall to her room, where immediately upon closing the door, I began to cry in relief. She and Tom and I sat on her futon. I think she cried, too.

What about? I didn't even conjecture at the time. Relief? The hardships she thought I'd face? I worried the next day that perhaps my parents had missed the point. I hadn't actually said, "I'm gay." I had said, "I haven't had any girlfriends and I think you can guess why." "Maybe they just think you have a fear of intimacy," she joked. I moved to Tokyo a few weeks after that, and she to Tel Aviv with her boyfriend. When we reconvened in Canada, it seemed my being gay was immaterial and not germane to the matter at hand. It seemed merely a newly acquired and slightly irritating trait—like a bogus English accent acquired after a summer term at Oxford—that, at best, was something to be disregarded in the climate of illness that demanded cooler heads unclouded by issues of character. At worst, before I was diagnosed with cancer, I feared my sexual orientation could be the cause of my illness. I treated my sexuality upon my return like a too-loud shirt bought on holiday in the Caribbean that gets stowed in the bottom drawer. There was nothing so desexualizing to me as the total betrayal of my body.

When I found out that it was not AIDS but a highly curable form of cancer, my relief was alloyed with a sense of being a sham and a charlatan—doubly so, since I could not justify for myself a place within the hierarchy of suffering that belonged to either the gay community or those who had had to live through, or die of, truly serious cancer. I was embarrassed by having gotten off scot-free, and so I shut most everybody out. Without a career or, to my mind, a legitimate reason not to have one, I clung to my sister for support and shelter. Each day she drove me to the hospital, where I, depleted, slept for hours. I did not have many friends left in Toronto, and certainly no gay ones. Time accordioned, and I was as sexless upon my return as when I had originally left Canada to go to college.

If I was going to show someone my ass, it was to have a bone marrow test.

Ruth became my ally. Her boyfriend was thousands of miles away in Israel, so she, too, was profoundly single. We resembled nothing so much as two aged celibate siblings, a fantasy bolstered by my geriatric infirmity as we walked down the street, me leaning on her arm. We had never lived together as adults in our parents' home, with time on our hands and our needs provided for. In solidarity with me, she became as useless a member of society as I. We tooled around in my mother's car looking for fun food, cheap pajamas, kitchenware. Occasionally, even we were overcome by our lack of achievement and found ourselves in a bakery, where Ruth, a cook by trade, would expound to the staff on sorbitol sweetener while I declared in a loud voice that I had never had anything so tasty when I was *living in Tokyo*—octogenarian football stars desperately waiting to be asked to recount the final minutes of the big game of 1927. We went to the movies in the middle of the day. "My god," Ruth exclaimed in a crowded theater at midday, "does everyone in town have Hodgkin's?"

We fought only once during that time, to my recollection. It involved an errand she had wanted me to run on the way to treatment that I did not do. I snarled something about her letting me out of the car, that I'd make my own way to the hospital. We both knew this was impossible, since I was very weak and, having no real need of money, carried none. I sat in my seat, seething and impotent, unable to make good my threat to get out and walk. Silence in the car. This was the first fissure in the veneer of total politesse that had existed between us during the illness. I felt closer to Ruth than anyone else at that time, but I had not discussed my feelings with her. I had no feelings to discuss, and she had not pushed or pried. I was shocked by my sudden impulse to make a claim to goods I clearly couldn't deliver. I hated my sister at that moment for being witness to that kind of impotence. She hated me, however briefly, for being ill and therefore requiring her to rise above the altercation and take the Moral High Ground. But take it she did. As we drove by Maple Leaf Gardens, the hockey arena, she said, "I bet people who buy their skates in that sports shop think they're really much better quality because they bought them at the Gardens." We both laughed, sports and sports enthusiasts being an endless source of derisive amusement in our decidedly unathletic family. She put her arm across the back of my seat and rubbed my neck.

When she went back to Israel after a month to reclaim her job, Ruth started to cry at the airport. "You really have to get out more," she pleaded. I, for one, had no intention whatsoever of getting out more. With Ruth, I didn't have to be charming or a professional invalid. I did not have to answer the inevitable party question—"What do you do?"—with, "Vomit and sleep, and yourself?" My recent time in Tokyo felt distant and abortive. To talk about it was, to my mind, grandiose and pathetic. The drugs puffed up my face and I was unattractive. Such was my level of emotional strangulation that I was truly baffled by Ruth's tears. She, in turn, was baffled by my lack of self-esteem. She found my capacity for steely reserve alarming. How wonderful to have someone like her around who still found me funny and smart. My sister was the ultimate no-pressure date, the husband who looks across the room at his wife of twenty-five years and still sees the girl he married.

Ruth and Tom, her boyfriend, came home that summer to be married. I was declared to be in remission but not getting better. I developed a wracking cough and lost thirty-five pounds. I had avidly watched Oliver North's testimony on television, but by the time John Poindexter took the stand I was in too much pain to concentrate. Some undetected cancer outside the field of my radiation had been growing steadily, and it was determined that I was in fact much sicker than when I had first presented with the disease and that I would have to have chemotherapy. Ruth became my caretaker again. Because of my extreme weight loss and the constant pain I was in, I was swinging wide and free emotionally. On good days, I was the aesthetic arbiter of her impending wedding, tyrannically deeming things either timeless or vulgar. On bad days, I would cry uncontrollably, once while watching *Sleeping Beauty* in the middle of a sticky-floored theater full of children, Ruth with her arms around me, comforting a child of her own.

I resumed my role as cancer patient rather than unmarried gay sibling. I joked to my family that if anyone was stupid enough to ask me when I would be tying the knot, I was going to turn to them with tears welling up in my eyes and say, voice cracking, "Well . . . if I live that long." It occurs to me now that these assembled friends and strangers found me far more sympathetic as a man with cancer than as a queer. Perhaps some of them thought that Hodgkin's was merely a cover-up for what was really wrong with me. I had, in fact, been denied an invitation to a friend's engagement because her father-in-law, a physician no less, thought I had AIDS. At that point, however, being gay and being sick were ineluctably joined. My sense of self at my sister's wedding depended on both things being manifest. I burst into tears a few weeks before the wedding, saying, "I'm in too much pain to be nice to anybody. No one's going to like me." Ruth spoke of her wedding as something that might be a nice break for all of us from the utter joylessness of my illness, the true concern for the family. I had known my brother-in-law since I was twelve, and the three of us, Ruth, Tom, and I, had been a contained unit for some time. I was made to feel that it was a party as much about their union as about my eventual recovery. I have a photograph of the three of us from the wedding: Ruth, Tom, and me. We all have linked arms, and it's tricky at first to pick out the bride and the groom, since we all look like we could be related— until one sees that they are the ones whose faces have broken out from nerves like adolescents'. I can't remember, though, if I'm standing in the middle or on one side.

At my nadir, about two days before the wedding, Ruth and Tom had tried to take me swimming to relieve some of the intense pain in my back. It was too cold for me and I started to weep. They sandwiched me between them so tightly, I could no longer feel the water.

I have now been in remission for well over three years, and it is likely that I will make it to five and be deemed cured. I have since moved to New York, where AIDS is now the illness that pervades every aspect of my and my friends' lives. Ruth and Tom are now endlessly solicitous and supportive about the illness of my friends, forever asking after their health. When newly returned from Israel, they came to visit me. Ruth had asked me a great many times, when we had seen my gay friends, "Is he positive?" (having just learned from me the difference between being HIV positive and full-blown AIDS). She was slowly beginning to understand both the invisibility of HIV and its seeming ubiquity. When I decided to be tested, Tom was the only one in the family I told. When I found out I was negative, I gave him separate permission to tell Ruth. The illnesses and deaths of my friends have separated me from Ruth in a way. I have my worries about the people who are my fictive family here, and she has her worries about me and my health, fears she does not speak of with me.

Tom, Ruth, and I are still very much a unit of three within my family. I now wait anxiously for them to have children, whom I, perhaps unrealistically, will consider to be partly mine, something Tom and Ruth have not denied. To this day, I still look at my sister and see a female version of myself with long hair and breasts. Ruth does not see the same strong resemblance, and never has. I see something in my sister's dark Semitic face as vital as a kidney, as untraceable, yet present, as the phantom pain from a limb long since gone.

[*Published in* A Member of the Family: Gay Men Write About Their Closest Relatives, *edited by John Preston, Dutton, 1992]*

Sagrada Família

When she sees her son get off the bus, Ellen chokes a little bit, suddenly. A discrete fistful of air comes up and punches her in the mouth, although the windows of the car are all closed. She has last seen him on Memorial Day and now, mid-July, she can see how much weight he has lost. In fact, she can scarcely believe he has made the trip alone from New York to Truro. These two-month gaps in contact serve only to shock and mortify her.

Leo stirs from his nest of newspapers in the driver's seat and says affectlessly, "There's Marcus. He looks good."

Ellen turns in her seat to look at him. Who is this interloper in her family car? Is she the only one who sees this wraithlike creature moving across the parking lot on his spindly legs? The slight breeze outside is blowing his jeans as if they were made of the flimsiest silk.

Leo has relinquished his anguish and worry in favor of powerlessness. When Marcus was first diagnosed, they both got on the phone and screamed, literally screamed at the tops of their lungs into the receiver, that Marcus should move home to Cambridge. Marcus calmly told them (he had clearly rehearsed this scene many times before calling them) that his life was now in New York with Tom.

"So stay with Tom! Die and go to your grave in New York with Tom!" Leo yelled, and smashed down the phone, the force of his anger pulling the whole unit out of the kitchen wall. The next day, Ellen went out and bought a table model and plastered the hole. She hung a small framed print over the unpainted spot. Three years later, Leo is resigned—almost punch-drunk with impotent anxiety. Now, when they get off the phone with Marcus, Leo nods off immediately, like the narcoleptic puppy in that film clip, who frolics around on the grass only to crash to the ground like a fallen stone, having fallen asleep mid-leap. Ellen doesn't sleep. She either cooks or drafts at her desk. Sleep has become an untrustworthy friend these last few years. Like someone who has been slipped an un–Mickey Finn, Ellen finds herself suckered each night into bed by the promise of rest only to be up and in the kitchen not two hours later.

Ellen watches her son through the windshield and thinks of his lover, Tom, and is reminded of a story about an anthropologist who proposed an eternal, unsolvable dilemma to some people in Micronesia. In an attempt to gauge their feelings of loyalty, kinship, and fealty before and after marriage, he asked them, "If your mother and your wife were both drowning, who would you save?" What he amassed, instead, was extensive data attesting to the utter absence in the Micronesian lexicon of the hypothetical case, as almost everyone answered, "But they are not drowning. They are alive. There they are."

"He is not drowning. There he is," she whispers, glancing back at him in the sunshade mirror.

Marcus opens the back door of the car. He falls back against the seat, tired out from his short walk from the bus, and closes the door. He looks from Ellen to Leo, gulps a smiling, breathless "hello," closes his eyes and leans his head back, allowing his father to drive.

Ellen talks at her son animatedly from the front seat. These first few minutes of reunion are always the hardest for her. Until she can recover those Marcus characteristics, she barely recognizes this generic, cadaverous man. She tries to elicit facial reactions from him: arching eyebrows, a smile, a considered frown, anything that will motivate this sunken, drum-tight skull into some identifiable trait of her boy.

Marcus is exhausted and asleep in the backseat. She cannot stand to look long at his shallow-breathing head with its rattling snore. She is sure his soul is dissipating out of his slightly gaping mouth, like the plume of fog from an opened bottle of champagne. When he was a child, she used to thrill to see him asleep, he was so beautiful. Thinking back on it, Ellen feels that it was the only time in her life when she had been calm, or at least stopped thinking while conscious. She now wants to clap and shout and shake him out of sleep before death takes him, before his pigeon chest just gives up and folds in upon itself. She fiddles with the radio, looks out the window, pressing her forehead against the sun-heated glass, trying to fry her skin.

Their summer house was always too big for just the three of them. At least when they were younger and Marcus just a little boy, there had been a vital community around, and the house was a hub of sorts. There were the inevitable Cambridge therapist/architect couples like themselves, scientists from the Woods Hole Institution, artists. They used to congregate on the wide, wraparound veranda. Ellen would cook elaborate meals that would be washed down with too much liquor. The same jokes would be told, the same wit trundled out. It seemed that Ellen was forever punctuating some pronouncement of Leo's by saying to the group, "What you must all realize is that Leo is at an advantage—in addition to being an adolescent psychiatrist, he is an adolescent psychiatrist," to much laughter and drunken cries of "touché." Then, invariably, the guitar would be brought out and they would sing the work songs of their preaffluent days until the final, staggering three A.M. march down to the beach for a group nude swim and perhaps some furtive, unproductive, extramarital gropings in the beach grass.

Ellen was lots of fun back then; heightened, bright, edgy. Years later, she recognizes that showing her quick wit, her ease with the verbal barb, is the only way she knows how to react anymore. She is burning too brightly. When she sees her friends lately, she silently agrees with herself beforehand that she will shut up, but there she is, maniacally interjecting, filling up the tiniest silences with her voice. Friends tell her of the deaths of other friends and she cannot resist—she says:

"Well, she was the meanest woman who ever lived and I say that with no fear of contradiction." Then she laughs her short silvery laugh, sharp and thin as water from a pistol.

People move away, summers are spent elsewhere, marriages break up, and Ellen and Leo rattle around in this extravagant house. This luxury makes Ellen feel guilty, but she is actively pursuing her materialistic impulses lately. She found herself downtown the other day buying black marble figs, cast-iron-snail paperweights, alabaster eggs; small useless things with heft that she can try unsuccessfully to crush in her hands. Her knuckles can go white and her teeth can ache with the effort.

The house has a main staircase inside with a gentle curve and a cool, dark underside. The bedrooms all face the sea; they all have sloping ceilings. The kitchen was done up by the original owners like Monet's at Giverny—all periwinkle-blue-and-saffron tile with an open hearth—with glass-fronted cupboards now full of haphazard stacks of Ellen's expensive multicolored dishes. In preparation for Marcus's arrival, she went out and bought so much food that, even if he were well, there is no way he could eat any significant portion of it. She woke at three in the morning and began cooking. There is a leek soup chilling like a green ocean in a tureen in the fridge. She has arrayed the kitchen table like a circus: three perfect peaches in a blue bowl, black grapes on a yellow plate, six greengage plums, each in a separate teacup. She went down to the beach in the middle of the night and brought up bowlfuls of sand, which she has piled up in little hills between the dishes. She tore the buds of garlic from their braid and placed them around, too. The rest of the surface she has festooned with whole and cut fruit. It looks like an aerial photograph of a carnival. She will just have to keep her husband and her son out of the kitchen until she is finished. She might not even show them her handiwork at all.

"It's a Roman Jewish dish," Ellen says of the cold sliced tongue marinated in vinegar with golden raisins. They are eating on the veranda.

"The acid is a bit much for me. I have some lesions in my mouth."

"The last time we were together you wanted concentrated flavors. 'Concentrated flavors' you said. Hard salami, cranberry juice, plums. I thought this would be nice for you."

"I have some lesions in my mouth. I'm sorry. Actually, I'd love something nice and bland, like a potato, if you have one. I'll make it."

"Don't get up." Ellen cuts off his access to the kitchen. "I'll be right back."

Of course Ellen has potatoes, all kinds. She will make him every potato in the house in every way. She will press them up against him still warm, covering him in potato armor. She will work them under his skin. She will make him fat.

She finds some small purple ones lying here and there around a sandpile and some strawberries. The fragrance rising from the soft fruit in the display is warm and sweet with the incipient promise of a vinegary sharpness. The watermelon she had sliced up is no longer so wet, now more syrupy. She boils the potatoes, removes their black jackets, and mashes up the violet flesh. She puts them in a yellow bowl and takes them out to Marcus.

"There. You can watch the sea while you eat."

Marcus looks up at her and screws his mouth sideways in an apology.

"I'm sorry. I can't eat anything right now. I really must have a nap." He gets up and slowly walks into the house. Ellen can hear his soft footfalls negotiating the stairs. The bowl of potatoes is warm in her palm. She watches the waves for a while, thinking of nothing. Feeling the warmth in her hand, watching the waves, hearing Leo snore under his blanket of newspapers on the swinging sofa. She comes to, puts the bowl down, and goes up to see how Marcus is getting on.

In these past few minutes, he has only just made it to his room and undone two buttons on his shirt. Without a word, Ellen turns down the covers on the bed and helps her son undress.

He is indeed thirty-seven, she sees. In addition to being sick, he is no longer a young man. His hair is sparser now than ever and there is a lot of gray. It tufts out of his ears and falls out of his head and grows in isolated regions on his back like his father's. She can see the short tube of his Hickman underneath his undershirt. He no longer needs to be infused for hours at a time, but Ellen has neglected to ask him when he stopped or why this is so. When he undoes his belt, his trousers fall all the way down, the keys in his pocket clanking loudly on the floor. He puts his hands on her shoulders as he steps out of his pants. His underwear and socks gape at the tops and bottoms of his skinny legs. She pats his rear end. She can feel his tailbones.

"You've lost your ass, Marcus. We're going to have to fatten you up."

Marcus says nothing. He smiles a little bit and gets into bed, facing the window, away from her. She pulls the covers over him. He makes almost no bump at all in the blankets except for his hip bone, which sticks up like a jagged rock or a shark's fin.

He is asleep before she leaves the room. She is glad to have this time alone with Leo and Marcus both asleep. She no longer sees her son's character. Marcus, once so verbal and engaging, is now so deadened and tired all the time. She does not know if this is dementia or the result of constant pain and starvation. Whatever the cause, although she knows the alternative will be much worse when it comes, she does not find Marcus to be good company anymore—something he most profoundly used to be. For a moment, she wants to go back into his room and shake him awake by the hipbone and tell him so—"You are not good company anymore, Marcus"—the way she used to discipline him when he was younger: "Stop showing off, Marcus," or "Show a little stoicism."

She walks downstairs, passes by the kitchen, and surveys her landscape from the doorway. The whole room is smelling green and hot, as if she were baking the houseplants. She takes the tureen out of the fridge and places it in the center of the table—it is a high mountain lake.

She stands in the shadow under the staircase for a while,

feeling the wood. She walks outside. Leo sleeps still. She walks around the veranda on tiptoe, placing the balls of her feet on each narrow floorboard all the way around the house. She goes down to the beach, piles up wet sand, and begins to carve away at it with a mussel shell. She is extremely adept at making sand buildings. She once made a near-perfect replica of Gaudí's cathedral in Barcelona, Sagrada Família, using corncobs rolled in sand for the towers. When he was young, Marcus, as might be expected of a little boy, made piles of wet, dripped sand as his castles. "That's wrong, Marcus," is what she had said to him. What she really wanted to express was that, although his structures resembled Gaudí's, they lacked an underlying logic or structure, a controlled anarchy of form. She knew that it was too harsh, but she had always felt so strongly about architecture. Marcus reacted by creating even more juvenile mounds. She, in turn, declared war and produced sharp-edged Bauhaus sand models, all the while exclaiming, "Look how nice and neat, Marcus. And my hands are so clean from using my tools!"

What Ellen likes best about architecture, and has always liked best about architecture, is this: An arch, even one made without mortar (and thousands, millions were made without mortar), can be as thin as a sliver or as long as a train tunnel. No matter how hard you press on an arch, you cannot break it. It has an empty underside and still cannot be broken, regardless of the force used. That an arch can be broken by the slightest push upward or from the side concerns Ellen not at all. It is that needful marriage of stress and strength she loves. When she is aligning floor levels of preexisting living rooms with proposed sunporches, when she is drawing plans for skylights and fireplaces, recessed bathtubs and glass-brick kitchens, she thinks of this arch. When she is designing the happiness of other people's lives, this ever-beleaguered, ever more tenacious arch is what she likes best.

Ellen pounds the meat for veal marsala so hard that she is emitting short, yelling bursts as she makes impact with the cutting board. Leo calls in, asking if she needs help. She does not and makes sure to continue quietly. It seems that the kitchen table is now giving off steam. Ellen's hair comes down in wet tendrils as she cooks.

Marcus eats only some ice cream, to soothe his mouth. They eat again on the veranda, this time on the other side of the house, away from the ocean, toward the sunset. The failing light and its colors replace conversation adequately, but now, with night fallen, with Marcus's slow, studied progress weakly licking the ice cream from his spoon, with little or no speaking, the silence seems amplified. They are outdoors and it is airless. Ellen's lungs are made of lead. When the phone rings, she feels she has broken to the surface and starts to breathe again. She fairly flies into the kitchen to answer it.

"Hello?" she breathes heavily into the phone. She doesn't care who is on the other end.

"Hello, may I speak with Valerie, please?" asks the voice.

"Valerie who?"

"Is this Valerie's house?"

"Let me check," says Ellen. "I'm just visiting. Hold on."

Ellen holds the phone for a while against her chest. She must calm down. Eventually she must let this woman on the other end off the phone, but she cannot slow her heart. She is sure the woman can hear it on the line.

"No, I'm sorry. No Valerie," she says with such hopelessness and apology that the other woman reassures her.

"That's okay," she says. "I'll check the number again."

"I am sorry."

"Who?" Leo asks when she returns.

"Wrong number." She scowls at him as if it were obvious.

"Do you know what I was thinking about this afternoon, El?" Leo begins. "Remember Asher Korner? The biologist? That summer he made up '*Menteur menteur, pantalons de feu*'? Remember how we laughed at that, we thought he was so clever? We said it all summer, '*Menteur, menteur, pantalons de feu.*' Remember?"

"No, not really." Ellen speaks through the fog of an oncoming headache. "Anyway, that means 'Liar, liar, pants of fire.' I hardly think we would have thought it was so clever. It's actually wrong. It should be something like '*pantalons brulants*' or something like that."

"I remember it," Marcus says. "Tom and I say it sometimes."

"Ah, Marcus has joined us for the evening, I see," she says, looking at him sideways. "How's the ice cream, Marcus?"

"Fine, Ellen. How's your drink?"

"Fine, thank you." Ellen eyes him skeptically. "You remember that? I haven't heard you say that since you came. I haven't heard you say much, actually." Ellen wets her mouth with her wine. Her tongue feels thick and gluey in her mouth. She is drinking too much this evening and does not care. She is feeling the hard-edged, funny nastiness brought on by drink that she used to get at those dinners from the past. She is, truth be told, a little bit out for blood. The present company will do, she has decided.

"I do remember it; I do say it sometimes. Not all the time, sometimes." He rises. "I'm going to bed. Thanks for the ice cream. Leo, I leave you to your wife." Marcus pushes his chair back and walks inside.

"I just think it's interesting when you choose to and choose not to chime in, that's all. That is all. That is all I am saying. Never too tired to disagree with Mom! Never too tired to make a fool of Ellen, huh?" Ellen yells at his retreating form, eager for a fight.

She is swinging wide now. She focuses on Leo across the table. She can see that he is looking at her uncomprehendingly. He does not know when this shift in her took place, at what point pleasantly-buzzed-at-twilight turned into shrewishly-soused-for-the-evening.

"Fuck him if he can't take a joke," Ellen says and looks out into the night.

She dreams she buys a bottle of water in a shop. The water is so high-tone that it contains caviar. When she tips the bottle to her mouth, the fish eggs block up her throat like small twigs in a sieve. Her thirst remains unquenched. She cannot find another shop to make a different purchase.

Ellen finally wakes and rises to get a drink. She feels like a salted plum—desiccated and crystalline. Her fingers will ping and snap off like stalagmites if she bangs them against the sink. She watches herself in the bathroom mirror. She thinks she can see her cells moistening and swelling as she drinks water. Her pores are wheezing and creaking at the effort of replenishment. They stop, gasp, and wheeze again. She is a ship rolling and creaking on swells of water. She is watching her unmoving face all the while, fascinated by the labored sounds her body is making as it fills up, as the water races through her channels. Wheeze, rattle, gasp. This has never happened to her before. She must either have drunk more than she thought or her metabolism has changed radically with aging.

Things slowly focus and she sees her mouth is closed, her breathing even. She checks the taps for the sound. She lays her forehead uncomprehendingly on the porcelain edge of the sink.

"Not me," she thinks, "not the sink." She is sniffing around, eliminating possible sources of the noise. She fingers the folds of the shower curtain. She feels like a stroke victim, only getting it partially right, or one of the blind men with the elephant. The knowledge dawns on her before she is even fully awake. She has walked to Marcus's room before she even remembers she's at the beach house.

She turns on the light, touches her son, pulls her hand away, wakes Leo and tells him, "Marcus is on fire. Call Tom and tell him to call their doctor. We'll drive him to New York." She is weary and somewhat relieved. The way one greets rain after a day spoiled by an oppressive, threatening sky.

"Why don't we just take him to the hospital in Cambridge?" asks Leo.

"Because he doesn't live in Cambridge."

She has practiced these steps, this actuality, so often. All these actions feel apart from her and automatic. She is performing in a play she has rehearsed in her sleep for years. The anthropologist was wrong—there *is* a hypothetical case, although the scenario is reversed here: If a son is drowning and the mother and the lover are on shore, who will save him? And what if the sun is shining on the waves and the gulls have voices like razors and she can't see if it's even her son out there, or what if she's already too damned tired and she knows he'll just end up back in the water anyway? Ellen will drive him to New York.

It is three A.M. She has pulled on jeans and a sweater and is tending to Marcus. She sponges him down and looks at the naked body of her son—it is already vestigial. When her father was sick and dying, she bathed him, too. Seeing her old father's penis bobbing in the bathwater as she washed his back made her strangely nauseous in the base of her stomach. Looking at Marcus's penis, she feels nothing. It is a dewlap, a soft ear. When he first came out to her, Ellen had a dream of Marcus. His penis was huge and red as he held out a crooked bony finger to an unseen figure. She had woken shaken and sweaty and angry with her son.

Leo stands outside in the hallway, naked as well but for socks, talking to Tom on the telephone. Her own clothes feel ludicrous to her.

This is the time years ago when we'd all be skinny-dipping, she muses.

The night smells uncommonly good to Ellen as they drive along the Cape toward New York—like crackers. She opens her window only an inch at the top. If she opens it the whole way, she'll gorge herself on the night air and be sick. Marcus is wrapped in a blanket in the backseat. He had whispered "I'm sorry. . . ." once as they locked up the house and Leo carried him out to the car, and then he dropped off.

When he was eight or so, he broke his leg in a hockey game. Leo had gone down to the hospital to pick him up. When they returned, Marcus was in Leo's arms as he was now, wrapped in Leo's overcoat. His face shone with pride. "I broke my leg!" He beamed at Ellen. She had felt embarrassed, at the time, in the presence of Marcus's masculine pride. It felt oddly sexual and private to witness the pleasure her son was taking in his physical injury. She had the same feeling when, years later, she met Tom and Marcus for a drink in New York. When the pianist began to play "But Not for Me," Tom, who had been saying something to her, took Marcus's hand in his and placed both of them on his knee and continued speaking to Ellen. She did not want to be privy to this aspect of Marcus's life. She had been glad to get back to Boston after that. "I'm sorry. . . ." her grown-up son had said. I'm sorry what? she thinks. *Sorry's not good enough.*

Leo puts in a cassette of the Weavers. Pete Seeger tells the audience at Carnegie Hall to harmonize, and they do— spontaneously, beautifully. Ellen sits in the dark listening to them sing "Goodnight Irene." She wonders if they all knew one another that night in 1955, if they were professionals sitting out there. Or was that one of those instances where life doesn't disappoint? Why not be a communist, she thinks, if it means that kind of belonging? The road is bone white under the headlights.

"No one opposes Commissioner Moses. Even the fishes do as he wishes." Growing up in New York, Ellen recited this in primary school. She thought Commissioner Moses must be a very mean man, bullying everybody, even the fishes. Ellen had never liked the city, her whole life. It all seemed too crowded and squalid and she couldn't help feeling that Robert Moses had imposed his despotic will on everything. Parks, beaches, roads. It all felt so much like what her own father did with his loud, autocratic hectoring. As a young child, she had conflated the two of them; Moses was in the Bible, her father was Jewish. "Don't tell your father," her mother said about the most minor infractions of his will, usually involving something as inconsequential as a new pair of shoes, or the two of them having an ice cream at the Woolworth's counter before they returned home from shopping. The kind of man who yelled at fish: Swim faster! Swim slower! Go through the fake sunken castle! New York doesn't thrill Ellen even now. Even though she successfully got out, she despises it and fights the panicked feeling that she will be detained whenever she has to visit. So much garbage everywhere. How does a sofa land on the side of a highway with no buildings in sight? The traffic creeps, radios cut out in the tunnels, everything is covered in graffiti, people wear the paucity of quality in their lives like a badge of honor, laughing ruefully and contentedly when their subway tunnels fill with smoke. Ellen hates New York and New Yorkers. They are everything she was thrilled to leave behind when she left to go to college over forty years ago.

It is seven A.M. when they reach the city. There is construction all the way down the West Side Highway. The Weavers sing for about the tenth time during their trip "the Rock Island Line it is a mighty good road." Marcus is still asleep in the backseat.

"When the stores open in New York, we can buy some underwear and toothbrushes and stuff," Leo said when they had just passed Boston.

"You can do what you like. I'm coming back to the Cape tonight."

People have been asking the same thing of Ellen for the past twenty or so years, ever since the culture got its paws into psychiatry: "Oh," they will say, "your husband's a psychiatrist? What must that be like? Does he analyze you just all the time?" Or they ask, "So, are you all crazy?" as if it were the funniest, most original joke that could be made. But the answer (the answer Ellen never gives—generally she will chuckle and say something like "Absolutely. As proverbial fruitcakes"), is quite simple: "He wouldn't dare." Ellen knows that she has become, amazingly enough, not her mother, whom she defended and vowed she would never treat with anything but respect and compassion, but her own father. She bullies, she lectures, and she has kept her husband at bay almost since the day they met. She has come to think of her mother's passivity in exactly the opposite terms she used to. It sickens her. It makes her wish she had lashed out more at her when she was alive. There are some days when Ellen would like nothing more than to have her mother back for even just an hour, but the fantasy always turns into Ellen dressing down her risen mother for some stupidity. By the time Marcus got sick, the lines had been drawn between Ellen and Leo. Maybe once over the years had he tried to get her to probe or question her feelings about something—perhaps he had commented on her extreme efficiency in dealing with her father's estate after he died, she could not remember. She had leveled a gaze of such murderous censoring on him that he had retreated immediately. Leo's analyses of her and Marcus, whatever they may be, remain unverbalized.

"Yes, well then," Leo says in a tiny voice, "I think I will stay and you can go wherever." And then her husband begins to cry.

She does not even need to ask him to pull over; he is already swerving across two lanes. He stops the car and leans on the steering wheel and cries in earnest, the ribs in his back furling and unfurling under his dirty T-shirt.

Ellen almost puts a hand on him but stops herself at the last moment. She is overcome with the thought that this scenario ought to have the windshield wipers going as well, for maximum effect. She hoists her purse onto her shoulder and gets out of the car. Marcus has still not woken, lying across the backseat like a suit on a broken hanger.

Standing on the side of the road, Ellen thinks of her table display. Now nobody will get to see it. She hopes that when she gets back it is blanketed with a carpet of flies. She hopes a family of mice are nestled into the hillocks and eating the soft rot of it.

In the distance, Ellen sees a cab. Leo's car still idles twenty feet behind her. The cab comes closer. A barreling yellow sun, its lights and grill smiling a greeting. Ellen raises her arm and opens her mouth to call and the air rushes in.

[*Published in* Men on Men 5: Best New Gay Fiction, *edited by David Bergman, Plume, 1994*]

My First New York

Arrived: 1982

My mother's purse was stolen about an hour before my parents left me in New York to start my freshman year of college. She noticed it missing from the back of her café chair just as we were finishing up our lunch at an outdoor table at a now long-disappeared Italian place at 111th and Broadway. The handbag had probably been gone for a while, but like cartoon characters who wander off cliffs but only fall once they realize they have done so, I felt the solid ground disappear from under my feet and my life in New York begin.

Truthfully, I found the theft thrilling, even as it sharpened whatever anxiety my folks must have been feeling. The robbery conferred a modicum of street cred with zero injury, and I needed all the help I could get. I was a sophisticated sissy, having grown up near the center of Toronto, a cosmopolitan city of three million people. But displaying cultural literacy and knowing the difference between shit and Shinola are two distinctly separate realms. Being able to quote entire scenes of *The Philadelphia Story* from memory or paint a good facsimile of Van Gogh's *Sunflowers* (large, on my dorm room wall) won't do you a bit of good in the real world. At seventeen, I knew nothing, and I looked it. A whelp of barely five and a half feet, I was markedly shorter and less developed than the boys I saw unloading boxes and suitcases. Compared to most of them, I was a tentatively pubescent cherub, encased in puppy fat, with a face open to experience that seemed to beg: Please hurt me.

I looked at the purse-snatching as an early and painless inoculation from violence, no small matter in the city back when the prospect was still real enough. New York in 1982 was only beginning to shake off the traces of its "FORD TO CITY: DROP DEAD" near bankruptcy. Infrastructure was still crumbling, the subways were still covered in graffiti. The term *yuppie* would not be commonplace for another few years (and it would be at least that amount of time before the city opened its first Banana Republic or Cajun restaurant to clothe and feed them). Coffee still meant a paper cupful from Chock full o'Nuts. There was a remaining franchise at 116th Street and Broadway, probably unchanged since 1961, still boasting its undulating lunch counter in buttercream Formica, while one block down, a warning shot across the caffeinated bow of the neighborhood, was a doomed black-lacquer establishment with the almost parodically striving name Crêpes and Cappuccino. The owners had wrapped the sickly tree out front in bright blue fairy lights, which illuminated the empty interior in a dejected glow. It lasted less than a year. The colossus towering over this particular moment shuddering between decadence and recovery was not Bartholdi's Lady Liberty but the first of Calvin Klein's bronzed gods, high above Times Square. Leaning back, eyes closed, in his blindingly white underpants against a sinuous form in similarly white Aegean plaster, his gargantuan, sleeping, groinful beauty was simultaneously Olympian and intimate, awesome and comforting. Here was the city in briefs: uncaring, cruelly beautiful, and out of reach.

Not all of New York's loveliness was stratospheric and unattainable, but at street level it was mixed in with the threat of harm, which was ever present, if in a somewhat exaggerated and highly prized form. We had been warned that the neighborhood around the university could turn dodgy in a matter of footsteps, but there was a certain pride in having dipped one's toe into its scary waters. Morningside Park, for example: Not since the age of medieval maps—wherein the world simply ends, beyond which all is monster-filled roil— has a region been so terrifyingly uncharted and freighted with peril as Morningside Park in the early eighties. To venture in was to die, plain and simple. There were other terrifying rumors abounding, like the one about the boy in the hideous Gwathmey Siegel–designed dormitory who narrowly avoided the bullet that came through his window and lodged itself in the plaster above his head. The shot had come from—where else?—Morningside Park. Another boy, walking back to his room on upper Broadway one drizzling evening, had had his wallet demanded. He handed it over, and for his compliance had his teeth knocked out with the hard metal barrel of a gun. The-boy-who-was-pistol-whipped-in-the-rain grabbed us with all the cheap poetry and tamped bathos of a Tom Waits song. It was doubly satisfying to me, since whenever he came up in conversation, I could say, "Tell me about it. I was robbed my first day here."

Mere days into the school year, my floor counselor, an elder statesman in his senior year, knocked on my door and gave me a stapled Xerox of the Joan Didion essay "Goodbye to All That." The flattery of being singled out for such a gift is what made me read it immediately, with little comprehension. "All I could do during those [first] three days was talk long-distance to the boy I already knew I would never marry in the spring. I would stay in New York, I told him, just six months, and I could see the Brooklyn Bridge from my window. As it turned out the bridge was the Triborough, and I stayed eight years." I was immune to the humor or irony in this passage. What I took away from it was the hope—as unlikely as sprouting wings, it seemed to me back then—that I might one day be as old as twenty, or have logged eight years here, to acquire that youth-viewed-at-a-distance weariness, to be able to rattle off the names of the city's lesser-known bridges.

It was what I took away from most every encounter: an almost obliterating desire to "pass" as a New Yorker, to authentically resemble one of the denizens of the movie *Manhattan*. More than the Deco penthouse aeries of characters in old musicals, more than the moral elasticity and heartless grit of backstage Broadway in *All That Jazz*, perhaps on par with the gin-swilling savagery of *All About Eve*, it was the city as embodied in *Manhattan* I ached for. The high-strung friends with terrible problems, the casual infidelities, the rarefied bohemianism—ERA fund-raisers in the garden at MoMA, gallery-hopping followed by filling one's simple grocery list at Dean & DeLuca.

There was no one specific moment when the rigorous self-consciousness gave way to authenticity. It was more of a dim realization that the very act of playing the "Are we a New Yorker yet?" game means you aren't one yet. But it eventually happens, dawning on you after the fact, tapping you on the shoulder after you've passed it. It comes from an accretion of shitty jobs, deeply felt friendships that last, deeply felt friendships that end, funerals, marriages, divorces, births, and betrayals, and you wake up one day to realize that you passed the eight-year mark decades prior; that you are older than all of the characters in *Manhattan*, with the possible exception of Bella Abzug; that you have been to a party in the garden at MoMA and watched the sun come up over Sutton Place and the Fifty-Ninth Street Bridge and decided that, in the end, you'd rather stay home; that only a rich moron would buy his groceries at Dean & DeLuca; and that, as fun and Margo Channing as it might seem to be drunk and witty and cutting, it's probably better in the long run to be kind. These are all realizations endemic to aging anywhere, I am sure. It must happen in other cities, but I've really only ever been a grown-up here.

As for my mother's pocketbook, it was found later that evening, emptied of valuables and abandoned in a building lobby in Morningside Heights. Some Good Samaritan had gone through her phone book and found the number of a New York friend, who eventually tracked me down in my dorm room. It made the city seem like a shtetl, a fact that after the better part of three decades I realize is more true than not.

[New York *magazine, March 29, 2010]*

An Open Letter to
My Sisters

When my sister bought her first car—a Honda, I think—she became attuned to two things: the existence of cars in general and the prevalence of cars of the same make as hers on the road. She suddenly found herself in earnest conversation with other Accord owners, talking about mileage, parallel-parking difficulty, recalcitrant steering, and the like. Similarly, years later, she consults and instructs other young mothers in the rudiments and finer aspects of mothering. This proves a pretty mundane point, but worthy of mention, nonetheless. In short: When in doubt, consult the experts, or at least those with experience.

Now, I don't own a Honda; I don't even drive for that matter, living in New York as I do, and I don't have a child, but were someone to consult me on that matter I'd say something pithy like "Be very nice to them and feed them lots of food." So it is entirely understandable that nobody asks me these questions. But I do wonder why none of my many female friends have ever come to me for advice regarding one thing of which I do have intimate knowledge, namely, How to Make Love to a Man. (I can't really say that phrase without laughing or following it up with something like, And Leave Him Begging for More!) More succinctly put, imagine someone who both drove a Honda and was a Honda—wouldn't it stand to reason to ask them about trunk capacity, so to speak?

My female friends will say they never ask me because I am forever asserting that, although I am great company, I am lousy in bed. It's true that I assert this often, but for Glib Comic Effect (my middle name), not as gospel. Taking their reluctance to consult me to heart, however, I consulted my friends, all far more handsome, articulate, and eroticized than I. What follows is the expurgated, annotated, and highly embellished transcript of a symposium held recently at a Vietnamese restaurant in downtown Manhattan:

DAVID: Let's come to order, shall we? The question put to the table is, what can we as sexually active gay men tell women about making love to a man?

PETER: That they don't already know.

DAVID: Yes.

RICHARD: Why am I reminded of that joke about the homophobic waiter who says, "I'm sorry, sir, we don't serve homosexuals," and the customer replies, "That's fine, I don't eat homosexuals"?

SCOTT: What homophobic waiter where?

DAVID: Hey, let's not propagate stereotypes here.

JAMES: You're reminded of that joke because the premise of the discussion is the conflation of the darker realms of homosexual appetite and expertise. Essentially, we do eat homosexuals, do you see what I mean? We're being asked how to eat one. Or a man, at least.

DAVID: This is for *Mademoiselle* magazine, James.

PETER: Are they paying for dinner?

DAVID: I don't think so.

RICHARD: When you write this and we have our pseudonyms, can I be "Kyle, airline pilot"?

DAVID: No.

SCOTT: Seriously, do you think that women think of gay men as men? I mean, as translatable into straight men, if you see what I mean.

PETER: Men are men.

JAMES: No, Scott has a point. There are a lot of myths out there about what we do in bed or place stress on that would need debunking. Such as size . . .

PETER: Let's not get into size.

JAMES: Okay. Or more simply even . . . can I say this in *Mademoiselle*?

DAVID: Say it and we'll see.

JAMES: The anus.

RICHARD: Eek! Would that be the anus that Norman Mailer and Mel Gibson insist is an utterly nonsexual orifice?

SCOTT: I think that's the anus we're talking about.

JAMES: Well, I'm not really familiar with the literature, but do books tell women about it? I mean, even straight men have prostate glands.

PETER: Which are open to the same sensations.

JAMES: Exactly. I'm not saying strap anything on but . . .

DAVID: We're being awfully circumspect here.

JAMES: I'm sorry, I can't be more explicit about it on tape—my mother keeps *Mademoiselle* in the waiting room of her office. Just let them know that it's there, and it's sensitive.

SCOTT: Same thing with nipples.

RICHARD: Underarms.

PETER: The backs of the knees.

DAVID: Insides of the wrists.

RICHARD: This is sounding awfully like a fragrance commercial, isn't it?

PETER: How about telling them this? We don't all generally distinguish between what might be called foreplay and what might be called coitus. It's all sex, agreed?

DAVID: Yes.

JAMES: More or less.

PETER: And so, inasmuch as it's all valued and not just a means to a release . . . uhm, a finish . . .

RICHARD: An orgasm?

PETER: Yes. There's a quality of making the whole body a map to be explored.

DAVID: That's good.

JAMES: Yes. How about, there's more fun to be had than just down there.

RICHARD: Like learning to use all the attachments for your Cuisinart.

PETER: Ouch.

SCOTT: What a horrible metaphor.

RICHARD: Okay, how about all the applications on a computer?

[*Check arrives.*]

DAVID: That's a little better.

PETER: Let's recommend this restaurant. [*Reads fortune cookie.*] "Reprove your friends in secret, praise them openly." I think you guys are the greatest.

SCOTT: "Good things are being said about you."

DAVID: Let's sum up, shall we?

RICHARD: Respect yourself.

PETER: Shame has no place in the bedroom.

JAMES: Use condoms!

DAVID: And if he won't?

JAMES: Tell him to beat it.

And that, indeed, was the soundest advice we'd all heard that day, and every day. Drive carefully.

[Mademoiselle, *December 1994*]

Goodbye to All of You

There is an unwritten social code that I learned at university. It is uniquely suited to the architecture of a campus, with its walkways and quadrangles, but it has proven to have universal application. The law is the following: If, when you returned after the summer break, you ran into someone on the footpath whom you knew—anyone from casual-nod-hello acquaintance all the way up to and including actual-yet-temporary friend—and you did not speak the first time you saw each other that semester, you never had to speak to that person again. Ever. You could nod, you could suck in the necessary breath for the possibility of expelling it in greeting, you could even chuckle at each other in recognition, but if you actually didn't say anything, you were rid of that person. Thereafter, for the rest of your lives, you could engage in the most wonderful, revisionist estrangement; you had never known each other. You could allow yourselves to be introduced to each other at parties and affect a disingenuous, doe-eyed, first-meeting "Hi."

This capacity and desire to slough people off is no less a paradigm for real life than it was for college. Admittedly, in one's student days, it happened far more frequently, casting about furiously for identities as we all were. How embarrassing it was to have come back to school affecting an Urban Marxist People's Poet demeanor only to be confronted with one's old friends from the Gilbert & Sullivan Society. Life is like a flight. Sometimes you sit beside someone and tell them too much about yourself. Unlike a flight, however, life goes on and on and you can't change planes in Grand Rapids so sometimes you just have to change seats. There is no one more worthy of our contempt than somebody who reminds us of who we used to be. Conversely, a true friend is someone who knew you when and doesn't hold it against you.

There is also a less Stalinist reason for these passive purges: You run out of time as you get older. I have been accused by many friends, as well as by my therapist, of being "suspiciously social." This doesn't mean that they think I'm a climber, or an Eve Harrington manqué. They know I'm not that. What "suspiciously social" means is that I am perceived to know and maintain too many relationships with people. If one is friendly to everyone, one is friendly to no one. Of course, this is not actually true. I have a very significant core group of friends who, despite transoceanic migrations, etc., remain the most cohesive social network of my adult life. In fact, the bonds get stronger as my social world shrinks. There are, however, many people whom I consider friends who, due to their being single and miserable like myself, spin at high velocity and bump together about once every three months. There are laws that apply here, as well. If, for instance, you have a cold and reschedule once, add three months, and then if the other person gets food poisoning, add three more. There is a quantifiably infinitesimal chance that a third rescheduling will actually bear fruit. This is true for most grown-ups I know.

Like all good theories, though, there is a seemingly contradictory and simultaneous aspect to the rule. If you really want to get rid of someone, a friend who has revealed an unfortunate penchant for psychotic episodes, say, or someone who responds to "It's such a beautiful day" with "Thanks, I've been feeling really attractive," you cannot. It is said that tragedy is sympathetic but chronic problems are alienating. Late-night, ear-bending, soul-baring conversations with friends who tell you that "nobody understands me as you do" get hard to take as they move into their second decade. It is nice to be needed, but like shelter in a storm, not like dental floss or a really good vegetable peeler. And so, you call less. You reschedule and cancel. You try to create distance. You are a fool, playing a losing game. A game governed by the you-forgot-to-tell-me-that-you-switched-jobs-and-your-home-phone-number-but-I'm-glad-I-finally-managed-to-track-you-down principle.

I can hear the voice of Jane Darwell as Ma Joad here, wondering when I got so hard and mean. It's not meanness that makes me or anyone terminate relationships; I've been gotten rid of, too. Countless times. When I first moved to New York, I maintained my contacts in Canada steadfastly, but it's not true what they say: Absence doesn't make the heart grow anything. Absence makes you forget. I had a new life that was admittedly more exciting than my old one. I came out, which distanced me yet further, and my friends back home responded in kind, having lives of their own.

I did have one friend, however, who used to call me, her voice fairly sawtoothed with umbrage. The very existence of my new life constituted a betrayal. I superegotistically backslid and apologized for years, terrified that I was in fact guilty of her silent accusation that I now felt myself to be superior. I, in turn, would roll my eyes on the other end of the phone at her anecdotes about the same old people, her inertia, the smallness of her dreams, the Narrowness of her Worldview

(I really did use these terms—I'm not proud, I'm trying to be honest). But one day, I just stopped. I took the note of contrition out of my voice. I talked about my life without trying to mollify her by disqualifying its importance to me. It is only years later that I see that at the same time I stopped apologizing, she stopped trying to exact those assurances from me that our relationship had not changed. We both knew it had and we both were finally comfortable about it. Recently, on a trip home, I called her. Not to make plans to see her—I didn't have time, nor did she—but simply to say hello. After years of avoiding walking by her house when I visited my parents, I got over my narcissistic fantasy that she was inside, sobbing, lying in wait so she could heap upon me recriminations of neglect and heartlessness. For the first time, I did not feel like I had wounded her when I put the phone down.

A boyfriend once explained to me his leaving New York for Los Angeles this way: "You know when Joan Didion has that man say in 'Goodbye to All That' that there comes a time in New York City when you've slept with all the women in the room and borrowed money from all the men? Well, that's why I have to leave, but I've borrowed money from all the women and slept with all the men."

When he told me this, I could only focus on the part about him having slept with all the men, but I know now what he means. It doesn't necessarily make one a bad person to lose touch with someone or leave them behind, no matter what the emotional or carnal bonds once were between you. People get used up. It sounds horribly callous, but it's true. The term is "tossed aside like an old shoe"—not a bad shoe, just an old one. There's a false moral component operating here. It's hard enough to simply grow up; don't confuse the issue by not allowing yourself to lose contact with people who have now become strangers to you. The movies lie: sometimes you won't always have Paris, and what's more, you'll neither of you particularly care. Although there is an occasional attendant sorrow, it's evident the art of losing's not too hard to master.

I was recently walking one Saturday morning and passed a store I had been inside a few hours previously. I looked through the plate glass and there, like a flimsy plot device in a bad movie, I saw an ex-friend looking around. I don't mean an old friend, which is how I refer to people in Toronto. He is my only true ex-friend, and there he was in the housewares section of Barneys.

When we first became close, several years ago, he issued me a warning:

"I get tired of people after two years or so. I get really intimate, and then I get tired of them. I'll probably get rid of you, too." He laughed and covered his mouth, mock-shocked at his own cynicism.

I issued the counter-warning that he wouldn't be able to dismiss me so easily. I liked this banter. It had a Hepburn-Tracy antagonism that I enjoyed and it felt like he was laying down a romantic gauntlet to me, which may well have been the root of my problem. His lover was sick, and I felt needed and up to the challenge of proving him wrong and sticking around for the long haul.

We became good friends. We filled niches in each other's lives that seemed dangerously close to the role of soul mates or lovers. In very little time, our discourse consisted almost entirely of inside jokes, catchphrases, and partial aphorisms. I would pick up the phone at work, and he would be saying in his best Ruth Draper, "My dear, this is not for the children's ears. Meet me at the Royalton."

We cared for his dying boyfriend. I sat with him in the

church at the memorial service, when his in-laws would not acknowledge him. And then something soured. It was precipitous, this disaffection. Maybe it had been developing all along but, if so, it had been concealed, occupied as we were with caring for his lover. But suddenly, there it was: biting into a perfect-skinned apple to find it full of rot. Both of us felt unacknowledged, censored, unrespected, and unloved by the other. Perhaps, in the absence of a shared crisis, we battled each other. But I actually think I had reached a point of saturation with my role as the subordinate caring one. Or maybe I was just angry he hadn't fallen in love with me. We spoke about it one night and agreed we would have to work harder at the friendship. We came away from that evening unconvinced and dissatisfied. I then went away for a weekend. I didn't call before I left and didn't call when I got back. We haven't contacted each other since. I don't feel gotten rid of in this case. It is both our faults. His two-year prediction of expiry was merely an unfortunate coincidence.

I watched him looking around the store, unaware of me. I had no discernible feelings watching him, none of the nausea of seeing an old boyfriend, for example. I was Stella Dallas minus the rain and the handkerchief between my teeth. And then, as if he had seen me through the glass earlier that morning when I had done the very same thing, he stopped in front of a bowlful of red-and-yellow parrot tulips. Among shelves of overdecorated vases, trays, crystal, and other articles of household pornography, he leaned in to them, closing his eyes, concentrating on the one real thing that was there.

[Out, *May 1994. This is a longer,
unedited version of the published piece.*]

A Former Smoker Cheers

When I quit my two-pack-a-day smoking habit three years ago, I told myself that I would take it up again when I turned sixty-five. Thirty-five smoke-free years and then I could resuscitate a romance with my old habit and, as S. J. Perelman might say, go to hell my own way.

But unless I plan to spend my retirement years in Paris or Beijing, that might not be an option: New York is slowly becoming a smoke-free zone. And you know, that's fine by me. In fact, I cheered from my bed when I woke up Monday morning, switched on the radio, and heard that the ban on smoking had gone into effect.

Lest you think I'm one of those zealous ex-smokers, I assure you I am not. I still understand that feeling when one's next cigarette seems more important than food or shelter. I smoked through nine months of chemotherapy, after all, so why can't I just live and let live?

Well, for one thing, smoking can kill you. End of story. It's incredibly bad for you. But far more important, it can kill me. And, frankly, I'm already cranky enough without being endangered by people who are neither relatives nor friends. If we've never met and you increase the level of poison in my already toxic New York life, watch out.

Besides, we should finally have the decency to try to take care of one another. There used to be a billboard at Houston and Broadway that read WELCOME TO AMERICA. THE ONLY DEVELOPED COUNTRY OTHER THAN SOUTH AFRICA WITHOUT UNIVERSAL HEALTH CARE! Nelson Mandela was still in prison when that billboard was up, and here we are still grappling with people's right to universal coverage. How can we, as a society, say that we care about our citizens' health and not agree to remove this most visible and dangerous threat? Otherwise, we all put our lives at risk of being nasty, brutish, and short.

I've been told that, as an non-national (I moved to the United States thirteen years ago), I can't fully appreciate the ferocity with which Americans regard their personal freedoms, that it is a slippery slope from stopping people smoking in restaurants to installing Orwellian telescreens in their homes. But surely my right to avoid the increased risk of another bout of cancer outweighs my neighbor's right to blow smoke on my twenty-dollar entrée (except, bizarrely, in a space intimate enough to contain fewer than thirty-five seats).

Finally, smoking is just not as glamorous as it used to be. It's been a long time since Jean-Paul Belmondo and Jean Seberg langorously puffed their way through Paris in the aptly titled *Breathless*. And don't even mention that much touted cigar renaissance that has young and old blithely lighting up as if they had never heard the name Sigmund Freud. Smoking is somewhat passé, and surely in New York that has to count for something.

It does seem ridiculous to make Central Park smoke-free, and I feel doubly sorry for the waiters working in tiny restaurants; somehow their health has been deemed less worthy of protection under the new law, and now they're likely to see even more business from serious smokers turned away from everywhere else. But when I think of the acute nausea, pain, burned skin, side effects of medication, and hair loss of cancer treatment, I can only think: "Been there. Done that." And so I cheer from my bed.

[The New York Times, *April 14, 1995*]

Diary, 1998

Monday, April 27, 1998

Back from a weekend in Toronto. My father's seventieth birthday—the "New Middle Age," I've counterphobically labeled it. Weekends in Toronto are anticipated with no small amount of dread: that my life in New York will be deemed a hoax, green card revoked, adulthood rescinded, etc. (The problem with a diary so public is my knowing that friends are reading this—or perhaps not—thinking: "Oh, god. Is he really trotting out those tired old anxious tropes again? Tiresome queen.") Poor old much-maligned Toronto. Really a lovely city, actually. But it still harbors bad associations for me from a time, just over a decade ago, when I suffered a touch of cancer there.

On the way out to La Guardia, passing the vast Wood-lawn Cemetery, in Queens (it *is* Woodlawn, isn't it?), two balloons hover over the gravestones, two balloons—one black, one white—before they eventually float up and out of sight. An image with all the cheap, icky, maudlin poetry of one of those hysterical fifties ballads about dead and dying teens—on railroad tracks, in car wrecks—and their last, post-humous wishes that their undying devotion be conveyed to some hapless girl waiting in vain at some dance or party or bake sale.

I fly Air Canada. Somewhere over Lake Ontario, the plane dips precipitously and rather violently. I am woken out of sleep. A woman whoops involuntarily from the front of the plane. Glances are exchanged and knuckles whiten for just a moment. No announcement from the cockpit. *I hate Canadian reserve! On American, the ax-head-featured pilot would have come on to tell us what happened while flight attendants tried to win our confidence back by plying us with conciliatory nuts,* I think murderously to myself. I am regressing fast; Sullen Teen is taking over my brain.

There are two Mormons on the subway in Toronto. I recognize them immediately: "initially handsome and then not really on closer inspection" blond faces; short-sleeved, polyester, white dress shirts; surprisingly misshapen and fat asses. I'm proved right when I see one carries *El Libro de Mormón* in one hand. I remember them well from when I lived in Tokyo. They traveled on bicycles in pairs. At the only rich-Westerner expat party I ever attended in Japan, I was talking to a small circle of investment banker types about these missionary duos.

"It seems unfair," said a young woman with Crédit Lyonnais. "Space is at such a premium in Tokyo, and they make them room together." We were in an apartment in the Asakusa district that was huge even by New York standards.

Her English banker boyfriend explained, "Well, there's a reason for that. They're supposed to keep an eye on each other, in case one of them is tempted to masturbate."

"That seems reasonable," say I, drunken, twenty-two-year-old, arrogant wiseacre. "It's infinitely more fun to masturbate with someone watching." I was not invited back.

The parents now live in an apartment building downtown

that is filled with old people. Last June, when my father had a mild heart attack, I was walking past the security desk on my way to the hospital when a cleaning woman bounded down the stairs and told the guard to come quickly because she had just found the old woman for whom she worked dead.

On this visit I see that the old carpets have been replaced by a truly hideous and comically large-patterned broadloom. Suitable only for those whose eyes are failing and for whom it would be beneficial to really be able to see the floor rising up very quickly to meet them as their brittle spun-glass bones shatter beneath them. All the doors to the parking garage have large electronic opening buttons imprinted with the universal sign for a wheelchair. Indeed, the facility seems more and more geriatric each time I go, which freaks me out a bit. Tell Laura I love her!

Return to New York City on a cold, rainy Sunday evening. My very favorite weather, actually. Time was, upon returning from Toronto, I would dump the bags and go out in pursuit of libidinal activity. Oddly enough, this time I am sufficiently calmed and gladdened by my tasteful apartment and my many, many material possessions. Outside, a modest parade of about sixty Tibetan Buddhists with orange lanterns, drums, cymbals, and a five-tiered pagoda palanquin on a U-Haul flatbed drown out my Edith Piaf tape as they bang and clatter by my window in the rainy dusk on Sixteenth Street.

Tuesday, April 28, 1998

In a *Publishers Weekly* review for an upcoming reminiscence of Richard Nixon by his last confidante, researcher, and travel companion, Monica Crowley, the review notes Nixon's "wide readings ranging from Aristotle to Machiavelli." Stipulating to the charge that I think Richard Nixon is one of the worst people who ever lived, almost because of his posthumous reconstruction as a statesman, and because I am newly thrilled each day that I wake up to find that he is yet deceased (and so I might be a tad prone to finding lacunas in anything resembling a sympathetic portrait of him), I still must ask the question: SINCE WHEN IS ARISTOTLE TO MACHIAVELLI CONSIDERED "WIDE READING"? At its most charitable, it merely means he had been a college freshman somewhere. I hate him I hate him I hate him!

I'm reminded of that supremely dopey moment in *As Good as It Gets*—you know, the movie that clears up the mysteries of obsessive-compulsive behavior as being nothing more than a taste for lots of Evian and a penchant for sorting your M&M's by color—where Greg Kinnear's character (a less-aesthetically-driven-seeming visual artist has almost never been portrayed on the screen since Rosanna Arquette played Nick Nolte's highly adenoidal assistant/muse in *New York Stories*) looks over at Helen Hunt drawing her bath, her towel falling down her naked back in graceful drapery, and says, "Hold it!" Any doofus who's been to a museum gift shop can get precisely the same image, on place mats, note cards, ties, trivets, clock faces, and jigsaw puzzles, rendered by Matisse, Degas, Bonnard, Cassatt, ad extreme projectile nauseam. This is his big moment of inspiration? This guy shows? In a gallery? A gallery that doesn't also sell flavored coffee and balloon bouquets?

Talking with colleague editor Eamon Dolan. The conversation turned to nostalgia and what a complete load of shit it all is. Czarist Chic was all the rage last year, I'm just waiting for Pogrom Elegance to kick in. Unfortunately, both Eamon and I are unhealthily steeped in a certain kind of wistfulness about 1930s through 1950s literary New York. Despite the glaring truth of the matter that in any age but our own he'd be an excluded poor Irish Catholic boy and I an excluded Jew desperately trying not to have my faggot ass kicked to death. Although I bemoan the present state of publishing constantly, I am also quick to point out that a "gentleman's business" generally really works only in favor of gentlemen.

I told him of the fake Abercrombie & Fitch*–oid ad I had always wanted to create: "Return to a simpler time. A time of ice cream suppers and neighborly conduct. A time of unbleached cotton and natural fibers. A time where a woman could die of a botched abortion, blacks didn't have the vote, blah, blah, blah." We reminded each other of the fake Gap ads we were going to wheat-paste all around town: HITLER WORE KHAKIS. Today's idea was pictures of Charles Manson, Pol Pot, etc., with the Macintosh logo: THINK DIFFERENT.

Went to the radio taping of BBC 4's *Talk of New York*, a show meant to convey a kind of classic, rarefied New York cocktail party. Think Dick and Dorothy Rodgers's apartment, Cole Porter at the piano, Brooks Atkinson getting sauced, Nazimova holding court. Not quite, really. But Julie Wilson sang two songs magnificently. She is bone-thin and sharp-angled like a lightning bolt, in a black turtleneck with a boa, and of course a fake Lady Day gardenia in the LP-slick hair of her huge, *huge* head. The setting was strange and authentic—I think someone said it's in Condé Nast's original living room

---

* Weirdly enough, I came home to a postcard from the A&F catalog sent to me by Sarah. Unbelievably Arcadian homoerotic tableau of a bunch of boys grappling shirtlessly on the beach. All shining teeth, rippling abdominals, and that gay-porn, fake-o hearty, straight-guy energy. ("Oh, man, now look what you did! You tore my underwear. Well, I guess I better take them off." "Hey, coach. I think I pulled a muscle in my groin." "Well, hop up on the table, and let's see if we can massage it out.")

in a brownstone on Forty-Fifth. The drinks were free. A snootful of gratis Bushmills is a lovely way to ease into a new week.

Wednesday, April 29, 1998

Koko, the gorilla who speaks in sign language (and has been around a long time; I did a project on her in fifth grade with Sholom Kramer. I copied a whole article about her from *Scientific American* onto a piece of poster board. Then, I suspect, as always, we tried to get extra marks by serving the foods of Holland or something), took email questions on America Online the other evening, thus exponentially raising the tone of most chat room conversation I've ever logged on to. An unholy combination, to be sure, my worst nightmare made flesh: the Web and animals. When asked "Do you like to chat with other people?" ("Other? Other than you, do you mean?"), Koko, briefly channeling the soundtrack from *Shaft*, replied, "Fine nipple." It's really a virtual community!

A lovely walk to work. It's an exercise in maneuvering my body like a car. I suppose this is where I vent my male aggression, as I don't know how to actually drive. I swerve, I change lanes frantically, I pass, I run lights, my rage blooming as garishly and violently as a magician's pop-up bouquet; YOU HAVE WALKED IN FRONT OF ME AND FOR THAT YOU MUST DIE!!! I arrive at work, sweaty, energized, with a taste for blood.

I get a qualitatively different postexercise feeling from my lunchtime swims at the Y, which bliss me out and fill me, for a while, with the soy milk of human kindness.

Ad on the subway on the way up to shrink: THE SEEKERS CHRISTIAN FELLOWSHIP WANTS TO DECLARE MAY 7TH "J.D.," OR

"JESUS DAY." Why, that's a marvelous idea! His religion seems awfully popular; it should be marked with a holiday of sorts, don't you think? People could exchange gifts or something, have parties, sing some songs specific to the holiday (someone would have to write some, I suppose). Stores could decorate in a festive manner. I think it could really catch on.

Best friend Natalia in town for the evening from London on her way to an international human rights conference in Jamaica. Other best friend Erin and I have supper with her at Andre and Leina's (her parents) apartment. Talk turns to feelings of guilt toward the parents. Andre feels some, Leina feels none, Natalia none, Erin some. We keep it light, as we always do, but I am almost uncoupled by feeling like a Bad Son. The world is a tad too much with me in general these days. I am easily disappointed, irritated, insulted, hurt. I have the post-jaw-clenching, low-grade headache caused by keeping something under wraps. Skillful repressor that I am, I couldn't begin to know what it is. But it keeps me thin. All I really care about.

Erin thinks the subway car coming home smells funny. "Like feet," she says. I detect nothing. I offer her my bag of fresh asparagus as an olfactory diversion. She sticks her nose in and reels back as if slapped. I sniff, and indeed they smell of death and putrefaction. I tell myself hopefully this is just due to the close quarters of the plastic bag. In an Oe novel, *The Silent Cry*, the wife, who has just moved back to her husband's country village, remembers some houseplants that once rotted, and imagines all the vegetation, the huge forests surrounding them, smelling of decay.

William Carlos Williams's "Danse Russe" runs like a loop of tape in my head: "I am lonely, lonely, I was born to be lonely, I am best so!" Something about that final exclamation point just makes it impossible for that to be a depressing phrase to me. Or maybe I'm lying. Hard to say. . . .

Thursday, April 30, 1998

Despite the glorious weather—and it is glorious, if not two degrees too hot—truly New York at its most authentically *On the Town* photogenic (one can, for but a moment, almost forget the oppressive presence of the NBA store, Coca-Cola store, Warner Bros. store, Planet Hollywood, Hard Rock Cafe, mega Gap, Armani Exchange, Banana Republic, etc., all within a four block area), no one is happy!

Chris, Deb, Kristen . . . no one is having any fun. There are busloads of green kids getting off at the Port Authority terminal every day, desperate for the kinds of jobs these folks have: magazine editor, book editor, in film development. Kristen was wondering about career counseling, but I've always thought it was a crock. Questions set up around the dialectic "I adore foreclosing on or, failing that, setting fire to, orphanages" vs. "Nothing pleases me more than pressing flowers gathered in my provender basket."

Lately, New York resembles nothing so much as the court of Louis XVI and Marie Antoinette. This morning, *The New York Times*'s House & Home section had an item about a new wallpaper from Scalamandré called the "Rogarshevsky Scroll," named after the family that occupied the building that now houses New York's Lower East Side Tenement Museum. The design is a faithful copy of the fourteenth layer of paper found on the walls. I'm sure the Rogarshevskys would be thrilled. It must have been a great solace to them all, when returning from their fourteen-hour workdays in some sweatshop, to think, Piecework's a bitch, but this wallpaper . . . timeless! The paper is available for $84.75 per roll, to the trade. *L'élégance Pogromoise est arrivée!*

I also heard through the grapevine this morning that the editor of a major youth glossy, a man who packages precisely that kind of nouveau-swinger, martinis-and-cigars, major-schmuck Weltanschauung that we all hoped had disappeared a decade ago, has proposed teaming up his editorial staff, giving them all new VW bugs, and having them race across the country, like some Terry Thomas movie on testosterone. I could vomit.

Met up with my friends Jeff and Nathaniel, the most beautiful couple in North America, to go to Fez, on Lafayette Street, to an event called "Loser's Lounge." My friends Andy Richter and Sarah Thyre sang a duet (brilliantly), the Lee Hazlewood and Nancy Sinatra number "Some Velvet Morning." The entire evening seemed to be some sort of Nancy Sinatra Festschrift, as a matter of fact. Sarah was a psychedelic vision, resplendent in platinum fall, Pucci top, and paisley skirt. Much fun, laughs *à gogo*.

Two girls came out of a croissant shop on Third Avenue as I was walking home. "My pimples were sooo big!" Loud and almost proud, certainly unabashed. I lost my heart to both of them, pustules and all.

Friday, May 1, 1998

The city is like Jakarta today. Gray-skied, sultry, traffic at a standstill, cacophonous.

I keep on trying to put into words what so riles me about the changes of late in New York, certainly not just in this diary but each and every day in almost each and every conversation I have. I love the city almost more than anyone I know—I guess it's the reasonable response of the adoptive New Yorker—but it's been so eminently depressing of late. There's a creeping dullness afoot, a homogenization, an ersatz feeling. All the protruding nails are being hammered down.

This is all drivel, of course, and has been said millions of times before. I also think it's quite dangerous to wax nostalgic for a Times Square where a twelve-year-old runaway girl could find work as a whore. And being whacked on the head with a two-by-four by four teenage boys (as I was some eight years ago) is hardly my madeleine, but surely there's a happy medium between what we had and Giuliani's bizarre, authoritarian, and ultimately empty quality-of-life measures, along with this wholesale effacement of history.

A perfect, and perfectly heartbreaking, example is the Case of Nora Ephron: Recently, folks on lower Seventh Avenue were thrilled to find a new independent bookstore in what used to be Barneys on Seventeenth Street. Only to find out that it was a movie set, the bookstore where Meg Ryan's character works in an upcoming Nora Ephron flick called *You've Got Mail*.

Okay, now Nora Ephron was an incredibly funny, insightful, take-no-prisoners journalist (*Crazy Salad* and *Scribble Scribble* are books anyone would be proud to have written), and I still read *Heartburn* every summer and still laugh out loud. But now Nora Ephron makes these pallid, heterosexist, retrograde Date Movies, and her only relationship to her former life—i.e., words—is setting up some skillful simulacrum of a bookstore in the city that desperately needs its rapidly disappearing independent bookstores. They used to use Toronto as a stand-in for New York in movies, but now I think Toronto's probably too gritty and real.

Perhaps it's all just the clarion call of Money and Power. I've often joked that for two dollars a word, I'd happily write a column called "I Love Nazis," and I keep dreaming of all the art I'll buy when my eventual TV series, *He's the Faggot*, goes into syndication. So what do I know? But still, for Nora Ephron to go from being the kind of effortlessly iconoclastic writer that she was—a writer who so cleverly nailed it when she wrote how she wasn't buying what American legend Lillian Hellman was selling, in terms of all that pretentious, self-righteous drinkin' and fightin' and lovin' that goddamn Dash Hammett—to this purveyor of these middlebrow entertainments just makes me want to go to bed forever. And would I love to audition for a Nora Ephron movie? You bet I would. (Madam, we've already established what you are, why now quibble about the price?)

I meet Chris outside the Ziegfeld Theatre, on Fifty-Fourth Street, for a screening of the new Warren Beatty film, *Bulworth*. Suspiciously thin D-girls in DKNY are walking up and down the line announcing with great officiousness, "Please have your tickets out." I can't help thinking that freedom of assembly is guaranteed under the law, and I don't want to have my ticket out.

One of the girls comes up to the men behind me in line and says, "We're turning people away?" Ah, how I love the rising intonation of Up-Speak. The men look at her blankly, uncertain as to whether she means what she says. As it's turned into a lovely, high-skied, late spring New York evening, Chris and I defiantly throw our tickets in the trash, catch the N train (where we get priority seating, thank you very much), and head down to the Excellent Dumpling House just off Canal.

Pistachio ice cream at Ben & Jerry's and then home up Third Avenue.

The Empire State Building is lit up blue and white for Israel's fiftieth. But that would require a whole other week to talk about.

[Slate, 1998]

What's Up, Dike?

D ear Amazon.com customer," it begins. "Many of you know John Updike as the winner of two Pulitzer Prizes and the author of great American novels such as *The Witches of Eastwick* and *Rabbit at Rest.* This summer, get to know him as the author whose words open our 'Greatest Tale Ever Told,' the first-ever collaborative story written by Amazon.com customers."

Who could resist the invitation? No one, it seems.

Begun by John Updike:

Miss Tasso Polk at ten-ten alighted from the elevator onto the olive tiles of the nineteenth floor only lightly nagged by a sense of something wrong. The Magazine's crest, that great black M, the thing masculine that had most profoundly penetrated her life, echoed from its inlaid security the thoughtful humming in her mind: "m."

Dr. Seuss:

Then Miss Tasso Polk without further ado,
Went in to her boss, Miss Jane Watt-Wehr-Hu.
"Good morning, Miss Polk," Jane began with a smirk.

"If it's not too much trouble, let's get down to work.
Now first, I need donuts, 'bout six hundred million,
And coffee, two sugars, no, make that twelve billion.
I want a new wardrobe! In silks, wools, and leathers;
I want to grow taller, I want to grow feathers!
And finally," she sighed, "As soon as you're able,
Call up Four Seasons and book me a table.
Now tend to your duties, I'm 'fraid I must fly.
I've got an appointment with John Wenn-Howe-Wye.
We're meeting, you see, to decide if it's best,
To move the whole office to a large eagle's nest."
As Tasso prepared to go start her day,
Jane opened her window and flew right away.
"That's that, job well done," Tasso said to herself
While she dusted the Chum-Chum tree up on the shelf.
And waving good-bye, Tasso swept out the door,
Heading up to her office on the two-thousandth floor.

Jacqueline Susann:

Tasso just managed to catch the elevator as the doors were closing. "You must be new here," she heard a voice behind her, as smooth as single malt scotch. It could only be the managing editor, Lyman Braithwaite, ne'er-do-well wastrel son of the magazine's owner and founder, Brixton Braithwaite—now, tragically, confined to an iron lung.

"Actually, Mr. Braithwaite, I've been at the magazine for twelve years." He stepped toward her in the car. He was no fag, that was for sure. Weak-kneed, she stepped back until the pert melons of her backside brushed up against the rich mahogany veneer of the elevator.

"I see . . ." he said. "You know, the magazine needs a girl

on the cover. A girl people can look at and say, 'That's the magazine I need to read, by god!'"

"But this is a financial magazine."

"Never mind that. Have you ever modeled for a great deal of money before, and are you free for dinner tonight Miss, uh . . ."

"Polk. Tasso Polk."

"Tasso? Rhymes with 'lasso.'" He fixed her with his cerulean gaze, giving Tasso the distinct feeling of a roped calf waiting for a red-hot metal branding iron.

Isaac Bashevis Singer:

She took lunch every day at a dairy restaurant near the office. The people here argued, spitting ancient and potent curses, they wept tears of joy while they danced with their feet several inches off the floor, they rent their clothing in unspeakable agonies. On nights after eating there, Tasso was invariably tormented by dreams in which she found herself sporting the horns of a devil, the genitals of a man, and her own woman's breasts. She would awaken, heaving and terrified, vowing to never return.

Once, there came into the cafeteria a man in a dark greatcoat. He sat down and pulled from his mouth three black plums and a silver spoon. From a hole in his chest he produced a loaf of black bread and a golden-skinned herring. When he had eaten his lunch—augmented with a boiled potato and a plate of sour cream from the restaurant—he closed up his coat and flew away, leaving behind the smell of sulfur and fresh dung.

"A dybbuk," spat the waitress, clearing his dishes. "And a bad tipper." He had left behind him on the table a damp and faded note. "The man to whom you are mistress is not a good man," it read. "You must forget him."

J. D. Salinger:

If you ask me, there's nothing more depressing than some old guy with dirty cigarette-stained fingers handing you some goddamn note in some cafeteria somewhere, as if he was letting you in on some big secret. It could just about break your heart if you thought about it for even a second. A goddamn note telling you that the guy you were going with was nothing but a phony who said nice things to you, and maybe took you for dinner at the Yale Club every so often. Like you didn't already know that he was just some show-off from Groton or Philips who thought it was so damn original to ask the waiter his name and then call him by his name for the whole damn meal.

Tasso just couldn't face the thought of going back to the magazine just then, having to pretend like everyone was her best goddamn friend, so she headed off to the Museum of Natural History. Maybe in the Blue Whale Room she could look at the kids. That always cheered her up; the kids running around like they were drunk, so happy 'cause they hadn't found out yet that everyone would end up disappointing you and it was all a big bunch of phony crap and lies.

Joan Didion:

There had been a time in Tasso's life when such a note, with its glaring eccentricity and specificity, would have brought on the thrumming aura of impending migraine and sent her to bed. A time when she had dated interesting boys in broadcloth shirts from Rogers Peet who took her to parties where they would collectively engage in what was known back then, indeed what was a key metaphor of the Age, as "having fun," as in "You should call up Trudy. She's a lot of fun," said, perhaps, about a girl, perhaps, who was amusing to be with (the particulars are what fade over time). A time in Tasso Polk's life long before she could have imagined herself one day standing in an A-line dress on the tarmac of a jungle airport in an unnamed country.

Often, in lieu of pondering such things, Miss Tasso Polk took herself off to buy a pair of shoes or to have her teeth cleaned. But today, it was the Blue Whale Room at the Museum of Natural History, lying on the western edge of Central Park, Frederick Law Olmsted's highly designed expanse of sylvan contrivance that had nothing to do with, indeed was in no way affected by, the Space Program, the advent of highways—and consequently movie making—in California, nor the kidnapping of Patricia Hearst.

Woody Allen:

INT. MUSEUM OF NATURAL HISTORY. BLUE WHALE ROOM. TASSO POLK and her boyfriend, NATHAN KANTER, are sitting on a BENCH underneath a very huge PLASTER BLUE WHALE.

TASSO

Yeah, I mean . . . uh . . . it was really incredible. My analyst said that I never really got a note at that restaurant and that I'm just insecure about whether you really love me, and in my dream where I had the horns it was because you were Jewish, you know, and Grandpa's always talking about those "horned Jews."

NATHAN

Yeah, your grandfather's a real Norman Rockwell type . . . whittling a swastika on the front porch.

TASSO

And, uh . . . in the dream, my analyst said the male genitals part is clear, and I still had breasts because you're always telling me that I'm flat-chested.

NATHAN
(Agitated)

I am not. I . . . I mean, I think your chest is . . . dynamite.

TASSO

You do?

NATHAN

Absolutely. I . . . I . . . yeah . . . I . . . tch . . . really think you should lay off the white fish. That cafeteria . . . sounds like some sort of kabbalah drop-in center.

TASSO

I know, Nathan, but I'm trying to like Jewish food, you know, and, and . . . I read that Heinrich Böll story you told me to . . .

NATHAN

Hey . . .

NATHAN takes TASSO's face in his hands. They KISS.
SOUND: LOUIS ARMSTRONG'S VERSION OF
"YOU'RE MY THRILL."
CUT TO: NATHAN against white background.

NATHAN

(Directly to camera)

You know, I really loved Tasso and I miss her a lot . . . and I'm reminded of the old joke—I think it's Zeppo Marx—of the woman who opened her refrigerator and found a rabbit sleeping there . . . and . . . uh . . . the rabbit asks, "Isn't this a Westinghouse?" And the woman tells him yes, and the rabbit says, "Well, I'm just westing." And I think that's how it is with love. We're all just . . . uh, just looking for a place to west.

FADE OUT.

[Salon, *August 12, 1997*]

The Wizards of Id

Lifestyle features have heralded the Return of the Swinger and the End of Moderation for the better part of two years now. Apparently, collectively weary from decades of having to watch what we eat, smoke, drink, and, most especially, say, "we" are returning to a simpler time of boomerang coffee tables and pupu platters. A time when, at worst, "Mad Cow" was a frothy drink for the ladies. A time when chicks knew how to shut up and cats "swung." Think back to the old "What kind of man reads *Playboy?*" ads, high-fidelity systems, scotch, Sulka dressing gowns, the work of LeRoy Neiman, etc.

Restaurants featuring smoking areas with cute, retro names like the Havana Room—I'm still waiting for the Missiles of October Lounge—are springing up like mushrooms, or rather, metastatic tumors. Even my formerly staid neighborhood, once the elegant home to Washington Irving, New York's only private park, and the charmingly prim National Arts Club, is rank with the smell of the Death of Restraint: prime rib, Bombay Sapphire, Ketel One, tobacco, and, of course, the unfortunate result of all of these at the end of a long evening, vomit.

I hate the Nouveau Swingerati. I will freely admit it. I quite enjoy a good martini, and will occasionally still take one in the privacy of my own home, although I'd sooner eat glass than be seen drinking one in public. I am also fairly obsessed with Frank Sinatra. I know the words to most of his songs and can emulate the phrasing on the important recordings more than passably well, not to mention sing both the Betty Garrett and Frankie parts of "Come Up to My Place" from *On the Town*, thank you very much. But you won't catch me out in public singing "Angel Eyes" while swirling an olive through my gin.

Swingers have ruined my life. The martini is now tied with the cellphone as the leading semaphore for "Hello, I'm a schmuck." (The cigar, it should be noted, is something entirely more direct than a mere semaphore.) And my beloved Frank has been co-opted as the god of Cool by precisely the kind of thick-necked douche bags I've spent my entire life assiduously avoiding. Not yet even dead, Frank hovers, shimmering perpetually above us all, like a beacon, like Noah's dove.

So, it was with a mixture of trepidation and the anticipatory bloodlust of a hatchet job that I went to the Museum of Television and Radio to see *The Rat Pack Captured*, a ninety-minute version of a recently discovered 1965 kinescope of a benefit concert by Frank, Dean Martin, and Sammy Davis, Jr., hosted by Johnny Carson—allegedly the only known video recording of an entire Rat Pack performance.

The audience at the museum on the rainy Saturday turns out not, however, to be made up of the Date Rape–oisie at all. For the most part, we are men and women of a certain age who have come to see the boys sing. The evening is opened by a startlingly young Johnny, at that time only three years on the air, who explains a bit about the Dismas House of St. Louis, a facility for ex-offenders for which this event is a benefit. And then comes Dean Martin. I brace myself, having never liked his boozy persona. He is a caricature of dissipation; shiny-faced, eyes lowered to half-mast, beatifically stoned. But boy, is he adorable. Imagine my surprise that I come to you now as a prophet of the Church of Dino.

Dean Martin sings like an angel. And this came upon me in a blinding flash of light: In the same way that, despite the seemingly extemporaneous ease with which Fred Astaire danced, we all know he rehearsed doggedly, I realized Dean isn't really a drunk asshole! Actually, there's nothing assoholic at all about his drunk act.

Unlike with his former partner and icon of the French, Jerry Lewis, you're not waiting for the vicious undercurrent. Dino smiles in a vaguely surprised, ain't-this-nifty way throughout his set, as if the music pouring out of him was not his doing at all. Something else he shares with Astaire is a vocabulary of the tiniest physical gestures. While singing "King of the Road," that pre-hippie, sixties anthem to barefoot, boho insouciance, he gives it a nice little gender-fuck by punctuating a riff with a lock of the torso, a cant of the head, his wrist a relaxed teapot handle, and singing, "queen of the road." At a time when gay-baiting humor relied on the wide swish and the hostile mince with the unspoken promise of ultimately kicking someone's faggot ass, Dean, for just an instant, makes a surprisingly sympathetic and counterintuitively convincing bottom. I sit there, homo that I am, charmed and unoffended.

By the time he finishes his set and brings home "You're Nobody 'Til Somebody Loves You," he does so with such a touching sincerity that I am thinking to myself, "Yes, Dean. So true, so true. I am nobody."

Sammy, on the other hand, is a wraith of pure energy, a pipe cleaner man in a tuxedo, with his hair plastered against his head like an LP. He is also so immediately sweet and unctuous, so afflicted with the inability to refer to anyone without the Homeric moniker "My dear friend," that I almost sank into a diabetic coma. This is pure telethon Sammy—the sycophancy ripe for parody. But it's just opening artifice. Who knows, perhaps in 1965, in front of an entirely white audience, this ritual self-declawing was required of any black entertainer. It is when he sings that the façade drops away. He is being played as surely as any other instrument up on stage. It is a miraculous, intimate, personal act. He is still, for want of a better expression, Mr. Entertainment, but the music moves through him.

It had been so long since I'd actually heard Sammy that I'd forgotten the depths of his talent, and it is profound. His version of "One for My Baby" alone, which contains uncanny imitations of Billy Eckstine, Mel Tormé, and Nat King Cole—all dead-on and not remotely obsequious—would almost be enough to justify an entire career. When he demonstrates the latest dances—the Mashed Potato, the Frug, the Pony—for the glaringly unhip crowd, he is not unaware of their innate campiness, the dopey names, the prescribed, vaguely bogus looseness. But he does them so beautifully and with such graceful abandon that you're reminded of how marvelously sexy and free it must have seemed to be able to dance like that alone. If partnered dancing was a metaphor for love, watching Sammy shake his little can while doing the Swim must have seemed like a national exhortation to go jack off.

And finally, the Chairman of the Board, who is, at least as far as *The Rat Pack Captured* is concerned, the least compelling of the three. "Your hoodlum singer," says Johnny. True indeed. Sinatra is no longer the beauty he was and his face has taken on a leathern, thuggish quality, which is not relieved by a surfeit of smiling for the audience. There is a

Great Star Reserve in evidence, however justified, that I find simply threatening. Dino and Sammy, as it turns out, had not yet done enough to soften me toward Vegas-heyday Frank. Even his own goofiness—miming shooting craps way too many times on "Luck Be a Lady," substituting "St. Louis" for "Chicago" on "My Kind of Town" to the point where even a St. Louis native would scream "enough"—merely make him seem more unimaginative than human.

And yet, as my sister says, "They don't call him Beethoven for nothing." He is still Frank Sinatra. Even if he phoned it in, it would be worth it.

But none of the three do phone it in. These guys are all about talent. Transcendent talent. The ancient Greeks got it right; talent this prodigious becomes a moral virtue. So that by the time they spend the last half hour of the concert breaking themselves up in their not terribly funny, mildly punch-drunk, highly exclusionary frat-boy way, it seems entirely earned and materially different from the annoying roughhousing that goes on of a Saturday night on Park Avenue South.

It is only this last part of *The Rat Pack Captured* that I associate with the new Swinger culture. The unrelenting irony with which Rat Pack culture has been adopted entirely ignores precisely why these guys were allowed to behave the way they did. Because they were some of the greatest interpreters of the American Popular Song that have ever lived.

Moreover, they only behaved that way some of the time. There has been an effacement of the historical record. *The Rat Pack Captured* is, in the end, a benefit for a halfway house for ex-cons, as they used to affectionately be called. What mainstream white entertainer today, other than Susan Sarandon, say, would take up such a cause? Sinatra was a progressive long before he became a Reagan Regular. Even the original founder of the Rat Pack, Humphrey Bogart, was a vocal opponent to McCarthy and a supporter of the Hollywood Ten.

Facts all lost in the Rat Pack Revival. The recuperated aspects of that time, the drinking, the smoking, the wardrobe, are not only the least important as regards the Sinatra signature style, but they are also the very attributes that resonate of a time and a world that was far less hospitable, kind, or gentle. It's all a bit like going to Beyreuth and coming out an anti-Semite instead of an opera queen.

The Swingerati have ignored the gallery entirely and gone straight for the gift shop. They don't even know from Frank Sinatra that much, beyond the swagger. When the hi-fi gets fired up, likely as not it is the strains of Esquivel, or the camp-right-out-of-the-box lounge music of groups like Combustible Edison that one hears. I said earlier that I wouldn't be caught dead singing a Sinatra song out in public. But I've changed my mind. I could make it all the way through to the end of "Come Fly with Me" and nobody would even recognize the tune, let alone the words. And that's the saddest part.

[Salon, *June 13, 1997*]

Laura Bush

Not known as a cut-up, First Lady Laura Bush told an absolute knee-slapper when she said "There is nothing political about American literature. Everyone can like [it], no matter what your party." She was speaking about the literary symposia she's been hosting in the White House.

"Isn't it pretty to think so," to quote Mr. Hemingway.

No thanks to the Culture Warriors of her father-in-law's administration, or the power-ballad-singing attorney general of her husband's.

There is almost nothing more political than American literature. No more vivid and organic manifestation of our unique capacity for dissent exists than the works produced by the vast spectrum of our nation's writers, both native and adoptive. Portnoy, Lily Bart, Bigger Thomas, political figures all. That they are now canonical and unthreatening works that wear the consoling patina of the past does not make them less so. It would surprise the writers of the Harlem Renaissance to the point of astonishment—Zora Neale Hurston, Countee Cullen, and Mrs. Bush's own beloved Langston Hughes—that their work was free of politics. Indeed, their work was both a response to and a triumph over very real public policy. As an educator herself, a teacher and a librarian, Mrs. Bush probably knows a thing or two about librarians who have had to routinely stand tough in the face of overzealous special prosecutors, refusing to disclose the reading habits of private individuals. In Mrs. Bush's home state, the narrow-minded and disproportionately powerful Texas Public Policy Foundation routinely puts the fate of the entire nation's textbooks in a stranglehold, its list of objections over content extending to history and, yes, even American literature.

It's entirely laudable that Mrs. Bush thinks a symposium on the work of Truman Capote would "be fabulous." She's absolutely right, both in sentiment and choice of adjectives. Were Mr. Capote still alive, he would no doubt be thrilled to attend. He had a particular affection for the wives of powerful men who managed true subversion under the guise of docile complicity. This, then, is the consoling fiction I choose to compose about Mrs. Bush: that she knows full well how political literature can be; that she is actually trying to change things from within. It's a charitable analysis on my part, I know—a charity not routinely granted by her husband's administration. But if she truly believes what she says, then I, to quote Mrs. Parker, am Marie of Romania.

[The New York Times, *Op-Ed, October 2002*
(unpublished)]

The Love That Dare Not Squeak Its Name

Had E. B. White written his children's classic *Stuart Little* today, he would have a hard time portraying Stuart, the second child of Mrs. Frederick C. Little of New York City—a child who was "not much bigger than a mouse" and who also "looked very much like a mouse in every way"—as anything other than some freakish monster. That's precisely why the current film adaptation shows Stuart being adopted, rather than being born. In this post-*Alien* age, examining too closely how a boy like Stuart might be made by human parents immediately brings to mind images of a tiny, hairless rodent slithering horribly from his mother's loins with a viscous plop.

But White wrote *Stuart Little* in 1945, when the biological process was shrouded in anesthetized mystery. For those who were neither obstetricians nor women, childbirth must have seemed little more than checking into the hospital and, after three weeks of bed rest, emerging with offspring.

And Stuart is certainly no monster in White's vision. He is very much the Littles' flesh and blood—ultimately a human child, albeit one with "the pleasant shy manner of a mouse." But phenotype will out, and we are told that "before he was many days old he was not only looking like a mouse but acting like one, too—wearing a gray hat and carrying a small cane."

At age seven, having the book read to me in second grade by the sainted Mrs. Brailey, it was this initial confluence of traits—Stuart's unquestioned membership in a family despite one glaring material difference from them and his tininess only accentuating his courtly manners and dandy tendencies—that made me realize that I was somewhat like Stuart and that Stuart seemed, somewhat like myself, pretty gay.

This is not to say that Stuart Little necessarily sought the embraces of other boy mice. But had White, even in 1945, placed Stuart in his worsted blue suit with patch pockets anywhere near a schoolyard (there is an episode where he actually teaches school, but more on that later), Stuart would have learned conclusively from his human peers that he was, at the very least, a big fag, a sissy, a 'mo, and a poof.

Nor do I mean to claim the fine feeling and higher sentiment embodied by Stuart's rarefaction as the exclusive province of the gays. Heaven knows that we inverts contain within our ranks many who have no manners to speak of, either shy or pleasant. And certainly a gray felt hat and cane are not necessarily gay props.

But props in and of themselves are an integral part of a gay childhood, with its vigilance against exposure, its years of passing. As a gay child, your life essentially consists of writing checks your ass can't cover. The two remedies to this problem are either stepping back and remaining more an observer than a full-on, good-faith participant, or going in for more performative behavior (during more judgmental times, we used to call this second option "living a lie") until such time as one can move to New York.

Stuart's very mouse-ness—indeed, at just over two inches

tall—his intrinsic lack when push comes to shove, means that he must rely on props and costumes throughout the book, if only to face the exigencies of negotiating a human-sized (and human-faced) world. His use of visual aids hardly makes him a closet mouse. Quite the contrary.

As part of Stuart's quest for human straight-boy realness, White unwittingly has him repeatedly embodying gay stereotypes. And Stuart does so with the exactitude and heightened attention to detail of the drag artist, right down to the cinematic lexicon of each new scenario. Stuart has the patois down pat.

Donning his sailor suit one fine morning, Stuart sets out for Central Park. Boarding the Fifth Avenue bus, he tries to pay with one of the small tinfoil coins made for him by his father. The conductor is understandably patronizing.

"Well, I'd have a fine time explaining that to the bus company. Why, you're no bigger than a dime yourself."

"Yes I am," replied Stuart angrily. "I'm more than twice as big as a dime . . . Furthermore . . . I didn't come on this bus to be insulted."

"You'll have to forgive me, for I had no idea that in all the world there was such a small sailor."

"Live and learn," muttered Stuart tartly, putting his change purse back in his pocket.

A thoroughly modern Stuart might just as easily have appended a withering "Mary" to the end of that riposte.

He butches it up considerably by the time he reaches the boat pond, where he asks the owner of a toy sloop, the *Wasp* (what a fitting name for the vessel on which to earn some measure of societal acceptability), to sign him on for a position as a crewman on deck.

"I'm strong and I'm quick."

"Are you sober?" asked the owner of the *Wasp*.

"I do my work," said Stuart, crisply.

Like that first highly encoded meeting of Glenn Ford and George Macready in *Gilda*, or Paul Cadmus's paintings of shore leave, there's an almost pornographic quality to this waterside transaction; the young matelot's brusque cataloging of his physical prowess to the older gentleman. Even the clipped manner of the exchange, the grudging half-disclosure, has something of the Genet rough-trade encounter about it: Stuart of Brest.

White does give Stuart a love interest. A small, wrenlike bird named Margalo who stops briefly in the Little household. And Stuart's devotion is ardent to be sure, but not precisely romantic. It is closer in nature to Janet Reno's self-admitted "abiding fondness for men": somewhat theoretical and confusing. I'm not advocating that Stuart prove himself by engaging in a little hetero-normative trans-species loving; it is, after all, still a children's book. But even within that chaste context, Stuart is only playing at lover, as he plays at everything.

He is unable to resist stepping back in commentary, even as he is saving Margalo from the jaws of Snowbell, the Littles' cat. He grooves on the theatrics of the situation, casting himself in the Sydney Carton role: "'This is the finest thing I have ever done,' thought Stuart." But feelings of devotion and protective nobility are not love. Almost every gay boy I know had that awkward adolescent moment when he made his very close female friend doubt her own desirability because he displayed no interest in jumping her bones, even as he himself was thinking, "Well, lip-synching into hairbrushes to the Supremes in her bedroom . . . this is really romantic . . . right?"

Margalo eventually flies from the Little home, possibly tired of waiting around fruitlessly for a little action (the official White version being that the feline peril in the house has become too great). Stuart takes to the open road, ostensibly to find her and make her his own, although he doesn't entirely commit to the he(te)roism of that romantic quest, either. "While I'm about it, I might as well seek my fortune, too," he muses. It's a little bit like resignedly hoping that there might be some cute guys at your engagement party.

It is during these travels that Stuart volunteers to substitute teach at the one-room schoolhouse in a small town. It is perhaps his finest drag performance. As proof of his qualifications for the job, Stuart disappears into the bushes and emerges in striped trousers, a tweed jacket with waistcoat, and a pince-nez. There would be no epithets hurled by the schoolyard boys at his current incarnation.

Stuart has transformed himself into a forbidding yet ultimately kind, highly cultivated pedagogue. The children are rapt by his cunning size, his stern air of authority, and his common touch in talking to them on their own level about deep ethical questions. The subject turns to stealing and he has one of the boys steal a small sachet pillow from one of the girls. When the discussion is over, Stuart turns his attention to the pillow, which attracts him; it might make a lovely, fragrant bed.

> "That's a very pretty thing," said Stuart, trying to hide his eagerness. "You don't want to sell it, do you?"
>
> "Oh, no," replied Katherine. "It was a present to me."
>
> "I suppose it was given you by some boy you met at Lake Hopatcong last summer and it reminds you of him," he said to her, dreamily.
>
> "Yes, it was," said Katherine, blushing.
>
> "Ah," said Stuart. "Summers are wonderful, aren't they, Katherine?"

Everything but breaking out into a rendition of "September Song," by Kurt Weill. Who is this old queen, suffused with nostalgic yearning? Stuart is still only about seven and a half years old at this point, but here he is, suddenly transformed into Mann's Aschenbach, an aging roué, his summers of love and beauty all far behind him now, watching the epicene young Tadzio on the Venice Lido as the plague creeps in.

White gives Stuart one last crack at romance. As he passes through yet another town, a shopkeeper tells Stuart there is someone he should meet—a human girl just his size. Like Edward Everett Horton, the un–Confirmed Bachelor, Stuart doesn't even feign interest anymore. "What's she like . . . Fair, fat, and forty?" he cracks.

But he does agree to meet the tiny Miss Harriet Ames. He purchases a small birch bark canoe, he prepares a picnic. He runs over and over again the details of their assignation, how they will paddle to a lily pad, what swim trunks he will wear, etc. At almost no point in his fantasy does Harriet make much of an appearance. When their date finally arrives and some large, rude boys have laid waste to his toy canoe, he is disconsolate and cannot continue with the charade. Design Queen Stuart has taken control.

Harriet suggests they try to have a nice time just the same. "We could pretend we're fishing," she gamely suggests. " 'I don't want to pretend I'm fishing,' cried Stuart, desperately. 'Besides, look at that mud! Look at it!' He was screaming now." The aesthetics of the date—the true locus of his fixation—have been ruined, the amorous simulacrum has been destroyed. I don't speak with anything resembling personal experience, but surely a damaged canoe should not be enough to ruin a lovely summer night by a river with a willing young woman by one's side. If anything, it sounds like the aquatic equivalent of that old saw "Looks like we're out of gas (heh heh)."

Stuart once more lights out for the territories, again putatively to find Margalo. Even White understands by now that this is probably not a phase. Certain things might just not be in the tiny cards for some. And it was Stuart who taught me, in no small part, that this would be fine, too. Sitting on that classroom floor, legs crossed, I realized that I, like Stuart, might one day hope to walk down a big city street, a little mouse among many, "full of the joy of life and the fear of dogs."

[Salon, *December 21, 1999*]

David Rakoff: Essayist, Mountaineer, "Comic Saint"

TERRY GROSS, HOST: This is *Fresh Air*. I'm Terry Gross.

You may recognize David Rakoff as a regular contributor to the public radio program *This American Life*. He's the guy who spent one Christmas as the anti-Santa, posing as Sigmund Freud in the window of the department store Barneys. Rakoff also writes for *Outside* and *The New York Times Magazine* and has written for *Salon* and *Harper's Bazaar*. Now Rakoff has a new collection of very funny essays called *Fraud*. He's also costarring off-Broadway in Amy and David Sedaris's latest play, *The Book of Liz*. David Sedaris says about Rakoff's new book, "With *Fraud*, David Rakoff manages to successfully pass himself off as the wittiest and most perceptive man in the world."

Let's start with a reading from the first essay in the book.

MR. DAVID RAKOFF: (From *Fraud*) "I do not go outdoors, not more than I have to. As far as I'm concerned, the whole point of living in New York City is indoors. You want greenery, order the spinach.

"Paradoxically, I'm about to climb a mountain on

Christmas Day with a man named Larry Davis. Larry has climbed Mt. Monadnock in southwestern New Hampshire every day for the last five-plus years. I will join him on ascent number 2,065.

"The trip up to New Hampshire will involve a tiny plane from Boston. I tear my medicine cabinet apart like Billie Holiday and still only uncover one Xanax. The hiking boots the outdoor adventure magazine sent me to buy—large ungainly potatolike things that I have been trying to break in for the past four days—cut into my feet and draw blood as if they were lined with cheese graters. I have come to hate these Timberlands with a fervor I usually reserve for people. Just think, the shoes I wouldn't be caught dead in might actually turn out to be the shoes I'm caught dead in."

TERRY: That's David Rakoff reading the first piece in his new collection, *Fraud*. What were you doing climbing this mountain?

DAVID: Well, I was—there is this fellow in southwestern New Hampshire who was climbing Mt. Monadnock every day. And he had done so for five years. And the folks at *Outside* magazine thought they would send someone on the day that seemed most unlikely to climb a mountain, Christmas Day, you know, other than one's birthday or Mother's Day or your anniversary. And they thought "Well, who can we send on Christmas Day?" And, you know, certainly, I identify as Jewish and I don't celebrate Christmas, and, you know, I was free. And they also thought that it would be kind of funny, since they knew that I don't really—I'm not much of a mountain climber; you know, I'm not much of an outdoorsman at all. They like that disconnect as well. So they—they sent me off for a Christmas climb. And there was an ice storm in the middle of it.

TERRY: How'd you do in the ice storm?

DAVID: I did all right in the ice storm, although there was a little bit of a testosterone contest, which is once you get above the tree line, things—you know, above the tree line means there are no trees, so all there is is bare rock. And when ice is falling on bare rock, it tends to sort of glaze it in a somewhat dangerous, perilous fashion. And I had been outfitted by the fellow I was climbing with and his two friends with all this apparatus.

Among the things that were in my backpack were a pair of crampons, which are those, you know, clawed little things that you put on your shoes. And—and I was climbing. I ended up not wearing those Timberlands. I wore my own pair of shoes, which were from the Payless Shoe Source and they're made out of plastic. So they're not the greatest things you would climb a mountain in, but they suited me fine until we got to this glazed rock. And I thought "Well, terrific. Thank goodness for those crampons. Let's all put them on, shall we?" And they wouldn't. And there was this little bit of a— Am I allowed to say "pissing contest" on the radio?

TERRY: Go ahead.

DAVID: Oh, there was a little bit of a pissing contest that I didn't participate in. I never—you know, obviously didn't say, "May we put on our crampons?" Because I was also there as—ostensibly as a journalist. I was—it really wasn't about me. But we didn't put on the crampons and it got rather tough going right near the summit. Our progress was somewhat slowed down because it's hard to find purchase on icy rock.

TERRY: So is the piece that you just read from the piece you wrote for *Outside* magazine, or is this behind—the piece behind the piece that you wrote for *Outside* magazine?

DAVID: This is the—this is behind the piece. This is, you know, the—the highs and the lows behind the piece. This is more of an examination of being sent as an outdoor journalist when, in fact, I had no business doing so.

TERRY: What made you decide to write that?

DAVID: It was an outcropping—the natural outcropping of the fact that when I take notes, when I'm doing a story—and I do so voraciously—I can't stop the wisecracks. And it was also so much at the forefront of my mind. I really—I was far more—sad and somewhat arrogant to admit it—I was far more interested in what I was feeling at that time, it being my first piece, than in the actual mechanics of the reporting. It was so much on my mind that this was an experience that I had not had theretofore and that I should really try and document it. And I also thought that the jokes I was coming up with were pretty good and it sort of seemed like natural material.

TERRY: Now in—in the piece, when you're talking about, you know, how ridiculous you feel as a journalist covering this mountain climber, you say that you feel like a fraud. And you write, "The central drama of my life is actually about being lonely and staying thin. But fraudulence gets a fair amount of play."

DAVID: Yes.

TERRY: Now there are so many people, interesting people, in your acknowledgments that it's hard to imagine you as really being that lonely. Are you also a fraud at being lonely or is that really a part of your life?

DAVID: Well, you know, loneliness, I think, is an interesting thing, but it is not entirely a bad thing, first of all, being lonely. Moreover, I don't think it's the kind of thing that's entirely corrected by the company of other people. You know, one feels—and I certainly also haven't cornered the market on loneliness, but I think that you can feel untethered and adrift in the middle of a crowded room full of one's dear, wonderful friends. And, as you pointed out, I have—you know, I have been the recipient of extraordinary friendship over my life. And certainly in that sense, I'm well cared for.

But that doesn't really go the full distance in counteracting loneliness. But I don't know that that loneliness is eradicable in a way. I think it's something that will always be with one, like double-jointedness or good turnout.

TERRY: Now, in addition to writing, you act. And you've been, among other things, in several pieces written by David and Amy Sedaris.

DAVID: Yes.

TERRY: And you've also had some small parts in films and TV shows, though I think some of these parts were probably left on the cutting room floor.

DAVID: Oh, most invariably, yes. I've been cut out of some very august projects. So . . .

TERRY: One of your pieces in your new collection, *Fraud*, is about a small part you had in a daytime soap. And you say in the piece you know that soap fans would have killed to be on the set with you. But you don't watch these programs. You had no idea who the actors were. And so you— like, being in their presence didn't mean a thing to you. Isn't it strange to be with people who you know are really famous in some circles and you have no idea who they are?

DAVID: It's very strange, and they were extremely conscious of the fact that soap opera fame is fame of a very specific sort. It's actually not unlike public radio fame, you know? It's— there's a very strict subculture to these things. So these people were, to a man and woman, gorgeous New York acting folk. I mean, they were beautiful. They had attenuated limbs and perfect skin, and, you know, when we were in rehearsal room in the morning, all their signifiers were incredibly stylish and urban. There was one woman in a pair of black cigarette pants and a black beret. I mean, she looked like Faye Dunaway in *Bonnie and Clyde*. And she was just fantastic-looking. But there was this vague sense of apology for the fact that they seemed to understand that the nature of their fame was exurban, out there, you know, among a very specific group and, you know, multitudes, but a very specific group of daytime television watchers. And they didn't seem to comport themselves with the kind of "Well, I'm just terribly famous and you should have heard who I am," you know? They immediately saw me for what I was, which is—I mean, at that point, I guess I came in as an actor in New York City. It never would have occurred to them that I would have watched the soap opera.

TERRY: What was your part on the soap?

DAVID: I played a modeling agent from the big city. I think I played a modeling agent from New York City, in fact, or Chicago. I can't—I think it was New York, and I was passing through the town, the fictional town that this soap opera took place in. And, apparently, although I'd never been on the soap opera before, I passed through that town a lot, you know, because I'm always checking out what's happening there fashionwise. It seems to be a hotbed of fashion, apparently. And there was a fashion show, and I was at the country club, which is the main set, you know, the place where they all congregate to act out the little dramas. And there is a fashion show there, and I was just checking things out, and I see one of the town lovelies, you know, I can't remember her name. I think I gave her a pseudonym, obviously, in the book. I didn't want to incriminate anyone. And I see her and I am deeply interested in her in both a professional and, I thought, you know, it helped my character, a possibly, sort of predatory, vulpine kind of way. And I try—I'm insinuatingly unctuous and I try and get her to, you know, leave this Podunk two-horse town and follow me to New York City or Chicago, I can't remember, and participate in this small but terribly important fashion trip that I'm organizing. And she—she rejects my advances, but

I'm, you know, slitheringly immune to, you know, the cold-shoulder actress. I then leave.

I—I never appeared again, sadly.

TERRY: Did you have any great lines in the part that stick out in your mind?

DAVID: I'm trying to remember my lines. It was something like, "I feel like I'm discovering a new talent. I mean, the way you wear a dress, your look," just things like that, just fantastically good, slimy—yeah, he was a slimeball. And I was wearing my own clothes, of course, because they give you ten extra dollars if you bring your own costume.

TERRY: Oh, you're kidding.

DAVID: Yeah, so I was acting with my house keys on my person, which was . . .

TERRY: Huh. Now did you look different from the rest of the cast because they're all these afternoon soap stars and you're not?

DAVID: I looked so very different from the rest of the cast. It was really—you know, they're gorgeous. They're not just pretty. They're heart-stoppingly beautiful people. Their faces are mathematically precise, you know, cross-culturally beautiful. And I am, in a word, not. So it—you know, I—I also have a certain kind of ethnic look. I have a certain care-worn Jewish quality to my face. So, yeah, I did—I did sort of stand out in that way. Happily, there were a lot of extras at this particular episode, because they were playing the other people in the audience at the fashion show. And they all tended to be senior citizens, because there's this vast network of lonely seniors in New York whose kick is to go be extras at soap operas. They all knew one another. And they had all clearly worked on all the other soaps that filmed in New York. So they all knew one another. And then there was me and then there was this aesthetic super race.

TERRY: You write in your piece that the typical parts you get are either "Jewy McHebrew" or "Fudgy Packer." Would you describe each?

DAVID: "Fudgy McPacker," yeah.

TERRY: "Fudgy McPacker," yeah. Would you describe . . .

DAVID: They're Scots. They're two Scottish clans. Well, the McHebrews are your prototypical Jewish clan, so I was sent for one of two parts. I no longer really act with any frequency except for the Sedaris [play]. Otherwise, you know, I don't get sent on auditions. But Jewy McHebrew is generally a kind of a care-worn—I already said—oh, "care-worn" twice in the same interview. I'm so sorry. But he's kind of an inquiring, furrowed-browed, bookish-type who can either be the kind of guy who an— He speaks rather quickly with the kind of inquiring people-of-the-word, people-of-the-book. And he says things like, with dentated final consonants, so he says, *"Papa, I can't believe it. You sold the store?"* Or he plays the kind of humanist rabbi–type who says, you know, *"And so we eat the bitter herbs. Why? Because it is to remember the bitterness of our days in Egypt.*" You know, that's the Jewy McHebrew type, generally. Or he's a psychiatrist and like, *"How do you understand that?"*

Whereas Fudgy McPacker is, you know, the gay character, and he can take a various variety of forms. There's, you know, supercilious Fudgy McPacker, and he's generally a hotel concierge or a makeup clerk or waiter and he drolls. He's more like, *"No, we're not carrying that this season. Next,"* you know? And he's just like too bored, too cool for school.

But there's the other Fudgy McPacker–type who is gaining great currency right now culturally, and he is the lovable queen who everybody loves. He gets the best lines. He's replaced, for want of a better term, the fat girl within the dramatic pantheon, you know? Fudgy McPacker, the funny one, now gets the best lines, like, *"Did somebody say swim team?"* And, you know, that becomes his catchphrase, and they put that on T-shirts and then he's—you know, ten years hence, he's opening malls and he's a bitter, bitter, bitter sociopath as a result.

TERRY: A bitter McPacker.

DAVID: It's a bitter McPacker. Fudgy McBitter. And—or the other one is he's dispensing clear-eyed, you know, romantic advice, not being privy to romance himself because, of course, you know, he has no actual sexuality, and he says things like, "Can't you see he's in love with you? Just *tell* him." You know, and then they kiss and then it's cut to Fudgy McPacker and he sort of cocks his head—oh, I'm sorry, it's not cut to Fudgy McPacker; it's cut to the dog. And the dog cocks his head, goes, "Er?" And cue the dog or cue Fudgy McPacker. Either way, terrific, terrific parts to get and be sent on, which is, essentially, why I stopped being an actor.

TERRY: Well, what would you do when you were cast in a part if it was obviously a stereotype? You knew the voice of the stereotype, you could do the stereotype perfectly.

DAVID: And I wouldn't do it. And—and, resultantly, I didn't get many parts. And I also, you know, wasn't—I—I—I didn't—frequently when I would be asked to audition for things, I would decline to even go into the audition. And, you know, if you do that enough times, then you stop being asked, which is precisely what happened for me, which was okay. I mean, it was—it was essentially a conscious choice on my part, you know, not—not to do that.

TERRY: So what's the problem?—that when casting directors see you, all they can think about is Jewy McHebrew or Fudgy McPacker?

DAVID: Essentially, yeah. Essentially, I think—I think that it's their—and this is not to say anything against casting directors—I think there's kind of—generally a kind of risk aversion, less so onstage. You know, onstage, you can be a number of things. Currently, I'm in this play by Amy and David Sedaris that's running till June 1 in New York, and I get to play four different characters, and only one of them is, in fact, Fudgy McPacker. But because it's written by David, it's a joy to play. You know, it's a comment on that entire genre. But the other people that I play are, you know, a very stern kind of deacon in a quasi-Amish order. And the other one is a cockney football hooligan with a heart of gold, and the other one is the, you know, coverall-wearing Lenny from *Of Mice and Men*, soul of the working class, you know, sweetheart doofus. You know, so onstage there's a great deal more latitude.

But in television and movies, let's face it, there's an enormous amount of money riding on these things and so a certain risk aversion is only expected. You know, I—I don't blame them, but there's not, as a result, a terrible abundance of imagination in terms of casting.

TERRY: David Sedaris has a quote on the jacket of your book, recommending the book, you know, a blurb. And Sedaris writes, "On first meeting him, I was struck by his ability"— he's talking about you—"On first meeting him, I was struck by his ability to impersonate any living creature and retain long stretches of movie dialogue. He's a human tape recorder." Do you think of yourself that way?

DAVID: It's certainly always been something I could do from childhood. You know, and there—I think it's just one of those, like, double-jointed things. Yeah, I always managed to get dialogue for some reason. It . . .

TERRY: Where's—are there certain movie scenes that were really significant to you when you were young that you memorized and that just are a kind of permanent part of your memory now?

DAVID: Oh, sure. I mean, there's that scene where—I mean, and now, of course, I'm going to have to paraphrase and various *Double Indemnity* fans all over are going to be writing WHYY, "He got that wrong." But it's when Fred

MacMurray, as Walter Neff, comes to meet Phyllis Dietrichson, played by Barbara Stanwyck, and her wheels are turning and she's understanding, finally, that she has an out from this loveless marriage. She can make a lot of money. And he's, in turn, interested in her, because she's this sultry, blond pistol of a thing, you know, who's come in barely dressed by the standards of that time. And he's making a pass at her, and she finally tells him that, you know, her husband is going to be there tomorrow night when he can come back and see him.

And he says, "Your husband?"

She says, "You're interested in seeing him, weren't you?"

And he says, "Well, I was, but it's kind of wearing off, if you know what I mean."

She says, "There's a speed limit in this state, Mr. Neff."

"Oh, really, officer? How fast was I going?"

"I'd say about ninety."

"Suppose you get off your bike and give me a ticket."

"Suppose I let you off with a warning."

"Suppose you rap me across the knuckles."

Oh, *damn*, I got it all wrong, Terry. Oh, god. It's in my wallet, but I'm not carrying my wallet today because it's so hot, so I'm only carrying money and ID.

TERRY: It's in your wallet?

DAVID: Yeah.

TERRY: Why is it in your wallet?

DAVID: I keep—oh, you know, should I meet my maker in front of a bus and people can rifle through my wallet and see that I was the kind of terribly interesting person who kept a page of *Double Indemnity* dialogue in my wallet, and then they could say, "What a waste." I have no idea, actually, why it's in my wallet, but it is actually in my wallet, and I will occasionally take it out and, you know, read it like a little mantra. Oh.

TERRY: David Rakoff's new collection of funny essays is called *Fraud.* He'll be back in the second half of the show. I'm Terry Gross and this is *Fresh Air.*

(Sound bite of music)

DAVID: *(reading)* "If psychoanalysis was late-nineteenth-century secular Judaism's way of constructing spiritual meaning in a post-religious world, and retail is the late twentieth century's way of constructing meaning in a post-religious world, what does it mean that I'm impersonating the father of psychoanalysis in a store window to commemorate a religious holiday?"

TERRY: That's David Rakoff reading from "Christmas Freud," about the Christmas that he impersonated Sigmund Freud in the window of a Manhattan department store. It's one of the essays included in his new book, *Fraud.* I asked him to explain his brief job impersonating Freud.

DAVID: Well, there is a department store in New York called Barneys, which is a very fancy, trendy department store, and their windows are always—they're closer to artistic installations. And it was under the stewardship of this really brilliant art director named Simon Doonan, who turned out to be—who turns out to be an acquaintance of mine, a friend of mine. And I asked him one October what the windows were going to be, and he said, well, they were devoted to various things—blonds of the twentieth century, Frank Sinatra, the beat poets, Martin Luther King, and Sigmund Freud. And he said, "And we wanted to put in a live Sigmund Freud into the window, but we can't seem to find anyone." And, of course, my mind immediately—I all but pounced across the dinner table, you know, to volunteer for the job because it just seemed like such ideal material, and such a strange experience and just kind of a lark. And I volunteered. They didn't have any other volunteers, actually.

And, you know, as I described myself earlier, facially, I'm not unlike Freud, you know. And I grew my little winter goatee, and I sort of looked like a young Freud. And I sat for four weekends before Christmas each day for about four or five hours, sitting in the window of Barneys department store in a kind of a mock-up of Freud's study that was also, you know, artistically reified. There were video monitors, there was a baby carriage that had a video camera on it going back and forth on a mechanized track that was a large black-and-white spiral, like the old sort of alienist hypnosis things. I mean, there was just marvelous activity in this window, and then there was me in a chair. And I started doing it. It was fascinating, but terrifying because you're so exposed in this window, and I had nothing to do beyond read the paper and take notes of my experience and read from *The Interpretation of Dreams*.

And I realized I couldn't do that for five hours a day for four weekends from—you know, I just couldn't do it, and so I decided to start seeing patients. And all my friends signed up, and we took it fairly seriously. They were scheduled for forty-five-minute sessions. And because the couch faced away from me, in true psychoanalytic fashion, and because also it sort of was angled somewhat away from the window and because there was sound insulation, we couldn't really hear the street. There was something very close and cozy—not B&B cozy, urban-department-store-window cozy. And it was something very sequestered and cloistered about the window, and we had some actual conversations. And, you know, uncharacteristically, these weren't conversations where I was the focus. I really asked them about themselves. And it was actually kind of a strange experience because it stopped being entirely a joke.

TERRY: Now, you're the son of a psychiatrist and your other parent you describe as a doctor who also does psychotherapy. Were you brought up with the lingo?

DAVID: I was certainly brought up with the lingo, but only— it's comparable to children of plumbers being conversant with the components of a toilet, but I don't know that they necessarily know more about toilets than you or I. I was brought up with the lingo, but I don't know that it was entirely part of the culture of my family. I don't come from an overly introspective fa— It's not the sort of media representation of the psychiatric family.

TERRY: Well, you write that you've been in therapy for many, many years. Did you initiate it or did your parents?

DAVID: Oh, I did. I'll—you know, I don't—because I don't really write about my family so much, I'm a tad uncomfortable talking about my family, but I'll just say that it's not the kind of thing where—in my family, it's not a foregone conclusion that one would go into therapy. It was definitely my choice.

TERRY: What do you think has helped you more, talk or medicine?

DAVID: Oh, how fascinating. Do you mean psychically, emotionally?

TERRY: Psychologically, yeah.

DAVID: Talk or medicine? I think it's been a blissful combination of the two, Terry.

TERRY: You know, there's a couple of mentions of Xanax in your new book . . .

DAVID: Yes.

TERRY: . . . and this is a pill that you take for anxiety or for panic. And I was thinking, you know, reading your book, you have such a good, really funny grasp of every situation that you find yourself in, and you're able to really put it in a perspective, in either, like, an absurd perspective or finally maybe in a more moving, reflective perspective. And so one might think, reading this, that you just have the measure of things in such an adequate way that you wouldn't need something like Xanax.

DAVID: Oh, it should be noted I don't actually take the Xanax. I just—I keep it . . .

TERRY: Yes.

DAVID: . . . totemically on my person, not unlike a page of dialogue from *Double Indemnity*. The Xanax is a prophylactic, should I lose my mind. You know, if need be, if I really need to medicate, if I'm about to freak out, I know it's there, wrapped in some tinfoil in a little pillbox in my change purse in my right front pocket. So it's always there. I rarely take the Xanax. Frequently, I give the Xanax—I mean, I give it to people when they're in times of trouble, but I've essentially had the same seven Xanax for a long, long time. I rarely, rarely take it. But just the knowledge that it's there is enough to stave off a full-blown anxiety attack. Also, I'm pretty good at, you know, how to regulate my breathing, you know, when I'm freaking out. I know how to do that. But I probably wouldn't know how to do that as well as I do without the sort of—it's like those very allergic people who have those pens full of, you know, adrenaline in their wallets—or not their wallets, in their purses and stuff, you know, so they know that if they eat a peanut, they'll be able to just stab themselves with it? I'm like that.

TERRY: So what's something where you actually needed a Xanax?

DAVID: Oh, it's so embarrassing to admit it. All right. I had to take a Xanax—oh, my gosh. Here's where I had to take a Xanax. I was sent by *Harper's Bazaar* to attend the couture shows in Paris, which were extraordinary. It was like one long Pepé Le Pew cartoon. It was just so French and so stylish and fantastic. But what they don't tell you about the couture shows is they all start late, really late, they're all really crowded and you are really a pawn to the designer's vision. So there was one designer who decided that the École des Beaux-Arts Paris, the Grand Hall, needed to be red. It all had to be red, red, red, you know. So we're sitting there in this incredibly crowded train station–sized room, wherein to get to your seat, you had to go over the runway and up some bleachers—you know, you're trapped.

You're literally trapped in a room full of thousands of people. The temperature is climbing steadily. There is no fire exit. It's all red, so all the windows are closed, so you're essentially in an oven. You're a rotisserie chicken.

The crowds keep on coming in. The thing is not beginning and, it should be said, you're not allowed to go—even as a journalist, you're not allowed to go to the couture shows dressed in normal clothing. You have to wear a suit in July in Paris, in France, where air conditioning is not the kind of American obsession, you know. So the heat is rapidly rising, and I think, "I am going to lose my mind." And so I actually took a Xanax before that show, because I really needed one.

TERRY: But did the Xanax dim your powers of perception that you needed for the piece?

DAVID: Not even. And, you know, I think that I actually had the Xanax for so long that they didn't even work physiologically, but just the fact that I had actually allowed a bit of chalky substance to dissolve under my tongue—I mean, it could have been chalk for all I knew—helped me maintain and it didn't affect, impede my note-taking capacities either. So, in fact, I think that I'm traveling around with seven little pieces of water-soluble—saliva-soluble—gravel in my wallet.

TERRY: One of your pieces is about when you were in your twenties and you were diagnosed with Hodgkin's disease, which is a form of lymph cancer and you required chemotherapy and radiation. How are you at being sick and at dealing with pain, and weakness, and fear?

DAVID: Well, I am—how am I now?

TERRY: No, how were you then?

DAVID: How was I then? *Then* I was—and I say this in not a remotely complimentary way—I was adept at it. I was . . . iron-fisted and funny and bright and kind of adamantine in this impermeable way.

So to the world at large, I think I manifested as being eminently humorous and terrifically stoic. Internally, I was similarly so. I was not—I was never bored with myself. I mean, my mind was racing. I mean, that was really one of the astonishing aspects of it. I simply had something to think about *all* the time. You know, there was no staring off into space during that year and a half of my life. But in terms of the larger questions of possible mortality or illness or whatever, I really—they didn't come up. They didn't bubble to the surface. My pond, such as it was, was iced over *very* efficiently. And certainly, there was a—you know, the unfortunate dividend was that once it was over, I experienced a bit of a collapse. You know, I guess it's much like that old mythic story of the mothers who can lift cars off their babies? You know, it must be *hell* on their rotator cuffs the next day. You know, it's that kind of thing. It was . . . but I was very—I was very funny that year, in the worst kind of way.

TERRY: Did you see yourself as Camille at all?

DAVID: No, no. I'm not . . .

TERRY: Not that she was funny.

DAVID: No, you mean sort of languishing neurasthenically against starched white sheets while the wind blows through the curtains?

TERRY: And just being remarkably, you know, just like beautiful and adored and . . .

DAVID: The only Camille—I felt adored. Certainly, I was the subject of great adoration, and that was, in part, due to the fact that it's cosmetically far more attractive to be funny and stoic and brittlely witty than it is to be coughing and vomiting. You know, people enjoy being around somebody who makes, you know, Eve Arden–like jokes about their own illness. In terms of beauty, it's interesting you say that.

There was a point at which I was extremely thin. I'm five-ten and I was down to about a hundred and fifteen pounds. And at that point, the illness was fairly prog—

TERRY: That's skeletal; that's not thin.

DAVID: Yeah, exactly. And we didn't really entirely understand how progressed the illness was for various reasons. It's easy to sort of lose sight of goals and stuff like that. But I was so thin and also my brain was clearly, you know, decompensating in some certain way, but I felt so attractive. It's a terrible thing to admit. And it sends a terrible lesson to our nation's young people, but I really did feel—at five-ten and a hundred fifteen pounds, I thought I just looked fantastic. I couldn't stop looking at myself.

TERRY: That's kind of strange now 'cause it sounds like—I mean, because you were beyond thin. I mean, looking back now . . .

DAVID: Mm-hmm. You mean when I see photographs of myself do I get scared?

TERRY: Yeah. Well, do you think you still looked real good at a hundred and fifteen pounds?

DAVID: Yeah. Sadly, yeah.

TERRY: You do?

DAVID: Yeah.

TERRY: Well, you . . .

DAVID: I'm not proud to admit that.

TERRY: You write in your book one of the central dramas of your life is about staying thin. I thought maybe that would have mattered to you less after nearly wasting away.

DAVID: I would love to say that it mattered to me less, and it probably does matter to me less. Certainly I'd rather go on living than waste away and die, and to say otherwise would merely be glib reductionism. But what's really rather interesting about experiences wherein one—I guess, whether you like to admit it at the time or not, faces one's mortality—is that there is an impermeable membrane. You know, you're either in the land of the sick or you're in the land of the well. And for a good few months after I became well, you know, after the final diagnostic measure and they cut me open and took out a scarred, burntout lymph node that was, you know, like a used flashbulb, you know, that the chemo had worked its magic on it and it was now a vestigial *whatever,* no longer able to hurt me.

So I was deemed well. For a few months after that, or maybe a few years after that, I was capable of still understanding the world of the ill. You know, I could understand that. But even when you're in the world of the ill, it's not a twenty-four–seven kind of thing. You know, when I was first diagnosed, I thought, "That's it. I'm not engaging in any more of that social crap. I am going to call them as I see them," you know, all that kind of stuff. And then, you know—

TERRY: Yeah.

DAVID: —a day later, I was, like, "Great dress!" You know, so you can't not do that. You can't stop—it's too—I guess, the life force and all the artifices associated with it, it's a very powerful structure. So, you know, the impulse to be skinny, such as it is and for whatever bundled, you know, impulses and sicknesses that speaks to, you know, it's not entirely countered by the fact that I once was sick.

I also have a strange relationship to the nature of my illness.

TERRY: What do you mean?

DAVID: Well, it was, you know. I wasn't as sick as some people are or can get. You know, I had a highly curable form of cancer. I mean—

TERRY: Well . . .

DAVID: Even saying cancer, it sort of seems—I mean, it's in the book and I'm not joking when I wrote it. Saying that word seems melodramatic in a way.

TERRY: Well, you still were pretty darn sick and went through . . .

DAVID: Oh, sure. Yeah.

TERRY: . . . chemo and radiation and so . . .

DAVID: Yeah.

TERRY: Yes. No point in making too light of that. I have one last question for you. I think you're really funny. And I'm wondering if you can kind of mentally keep yourself amused when you're kind of alone with time on your hands.

DAVID: Oh, yeah, I'm terrific company for myself. I can just, you know, sit there giggling all the livelong day. No, it's— yeah, I do think—generally, my twin impulses of the two default directories of my emotional life are to either make jokes about something or to be sad about something and sometimes simultaneously. *Sad* jokes.

TERRY: And does your therapist ever say, "This humor is a defense mechanism. You must pierce through it and get to the emotion behind it"?

DAVID: Sure. Yes. Yes, definitely. And we—you know, but I will say with no fear of contradiction, I was his funniest client. And I essentially made him admit as much at one point. But, you know, that's only part of the work, you know, but, yeah, certainly humor is a complete defense mechanism.

TERRY: But that's okay.

DAVID: Oh, yeah, I mean, what are you going to do without your defense mechanisms? You know, that's what makes one human, I think.

TERRY: David Rakoff. His new collection of funny essays is called *Fraud*.

[Fresh Air *interview, WHYY Radio, January 14, 2001.
Translation copyright © 2007 NPR.*]

Fu Fighters

Glenn Close and I are head over heels. Ass over teakettle, we tumble from our raft into the spin cycle of the Rio Futaleufú. It is a perfect day: The sun is shining and the river is beautiful—a shimmering, effervescent foam that glints like a shower of sapphires as it closes over my head. Suddenly I'm hit with a preconscious instinct, my own reverse Elephant Man moment. I am not a man, I am an animal: Follow the bubbles to the surface!

The froth is disorienting, churning in every direction, with no clear way up. But flotation being what it is, the combination of our life jackets and the powerful arms of Robert F. Kennedy, Jr. (Bobby for short; president of the Waterkeeper Alliance, senior attorney for the Natural Resources Defense Council), does the trick. Glenn and I are hoisted, dripping, back into the boat, our ordeal all of five seconds from start to finish.

Cutting through the green, snowcapped Andes in southern Chile like a satin ribbon, the "Fu" is nirvana for paddlers. Along with mind-bending Class V rapids, the river has two unique features: On its 120-mile, 8,000-foot descent to the Pacific, the Fu's meltwater stops in several lakes, which simultaneously warm it—at 61 degrees, it is considerably more temperate than most glacially fed rivers—and filter out almost all the silt. This accounts for the Fu's supreme clarity. By the time the water reaches the riverbed, it's an astounding teal blue, more Caribbean than Patagonian.

This is our last day on—and briefly in—the river. Glenn, fifty-six, grins widely as we resume our positions in the raft, her already enviable bone structure somehow enhanced by this brush with mortality. I wish I could say the same for myself. I've traveled halfway around the world to write about celebrities behaving badly on an expedition meant to bring attention to an endangered river. But most of them—Woody Harrelson, Julia Louis-Dreyfus, Richard Dean Anderson—didn't show up. And the ones who did—Bobby; his wife, Mary; and their longtime pals Glenn and New York hotelier André Balazs—all brought their kids. So I'm heading back with new friends and a story of a dam development scheme that seems more sleeping giant than clear and present danger. But not before having the crap scared out of me.

Travel with a Kennedy and you occasionally feel like you're on the road with a major brand: Mickey Mouse, say, or the Coca-Cola logo. There's a surreal quality to meeting RFK, Jr., for the first time, at JFK. Kennedy, forty-nine, has assembled two dozen people for a trip that will be part adventure tourism, part consciousness raising: The Futaleufú is facing a proposed dam project by multinational corporation Endesa, Chile's largest electric company.

We are being led by Earth River Expeditions, which started running outfitted trips down the river in 1992. Based in upstate New York, the organization has been buying up property along the Fu to keep it out of Endesa's hands. Earth River currently owns about 1,500 acres—land goes for about $3,000 per—upon which about ten homesteaders live. The agenda behind a trip like ours is that we will return home and, through word of mouth, send others down the Fu, enhancing its value as a well-traveled ecotourist destination and making it a viable economic alternative to a hydroelectric dam. Or there's the best-case scenario, from Earth River's standpoint: One of the wealthier rafters in our group will buy a piece of land and put conservation easements on it so that it can never be sold to a power company. (Endesa is a corporation, not the government; it would have to own any land it proposes to flood.)

Earth River's co-founders are Eric Hertz, forty-eight, an American with the youthful, blue-eyed friendliness of Greg Kinnear, and Robert Currie, forty-four, a Santiago native of Scottish and Chilean parentage, with the physique and demeanor of a benign Hercules. Hertz waits in a cataraft for ejectees at the bottom of each set of rapids, and Currie is our trip leader. We'll be on the Fu for six days in three rafts, starting at Infierno Canyon—roughly twenty-five miles from the river's headwaters at Lake Amutui Quimei, in Argentina's Sierra Nevada—and descending forty-five feet per mile for the next twenty-five miles down to the rapids of Terminador. Glenn and I are in the grown-ups' boat, behind Bobby and Mary, who have been taking rafting trips together since 1977, before they were even sweethearts.

Currie mans the oars in the back and precedes each run with a few minutes of river reading. On our first day, as we near Alfombra Magica ("Magic Carpet")—our first Class IV challenge—he points to the geography of chaos roiling below.

"We'll ride down that ridge of water and then we'll typewriter across and back up when we get to the second drop," he says. "Then we'll paddle over to the eddy, which will stop our drifting."

"I knew an Eddie once who stopped my drifting for a while," Glenn deadpans.

As we sit at the top of each rapids, I can always see exactly what Robert is talking about. Once we're in it, though, it's a barreling spume of foamy white and Scope green. Where are those watery landmarks he described? I have no idea. It doesn't matter, really—he can see them, and that's what counts. As his crew, we have only one job: to do what he tells us. More often than not, that means paddle like hell. And even though at times it seems impossible that our efforts could be doing much of anything—those moments when our paddles stew nothing but the air as the river drops out from under us—we are apparently Currie's power source.

And his mouthpiece. Kennedy is somewhat deaf in his left ear, and the river is loud. It falls to me to scream out Currie's instructions. "Back it up! Stop! Okay, dig in, dig in, dig in!" Later, when I get back home, I'm sent a copy of the video of our trip. I am talking in every shot, as if spooling out a monologue of fear. But there's no way to run the Fu without making a sound of one sort or another. Glenn laughs exuberantly, while I opt for yee-hawing in what I hope sounds like an approximation of "Isn't this fun?"

It *is* fun, in large part because I'm not steering. Currie's skill gives the danger a virtual quality; it's more like watching an exciting but consequence-free film of a river than being on one. I start to feel downright cocky.

Earth River has three camps on the Fu, where we will stay over the next six days. The first is Camp Mapu Leufu, a rolling meadow that ends abruptly at the edge of a cliff, its springy grass littered with ox pies. Our routine is less than strenuous: Each evening we peel off our wetsuits and head for the hot tub. There is one at every camp. What initially seemed like so much Marin County nonsense proves indispensable, our best chance to get warm after a day spent on a chilly river. We're treated like true adventure pashas—beer, snacks, excellent meals. We can even schedule a massage in our tents. With about a dozen children, ranging from seven to eighteen, we spend hours telling stories around the fire every night.

"A man checks into the Plaza Hotel in New York," Kennedy says one evening in his gravelly Jimmy Stewart–like sob. "He eats too much for dinner and goes to bed. He wakes up a few hours later to find himself marinating in diarrhea." That line is a big crowd-pleaser. Kennedy goes on: Horrified, the man throws his sheets out the window. They land on a wino, who wrestles them off and confusedly tells a cop he thinks he "just beat the crap out of a ghost."

There is grown-up talk as well. A good deal of it about politics and, not surprisingly—given that we are traveling with Kennedys and a bona fide movie star—some really choice gossip. I'm sworn to secrecy, but it doesn't really make a difference: I don't recognize most of the names. By the time I'm back in my tent, all I can remember are "World Bank" and "*Vanity Fair* airbrushed his Speedo bulge." Our wetsuits are hung overnight near the fire. By morning, the neoprene isn't exactly dry, but it's taken on a comforting bacony quality. The white noise of the Futaleufú is good for sleeping, though it also serves to wipe clean whatever confidence I gained the previous day. I wake newly terrified, as does Glenn, I'm pleased to find out. This is as it should be, according to Currie. Especially because today, our first full day of Class V rapids, we are running Infierno Canyon.

"The day you think about Infierno without your hands doing this"—Robert shakes his like Al Jolson singing "Mammy"—"is the day to quit rafting the Fu." This is no place for false bravado, he tells us, and seeing the sheer rock walls of Infierno up close, it would be hard to muster any. Even the names of the rapids suggest meeting your maker: Purgatorio, Danza de los Angeles, Escala de Jacobo. Once in, the only way out of Infierno is by running it. We couldn't portage here even if we wanted to. Yesterday I was aware of the river and others in the raft; today my peripheral vision narrows to nothing. It's just me and the end of my paddle.

The rapids don't take very long—or at least they seem not to. Time accordions when you're on the river. The water widens out and quiets. Vegetation creeps back onto the cliffs, which get lower, opening out to gently sloping forest and pastures in places. We throw a Nerf football from boat to boat. (Well, they do; over the years I've perfected my "Please don't throw the ball to me" face.)

Kennedy fly-fishes off the side of the raft and catches a ten-inch rainbow. When he removes the hook, the trout slips out of his hands and into the limited freedom of our boat, where it spends the afternoon swimming back and forth in the bilge. Sadly for this fish, the Fu is not a catch-and-release river; by nightfall it's headed down one of the most famous intestinal tracts in America.

It is one of only two fish I see the whole week. The other is an ancient bull of a salmon, easily forty pounds, which swims unmolested through the frigid waters. I also see two birds, kingfishers both. And that's it. Not one insect, rodent, or small reptile. The Fu's food chain appears to be as exclusive as our group: crowded at the top. There are apparently two types of deer, one subspecies of puma that eats the deer, and an alien population of wild boar brought over from Africa by the Argentinians. The pigs, huge omnivores with no natural predators, are of such mythic proportions, Hertz tells me, they can upend a man on a horse.

Such a preternaturally shy ecosystem wouldn't seem to encourage living off the land. This might account for the short history of the region, which was only settled in 1905, when the Chilean government offered its citizens land grants to stave off annexation by Argentina. Chilean settlers found no recent evidence of inhabitants, but indigenous people must have lived here at one time or another—Futaleufú is, after all, a Mapuche Indian word meaning "great waters" or "grand river." Until Chile blasted a road through the region from the coastal fishing village of Chaitén, in 1986, the only way in by car was via Argentina. Even today, a scant eight hundred people live along the Fu—five hundred of them in the hamlet of Futaleufú and the rest on small farms or backcountry homesteads. All of which makes it an easy target for a dam project.

The vibe on our trip is fairly urgent—well, as urgent as you can get sitting in a hot tub, sipping Chilean cabernet—fueled as it is by the cautionary tale of the Bío-Bío. Home to Chile's indigenous Pehuenche people, the Bío-Bío River valley was once the Chilean equivalent of the Grand Canyon and one of the world's premier whitewater destinations. Endesa—with the Chilean government's blessing and a loan from the International Finance Corporation (IFC), a subsidiary of the World Bank—planned a series of six dams on the river, starting with the Pangue, a 450-megawatt operation that would create a 1,250-acre reservoir.

In 1992, Kennedy, along with lawyers from the NRDC, pointed out to the IFC the major flaws in Endesa's plans, including the fact that the dam was to be built in the middle of an earthquake zone at the base of two volcanoes. The World Bank, already under scrutiny for funding some environmentally questionable projects, launched its own internal investigation. In the end, an international coalition that included the NRDC, the Chilean Commission on Human Rights, and

Grupo de Acción por el Bío-Bío, a grassroots organization, managed to keep Endesa from building all six dams. However, the Pangue devastated much of the Bío-Bío's whitewater.

Endesa wants to build two dams on the Futaleufú that would bracket the river like concrete parentheses. The 800-megawatt La Cuesta facility would sprout up about nine miles from the village of Puerto Ramirez, our take-out. The 400-megawatt Los Coigü dam would sit just below Infierno Canyon, gateway to the river's prime whitewater. Above that dam, local farms would be flooded under seventy-five feet of water; below the dam, there's a distinct possibility that the rapids could slow to a trickle. As for the power generated, a good portion of it would probably be sold to Argentina.

In addition to trying to keep property out of Endesa's hands, Earth River is waging its battle in the court of public opinion. One of the perks of being a river pioneer is getting to name rapids, and in 1991, when Hertz and Currie made their first descent of the Fu, they were vigilant about giving them Spanish or Mapuche names. (Endesa had tried to characterize the campaign to save the Bío-Bío as an affluent gringo insurgency, pointing out that some rapids, like Climax, were identified by English vulgarities.) The harsh reality of eminent domain, however, is that if the Chilean government really wants to hand over the Fu to Endesa, no amount of privately held riverfront property will make a difference.

Which makes it hard not to feel like a play-acting gringo insurgent. I had envisioned a trip where the whitewater thrills would be mixed with white knuckles of a different sort, as we bravely faced down bulldozers and sand hogs, blocking their way with our bodies, making us truly worthy of those long hot-tub soaks at the end of the day. But when I ask Hertz how dire the threat is, he puts it at about ten years off.

"Endesa hasn't been buying up the land, and they need every piece they're going to flood," he tells me. "I think the fairest thing to say about the dam is that it's in the future. People shouldn't think they have to race down here, because it's not true. But the more people who see the river . . ."

He's not being a Pollyanna. When I call Endesa, in Santiago, I hear much the same thing. One energy planner guesses that getting these dams built by 2020 would be "optimistic." "These projects are not confirmed," adds Endesa communications manager Rodolfo Nieto. "They are only a far, far, far possibility."

Perhaps, but it can't hurt to get a seventeen-year head start when trying to halt a multinational hydroelectric concern. Kennedy certainly seems to think so.

"I've just seen this so often that it's not even a question to me," he says. "The locals get trampled. Dam projects like this consume their economies, devour them, and essentially liquidate them for cash. I'm worried about losing the Futaleufú."

I'm worried, too, but mainly because it's our last day on the river and we're about to run Terminador, the most challenging rapids of the trip. We take on some preliminary Class IVs in the morning—Caos and La Isla, which is where Glenn and I take our spill. It shakes me up more than I care to admit.

"How are you feeling?" Currie asks as we wait in an eddy above the rapids. Scared, we tell him. He demonstrates a Chilean gesture for our fear, bringing his fingertips together like a blossom closing up for the night.

"Get it?" he asks.

Kennedy guesses that it's our balls shrinking down to the size of cocktail peanuts. No, Currie corrects us, it's a sphincter tightening.

"That's not a sphincter!" I shout. "A sphincter goes like

this." I make a fist and close it up tight like Señor Wences from *The Ed Sullivan Show.* S'alright?

Not really. I can't remember much about Terminador, except that the force of the water seemed much more aggressive than on the other rapids, as if it were holding a grudge—the difference between a schoolyard bully and a Teamster with a baseball bat. It moved with such speed and magnitude that we had to stay close to the bank, which meant negotiating a steep drop backward at one point. Thankfully, Kennedy waits until we're through it to tell me that it's the most dangerous commercially run rapids in the world.

No matter, we're alive and on to Himalayas, which is, by comparison, quite safe but possibly more thrilling. The waves are solid slopes of water easily twenty feet high, judging by our eighteen-foot-long raft. We ride up and down three or four of the aqueous mountains and we're out, drifting safely in the eddy—wet, exhilarated, and done. Our last night in camp is a traditional Chilean asado. Two lambs—recently gamboling on the meadow near our tents, no doubt—have been slaughtered, butterflied on racks, and roasted on an open fire. The portions are medieval: great haunches and joints. We sit around a large square table, tearing into our food like Neanderthals.

After dinner, standing in the meadow at Mapu Leufu, there are more stars than I've ever seen, and that includes the pot-enhanced heavens of the "Laser Floyd" show at the planetarium. "Wow, wow, wow," I whisper. I can't even hear myself over the rush of the river.

Here is what I lost on the Fu: two pairs of sunglasses, a water bottle, a carabiner, and my useless quick-dry towel, which swings, probably still damp, on a line somewhere.

Here's what I didn't lose: my life.

Here's what I got: a new hat. When we pull the rafts out

at Puerto Ramirez, Kennedy presents me with a baseball cap bearing the crest of the Swiss flag with an image of a tiny airplane clearing an alp. An adventurer's cap.

"You don't like my Krispy Kreme hat?"

"You're so much more than a donut," he replies.

He's wrong, of course. I'm so much less.

The following letter was from David Rakoff, the author of the above article, on his return from the trip.

DEAR ERIC,

Even though I'm a correspondent for *Outside* magazine— I'm on the masthead—I am frightened of everything. That's my bailiwick at the magazine, in fact; they send me to do things that scare the hell out of me. But nothing seemed as terrifying to me as rafting the Futaleufú. The minute I accepted the assignment, I regretted it. I spent the weeks leading up to my departure crossing Manhattan streets a little less energetically, in hopes that a cab might hit me and break my leg and get me out of it. Then, in the lobby of the hotel in Puerto Montt, someone hooked up their computer and showed me a video clip of Himalayas, which would be one of the rapids on our trip. The waves were fifteen to twenty feet high. The raft would crest and then disappear from view entirely. I thought I would pass out and seriously considered hitchhiking back over two continents.

So how extraordinary is it when I say what an amazing trip I had on the Futaleufú. The word I had heard over and over was "exhilarating," and it's apt, certainly, but actually not strong enough. The Futaleufú is an astonishment. The color of the water, its crazy volume, the roar, the velocity of the ride—and through it all, the absolute mastery of Robert, in the back of the raft—made every element seem heightened, perfected, colorized, almost virtual. And incredibly fun, it must be said.

There was also a great variety to the week, the camps all different from one another, but all surprisingly and ingeniously comfortable—from the arcadian, lost-boys hideaway of Cave Camp to the truly fantastical dwellings up in the canopy of the forest of the Tree House Camp—and the food was great. Now, when I watch the video of the trip, I can still pick out my face in the raft, against the barreling froth. I frankly can't believe I ever managed to do it, but I'm supremely glad I did. I'd go back for a view of the stars alone.

Sincerely,
David

[Outside, *October 2003*]

Evergreen Safari

The ten-minute ride by minivan from Vancouver's main airport to its south terminal—home to the tiny carriers that serve nearby Vancouver Island—is a trip back to the days before multiculturalism. Everyone in the south terminal seems to be white. And male. Many appear to be on their way to fishing adventures. Almost to a man, they wear baseball caps and nylon shells, and display that signal physiognomy of potbelly cantilevered out over counterintuitively skinny legs. The place looks like a casting call for *King of the Hill*. Or, more appropriately, for *The Red Fisher Show*, a television program from my childhood years in Canada in which the eponymous host and his guest—invariably some hockey hall-of-famer I didn't recognize—sat watching silent Super-8 footage of a recent fishing trip the two had taken together and narrating desultorily. Mr. Fisher's was a program of such magnificent stultification as to border on the conceptual.

These are the associations I have when I hear the words "Canadian fishing lodge." I think precisely of that Red Fisher scenario of a group of men out in the wilderness, standing in waders and drinking beer, or sitting in a boat and drinking beer, as they effortlessly pull in fish after fish from the bounteous waters. There is even a term for these places: whack 'em stack 'ems, rude dwellings with only the most cursory relationship to decorum, amenity, or hygiene; a weekend of corned-beef hash from a can and the necessary emulation of that timeless rhetorical question about bears in the woods. So, if the south terminal does not enchant me, neither does it surprise me.

I am on my way to Vancouver Island's western coast, to the town of Tofino (population 1,200). Rather, to the Clayoquot Wilderness Resorts, just outside it. I am not a fisherman by any stretch of the imagination, but that doesn't matter: The new lodges in British Columbia that I've come to visit cater to the all-around ecotourist looking for high-end outdoor adventure.

The sheer size of my native land never fails to overwhelm me. Canada is enormous—way bigger than the continental United States (something that was drilled into us in primary school). This is made abundantly clear during the one-hour flight to Tofino on a small seven-seat plane. Although just off the coast of the mainland, and serving as a bit of a bedroom community for Vancouver, Vancouver Island is in no way Brooklyn. It is almost the length of England and seems to go on forever. Ridge after ridge of mountains recede into the distance. When, one wonders, is the continent going to run out as advertised? Run out it eventually does, and all that's left is the even more overwhelming hugeness of the Pacific.

From the airport it's a twenty-minute drive to Tofino itself, a hodgepodge of surf shacks—nearby Long Beach is said to have world-class waves—and summer beach-town gift shops. The overall feeling is both twee and stoned. (The reputedly primo bud grown all over British Columbia is the province's largest industry, I am told by more than a few patchouli-scented individuals who speak with confidence-uninspiring slowness.

How astonishing, then, to find out that they're absolutely right. According to a December 2000 intelligence brief put out by the Drug Enforcement Administration, the province's cannabis cultivation yields a cool billion—that's U.S. dollars—per annum.) Then, from Tofino, there is a twenty-minute high-speed motorboat ride through a landscape of piney mountains coming down to meet dark water, all under blue sky and billowing Maxfield Parrish clouds. British Columbia is unfailingly, achingly, insanely beautiful. Over the next ten days, I alternate between regularly exclaiming an incredulous but direct "Holy shit!" and sounding like Bertie Wooster's insufferable erstwhile fiancée, Madeline Bassett, who was given to insipid pronouncements like "The stars are God's daisy chain!"

Clayoquot Wilderness Resort has two facilities: the main floating lodge at Quait Bay, where we stop briefly to take on supplies, and my ultimate destination for the next three days, the Wilderness Outpost, on the Bedwell River. The Outpost is Clayoquot's tent encampment, a woefully inadequate term to describe a place that looks like a nineteenth-century silver gelatin print of a gold prospectors' camp—the difference being that the gold has already been found, so to speak. None of the privations of the preindustrial gold panners for us. This is rusticating luxury. The tents, 150 years old in design but spanking new, are manufactured by the Fort McPherson Canvas Company of the Northwest Territories and outfitted with Persian carpets, antique dressers, torchère lamps, remote-controlled gas stoves, and beds fashioned out of alder branches. Individually accessible by boardwalks through the woods, each of the ten guest tents also has its own outhouse with an odorless compost toilet. My tent is in primordial forest, beside an old felled tree whose trunk has sprouted its own micro-ecosystem of moss, licorice fern, lichen, and countless new plants feeding off its spongy rot. Strangely, the place is absolutely silent, without even the tiniest bird call. The light is green and filtered, shafts of golden sunlight breaking through the canopy and illuminating huge prehistoric ferns and skunk cabbage whose leaves are the size of cafeteria trays. It feels sylvan the way a stage set for the second act of *Giselle* feels sylvan, except that there is nothing ersatz in these surroundings, complete perfection notwithstanding.

The staff are friendly and display a chastening ability to remember all of our names immediately. I am effectively adopted by a British family: Rob, Melanie, and their two boys, Nicholas and William, ages nine and eleven. There is no awkwardness to this unspoken transaction; we all seem interested in the same activities, the first being kayaking. We take out three doubles, teaming the boys with their parents and me with Dusty Sylvester, our guide. Dusty, who is twenty-one, works the season at the Outpost and spends the rest of the year traveling through Asia and Latin America. Self-possessed and unostentatious in his competence, which is multifarious, he's like Gary Cooper in fleece. He is knowledgeable about flora and fauna, pointing out a thousand-year-old western red cedar, the ubiquitous salal bushes (whose dark purple berries have a not unpleasant granular, puckering-mouth feel), and the analgesic properties of both the false lily of the valley, which carpets the ground, and the lichen known as Methuselah's beard. He alerts us to a white pin dot high in the green branches of a tree. Moments later, it takes flight: a bald eagle. Two harbor porpoises approach our kayak, near enough for us to hear the regular *chuff* of their blowholes as they breach and dive. Kayaking becomes my new favorite activity. From our brief paddle, I develop a raw pink blister on my thumb. I wear it as proudly as a Heidelberg fencing scar.

The Outpost experience is like a safari for those who sun-burn easily, with an almost one-to-one correspondence of attractions and absent the politically problematic colonialism of the original. Canada is a country with an enviably progres-sive social agenda—universal health care and a comparatively exemplary relationship between the government and the country's indigenous people, known as the First Nations, to name just two aspects. Even the dearth of lions is made up for by a local version of perilous omnivores: bears, albeit only black bears, which are much smaller and less aggressive than grizzlies. Still, the camp is patrolled at night by three dogs, and the wicker hospitality basket thoughtfully placed next to my bed contains not only Aveda products but also a Freon horn—one of those canisters with little megaphones on top that emit an earsplitting *braaaap* at hockey games and such. Just in case.

With only four of the tents occupied, the guests decide that it would be nicer to eat communally at one long table. The chef, Judy Walker, prepares huge and varied meals, with ample choices such as lamb chops, broiled halibut, Cambo-zola mashed potatoes, and berry crème brûlée. The food is unbelievably good, almost needlessly delicious given the fact that, after a two-hour kayak or a half day on horseback, one would readily eat the most rudimentary slumgullion from the roughest whack 'em stack 'em.

One morning, whose perfection is muted only by a bit of cranial thump—how can one not drink the freely flowing pinot gris amid such beauty and bonhomie—John Caton, the resorts' general manager, takes us on a five-hour horse-back ride. Clayoquot has 750 acres of land, purchased from a logging company specifically for ecotourism use. The for-est is a cathedral of aspens, dry creek beds, mossy trees, lush ground cover. We ride up and up a vertiginous hillside in the shaded woods, passing rusted old chimney flues and iron cots from mining cabins of a century ago. We venture about three hundred feet into the shaft of an abandoned mine to see the gold-flecked veins of quartzite. It is a terrifyingly dark tunnel, pitch-black beyond a certain point. My claustrophobia is a source of great amusement to William and Nicholas, who are determined to bring back ore-rich paperweights. I turn my flashlight in the direction we have come, and the beam lights up the eyes of our accompanying dog into two hellishly bright green spots in the darkness.

We make our steep descent from the mine—after which John tells us he generally doesn't bring novice riders here—and head to a suspension bridge, about thirty feet above the river. The water is a deep, clear navy blue. Looking down, John points out five sockeye salmon swimming about. The fish are visible only because one of them has been swiped by a bear, and the exposed white flesh of the gash in its side acts as a headlight under the water.

Originally built as a restaurant and bar for the Vancouver Expo of 1986, Clayoquot's floating lodge at Quait Bay has been turned into a lovely sixteen-room hotel, where I will spend the next two days and nights. The wraparound balconies are adorned with flowering baskets; there is a large stone fireplace and a barrel-vaulted glass ceiling above the dining room, all of it in gleaming repair. The building's subaquatic moorings are encrusted with sea anemones and crimson starfish. Translucent, ghostly jellyfish—ranging in size from Tic Tac to football—propel themselves slowly through the water.

The plan is to head out into the ocean to see whales. Before boarding the *Whale's Tale*, a high-speed Zodiac ringed with an inflated orange pontoon, we don orange jumpsuits, which provide both insulation and flotation. We look like snuggly convicts. Our driver is Cosy, short for Quoashinis. Born and raised on a small nearby island, she was home-schooled and has been driving boats professionally for thirteen years, more than half her young life.

We pass an island that turns out to be a favorite place for whales to beach themselves (if favorite can be used to describe suicidal behavior). When very sick, whales throw themselves onto dry land, where, once they're no longer buoyed by water, the weight of their bodies crushes their lungs and they drift into unconsciousness and eventual death, one a great deal quicker and less painful than lingering in the sea.

As for live and healthy whales, the first sign of any is the spray from a distant blowhole, which seems to augur a non-event, really, just a plume of white water against a misty white sky. But then the creature, a single gray, surfaces very close to us, showing its huge slate-dark back, followed by the twin shovel blades of its massive tail. "Holy shit!" I yell. There's really no being complacent about a whale.

Before heading back, we stop on Flores Island to walk the Wild Side, a trail where Dusty leads us on a long hike. The beaches are windswept and littered with bleached driftwood, mussel shells, and bull kelp, a plant straight out of Hieronymus Bosch, consisting of a central stalk, thick and sturdy as a garden hose. On one end is an air-filled bulb, like Harpo's horn, and on the other are multiple ribbons of bright-green seaweed.

Dusty suggests a shortcut, which involves fording a five-foot channel of freezing water. We have to strip down to our underpants to do so. Either because he has misunderstood or is too short to avoid getting them soaked, Nicholas takes his underpants off as well. His T-shirt rides up as his father, Rob, carries him; and as older brothers have done since time immemorial, William points and screams, "Bare bum!" William's day, at least, has been made.

There is something innately Agatha Christie about the King Pacific Lodge, fifty miles from the town of Prince Rupert, near the Alaska Panhandle. Perhaps it is the arrival of all thirteen guests, a cast of characters ready-made, on the same floatplane and the staff lined up to greet us. Or perhaps it is that, immediately after our arrival, the fog rolls in, effectively cutting us off from civilization (cue sinister power outage here). Or perhaps it is the intrinsically violent presence of the metal table right out front, where the lethal business of fish-gutting takes place. Whatever the reason, the place is an ideal setting for a murder mystery—and I mean that in the best way. After all, there's no great mystery called "Murder on the Long Island Rail Road." KPL is appropriately luxurious, beautiful, and sybaritic.

I go into the main mudroom off the lobby, where I find a cubbyhole with my name already on it; inside are a pair of rubber boots and a deep-sea-fishing insulation-flotation suit. Unlike Clayoquot's floating lodge—which is connected to land by a dock and a walkway—KPL is truly separate and accessible only by water, requiring a thirty-second boat ride to reach the edge of the forest (so much the better for a Hercule Poirot lockdown). I go on a hike with a guide, Jenn Dickie. She is twenty-nine and as beautiful as a car, with the sleek, aerodynamic quality of Carrie-Anne Moss in *The Matrix*. We ascend through the brush beside a barreling creek that the recent downpour has swollen to twice its previous size and force. KPL is situated in the Great Bear Rainforest, which extends north into Alaska and may account for fully 25 percent of the globe's temperate rain forest. The trail, such as it is, ends pretty quickly, and Jenn and I bushwhack through the wet, spongy, mossy woods. We stop often to eat huckleberries.

This is full-service guiding. Jenn carries the water and the cookies in her backpack. At a huge western red cedar, she says, "let's take your picture."

"I have no camera," I reply. She pulls out the lodge's digital camera and snaps.

She points out one of British Columbia's famous banana slugs—enormous, slimy creatures, yellow flecked with black; living tubes of toothpaste. She goes on to tell me that they are hermaphrodites and so they can mate with themselves. But when they do double-date, consummation can take up to thirty hours. Sometimes, rather than wait around for withdrawal, the banana slug simply gnaws its partner's appendage off and keeps it. My delighted crow of disgust is the only sound in the woods.

A brief word on fly-fishing, one of KPL's main attractions. I do not go. It requires use of the KPL helicopter, which costs hundreds of dollars more than I've budgeted. But I cannot return home without at least attempting to have one true Red Fisher experience. I try my hand at a little deep-sea fishing. There's so much gear and mechanics involved, starting with the Fish Finder, a GPS-like monitor showing small LCD fish shapes and their depth below the boat. The rods are set into holders, and the lines are baited with lures and weighted with ten-pound sinkers. I apparently get two bites but fail to reel in either fast enough. On the first bite, in fact, I simply stare at the bending rod, too confused by this new skill set to pick it up and start reeling. Still, it's pretty out on the water in the fog, and the waves are not unexciting. But the entire process seems at somewhat of a remove. I might feel differently if I had caught something. Certainly the other guests who've hauled in huge salmon glow with predatory high spirits.

Perhaps this is the true salubrious function of the lodge vacation: the controlled and safe release of our less attractive impulses. All that Hemingway bloodlust tempers into easy relaxation and friendliness by the evening. Time after supper is spent playing backgammon by the fire, games of cards, table shuffleboard. Standing with another guest on the veranda, I mention the whodunit flavor of the place. He agrees completely. We discuss the particulars, drinks in hand, collaborating on the screenplay we will never write. One of the other guests emerges and, looking around nervously for her staunchly anti-tobacco boyfriend, takes a forbidden Marlboro out of her pocket and lights up. (Plot twist! Motive!) We tell her our idea.

"It's probably easier to kill someone than to smoke a cigarette," she muses philosophically.

Clayoquot and KPL both illustrate the truism that one has to travel far in this developed world to find untrammeled wilderness. They are not easy to get to. But that many-legged journey, at least on the return, is a saving grace. Extrication from such otherworldly relaxation and beauty needs to be gradual. I'm grateful for this slow easing back into civilization (although there is one very unslow second or two when the floatplane drops thirty feet and we all scream in precisely the same way: an automatic, percussive "Whoa!"). From the float-plane, a short ferry ride across the water takes us to where the airport minivan will pick us up for our flight to Vancouver. We arrive at the dock a little before the bus. A bald eagle is perched on one of the wooden pilings, unbothered by our presence. By the side of the road are many thimbleberry bushes, their fruit like brighter, redder, fuzzier raspberries. I pick some and hand them out. The bus arrives. I toss the last few into my mouth, wipe my juice-stained hand on my jeans, and step aboard.

[Condé Nast Traveler, *March 2003*]

Northern Composure

It was a murderous summer heat wave that gripped New York City. The newspapers carried grim stories of people essentially cooked to death in their un-air-conditioned apartments. Con Edison, the power utility, was sending agents door-to-door, begging people to turn off appliances to forestall an inevitable blackout. Al Gore's direst predictions seemed to be coming true. How to escape this inconvenient truth? By getting out of Dodge, of course. But if my Northeastern home was now the climatic equivalent of Atlanta, what did that make New York's local oceanic respites, the Hamptons and the Jersey Shore? The Everglades?

The only solution was to go north. Hoping to avoid the throngs of vacationers who yearly overrun Cape Cod and Maine, I settled on the Canadian Maritimes. I had always wanted to see that part of my native land, my desire based almost entirely on a postcard I had received as a child depicting the lighthouse at Peggy's Cove, Nova Scotia. Possibly the most famous image of Eastern Canada, the bright-white beacon stands alone and proud on the smooth, bare rock, looking out to a gray sea that is cold and huge and cares not one jot for the lives and aspirations of man or beast. My kind of place.

The first leg of my journey on the ground—a two-hour

cab ride from Nova Scotia's Sydney Airport to Ingonish—
is as immediate and welcome a relief as a cool hand on my
forehead. I am driven through the misty, rugged Cape Breton
Highlands. Unlike, say, Rome, New York, or any other improb-
ably named place (O, whither your white nights, St. Peters-
burg, Florida?), the Highlands of Nova Scotia, literally New
Scotland, really do resemble their namesake, both topograph-
ically and spiritually. We cross the Great Bras d'Or inlet, a
narrow channel from the Atlantic bordered on both sides by
piney banks of forest. It is beautiful and harsh and looks like
nothing so much as Loch Ness. We pass signs reading CÉAD
MÍLE FÁILTE ("one hundred thousand welcomes"), an old
Gaelic greeting, just as we come upon the Gaelic College of
Celtic Arts and Crafts, an institution devoted to the culture
of the original settlers. There in the circular driveway stands a
young student playing the bagpipes in full kilted regalia. The
winding road up Mount Smokey climbs about eight hundred
feet in a mile, the Atlantic stretching out below us. I've said it
before—perhaps even in the pages of this magazine—but it's
hard to be blasé about an ocean. And there in the distance is
my first stop, the Keltic Lodge: red-roofed, Tudor-timbered,
perched on its rocky promontory. It is here that I am meeting
up with one of my best and oldest friends, Natalia, who now
lives in London, along with her husband, Philippe, and their
three children. We will be together for five days.

The Keltic Lodge sits, incongruous as a bowling green in
the cone of a volcano, paradisiacally situated on a peninsula of
protected provincial park. The sea roils below on three sides,
crashing against rocks that give way to wild forest that climbs
the hills. But the grounds of the hotel itself are sweet formal
English flower beds and rolling lawns dotted everywhere with
multicolored Adirondack chairs. Opened in 1952, it still has

that feel. Indeed, 1952 (in that innocent and retro sense, as opposed to that Red-baiting/duck-and-cover sense) will be the prevailing mood for days to come. A gentle politeness will suffuse every interaction. The Keltic is a Shangri-La of sorts. A reverse Shangri-La, to be precise: The place is peacefully geriatric. Golf culture and its attendant quiet prevail. And while I don't feel anything but completely welcome, the 1952 feeling also savors of a Canada before it became a multicultural haven. I do not see, for example, among the prevalent white hair and ice cream–colored wardrobe, anything resembling the sartorial exuberance of my own fellow Hebrews when they reach a certain age: the Matisse-bright loungewear accompanied by the ethnic clank of hammered silver jewelry purchased on the previous year's trip to San Miguel de Allende.

We get into the Keltic rhythm by doing not much of anything really. We walk to a nearby rocky beach, picking and eating raspberries along the way. We have our very good breakfast and supper nightly in the lodge's Purple Thistle Dining Room, with extraordinary views of the Atlantic on both sides, and we spend a fair amount of time sitting in the Adirondack chairs, chatting and taking in the astonishing scenery.

Rousing ourselves one morning, we tag along on a nature hike. We see two varieties of birch and some woodpecker holes in a fallen tree, but I can't really blame the kids when they get a little bored. There's just not that much going on in these woods, and our guide is a less-than-electric docent. We do manage to see a partridge slowly making its way through the underbrush, but Philippe and I peel off with the girls down to a rocky outcropping where we can at least watch the waves come in. And there, finally, wildlife! A school of jellyfish. (Does one say a "school"? Isn't their presence in multiples merely a function of currents? Can they be said to have social cohesion any more than one would describe the dozens of insects flattened on a car's windshield as a community?) The jellyfish are a very pretty dark bluey-purple. We skim one out of the water and bring it up on the rocks to get a closer look. While it's floating in water, we can see the flowerlike opening and closing of its body. But here on dry land, glistening in the soon-to-prove-lethal sun, it is a formless and shuddering pile of violet gelatin, absent of structure.

The irony is not lost on me that finding refuge on this roasting planet requires that I blithely increase my carbon footprint by hopping on a gas-guzzling airplane (two of them, actually: I had to change in Montréal) and, once here, further engage in that most traditional of fossil-fuel bacchanals: the driving holiday—and me a nondriver. My guilt is assuaged somewhat by the fact that the Maritimes are almost completely unserved by trains, except for one—about which more later— and that I am just one of six sharing a barely midsize vehicle. It is all very jolly in the backseat with the three children, who take up little room and are excellent company; but after an hour, the delusional monsters start complaining about the size of my backside.

Our Maritimes trip will describe an exaggerated circumflex that will take us from Cape Breton, Nova Scotia, to Prince Edward Island, and back to the mainland of Nova Scotia to Halifax. We leave the Keltic one morning and are driving off the car ferry onto Prince Edward Island by that afternoon. The lodge and its environs seem a distant dream. Maybe that's because the evergreen wilderness of Cape Breton stands in such distinct contrast to the flat patchwork of Prince Edward Island's fields. We drive past immaculate clapboard houses and small white churches, through towns with the most starchy Anglo names: Roseberry, Cardigan, and Point Prim. It might all be called Point Prim, given the pin-neatness of the land-scape. Even Charlottetown, P.E.I.'s capital, seems to be under the thumb of some despotic, flower-hatted gardening club. Its many small green squares are lovingly planted and maintained. Large shade trees line streets of restored old mansions—some once again private homes, some that house social services, clearly predating the area's revival, and some converted into B&Bs, like the Hillhurst, where we are staying.

At our breakfast table the next morning, we are joined by the inn's other guests: five grown women from Utah, Mormon sisters and sisters-in-law. They have left their many children back at home with their husbands. All very nice and chatty, Natalia asks what brought them here to P.E.I.

"Anne," one of them answers simply.

Ah, yes, Anne of Green Gables, the Lucy Maud Mont-gomery heroine who put P.E.I. on the map and has inspired mad global devotion. But in our little group, I, the only Cana-dian, don't care, Natalia and Philippe didn't grow up with the books, and the children don't know them either, so we count ourselves uniquely lucky in our imperviousness to the ubiqui-tous merch.

It might seem that visiting P.E.I. in the summer and not driving to the mock Anne of Avonlea village up in Cavendish, or seeing at least one of the two Anne-themed musicals playing simultaneously in Charlottetown, is like visiting Mecca dur-ing the hajj, but for the ceramics. Still, there is much here to delight the general traveler. We stroll along streets of restored nineteenth-century buildings, past outdoor jazz trios and ice cream parlors. It is both languorous and decorous. A beach town in white gloves. In a gift shop, I find the first in the line of Canadian Legends action figures: John A. Macdonald, the first prime minister. There he is in his dark frock coat, with his fearsome swivel table and two Chiclet-sized leather-bound volumes at the ready. *Biff! Pow!* Take that, foes of postcolonial representative parliamentary democracy!

In truth, there is no more fitting superhero for this place. Here is where the first talk of confederating the British North American colonies into present-day Canada began. In Province House, a lovely neoclassical building, we watch *A Great Dream*, a video about how this all came about. It seems there was a conference, and a lunch, and a ball, and some more talking. Just as I remember from my own Canadian childhood, our history is almost parodically uneventful. Then again, a country born of conversation might make for some dull classroom hours but seems a fair exchange for fewer burial grounds filled with eighteen-year-old boys.

In a nearby outdoor amphitheater, we watch a more exciting, musical-theater version of How We Got Here. First up: the natives, played by cute, muscular dancer boys—all Caucasian—in fringed chaps (with what look to be fetching suede Speedos underneath). They jump through feathered hoops with acrobatic grace, punctuating each routine with a very un-Ojibway-sounding "Oy!" Suddenly!—through the audience he comes. A drifter, drifting. He wears full-body buckskin, the traditional costume of a trapper, those fur traders who settled the New World. He sings an anthem to all souls who have ever left their homes in search of a better place—like a Broadway theater, for example. "What will I find in this newfound land?" he wonders. Time marches—and jetés—on, and here come the resolute men of the railroad "living on stew and drinkin' bad whiskey." Now a barn-raising dance, à la *Seven Brides for Seven Brothers* (minus the uncomfortable associations to *The Rape of the Sabine Women*). It is all energetic and well-danced and sweet. There are towheaded children in the audience waving little Canadian flags! Like I said, 1952.

"Each man stood at his post / while all the weaker ones went by, / and showed once more to all the world / how Englishmen should die," reads the headstone for Everett Edward Elliott, age twenty-four. At Philippe's insistence, our first stop in Halifax, before we even get to our hotel, is the Fairview Lawn Cemetery. It is here where 121 of the roughly 1,500 victims of the *Titanic* disaster are buried. The very modest black granite stones were provided by the White Star Line. The word TITANIC was only carved onto the stones after the success of the movie, but the sinking of the great liner has always been one of the nautical disasters imbedded in the collective memory of Halifax. The other was an explosion in the harbor in 1917, when a munitions ship crashed into another vessel and blew up, killing two thousand people and destroying much of what is now the north end of the city. I know a couple who were flying back to New York from Paris on 9/11. Their flight was rerouted to Halifax, where they were put up by a volunteer family for days. When one of my friends wondered aloud at the extraordinary and unquestioning kindness they were being shown, their hosts mentioned how it was the very least they could do considering how helpful the Americans had apparently been.

That a Haligonian would regard events that had taken place nine decades earlier as a potent pretext to do someone else a good turn doesn't seem surprising after spending as little as twenty-four hours in the Maritimes. I cannot say this too emphatically: The people of Nova Scotia and Prince Edward Island—or everyone I encountered over eleven days, at any rate—are among the kindest and friendliest I have ever met. Forget the achingly pretty towns, the ocean vistas, or the oysters and mussels so fat and briny you want to marry the shucker or cry, or both; it is the people who are reason enough to go there on holiday. Every interaction, whether getting my morning coffee or searching for children's car sickness lozenges, is like having my heart massaged.

And Halifax is lovely! The streets slope steeply down to the water. The worn cobbles of the Historic Properties—an area of eighteenth- and nineteenth-century buildings that now house the Granville campus of the world-class Nova Scotia College of Art and Design—suggest Paris. We walk along the waterfront, passing runty, muscular tugboats, those most anthropomorphic and sympathetic of vessels. There is a small island in the harbor, a rolling green hill with a lighthouse and two smaller buildings. Like many a prospect in the Maritimes, it seems toy-scale. We look at the sea stars collected near the pilings of the pier, we gorge ourselves on the free samples of rum cake in a shop and look in waterfront store windows. There are some very snazzy condominiums nearby with what must be astonishing views. Walking up the hill past the stately stone building where the farmers' market happens each Saturday, Philippe observes, "It's quite gentrified here."

"What's gentrified?" asks eleven-year-old Leo.

"Poshed up," his dad explains.

Leo thinks about it for a moment. "Oh. I like things that are gentrified, apparently."

In *The Children*, the Edith Wharton novel I have coincidentally been reading on the trip, Martin Boyne, a single traveler in Europe who becomes the unwitting guardian of a roistering bunch of kids, finds himself to have "been gradually penetrated by the warm animal life which proceeds from a troop of happy healthy children." That's exactly right. It is with great reluctance that I say goodbye to Natalia, Philippe, and the kids the next morning. But I have decided to spend some time alone in Halifax before heading off elsewhere in Nova Scotia, including—finally—to the place that brought me here: Peggy's Cove. That, at least, is a thought that pleases.

And a bonus: I will not be bereft of youthful energy for very long either. I have booked two days with Salty Bear Adventure Travel, an outfit that organizes driving tours through the province. Trolling its website, I see that I am a good deal older than its average customer. Indeed, this will turn out to be very, very true. There are thirteen of us on board the Salty Bear van. There are young men and women, early twenties, from Scotland, Ireland, Australia, England, Germany, and Canada. Plus Chris Penton, thirty-two, our driver and until recently the co-owner of Salty Bear. Originally from Ottawa, Chris has something of the blue-eyed, verbal quickness of the actor Matthew Perry about him. He kicks things off with an icebreaker: Who are you? Where are you from? And whom would you like to see naked? I haven't heard of easily half of the physical paragons the others invoke. I beg off. I have to spend two days with these striplings, and I am loath to scare them by responding with the only logical answer, really, given their taut poreless skin and the keening Doppler of their racing, turbocharged metabolisms virtually ringing in my ears: "Every single one of you."

In truth, over the course of the trip, they will seem less a monolithic storehouse of collagen and will separate out into a disparate group of some very charming individuals. But in this initial blush, I feel old, old, old. One of them passes around her iPod, inviting the rest of us to bestow upon its storehouse any of our own particular MP3 favorites. She hooks it up to the van's sound system. Scissor Sisters pours out of the speakers, and we are off. Quite an acceleration, from 1952 to the present in under four seconds.

The landscape of my childhood postcard starts only about

three hundred yards from Peggy's Cove itself. It is an abrupt change from forest to gently rolling earth with low ground cover, scattered with boulders that seem as though they've been dropped from the sky. The fishing village is ridiculously picturesque, with clapboard houses nestled among the famous rocks. There are signs advising us not to stray too close to the water's edge or onto any darker (read: wet) rocks. Someone gets swept out to sea every year, we are told. But the water is placid today. The lighthouse glows against the clear blue of the sky. Even with the hundred or so tourists here at this moment, it doesn't feel crowded. The bare, rocky expanse is big and austere, affording each of us our contemplative space. We amble over the boulders, each lost in our isolation, a musical version of that last extended sequence in Antonioni's L'Avventura. It is everything I'd hoped for, if not a tad upbeat.

But for cheerfulness, nothing is as warming as the town of Lunenburg. In centuries past, it was a global center of shipbuilding. In its preindustrial form, it was an endeavor that involved lots of photogenic he-man arts and crafts: much hewing and bending of majestic trees into the upended cathedral skeletons of schooners; mutton-chopped stevedores and dignitaries staring out from ship-christening tintypes. Lunenburg's Old Town, with its historic waterfront, has become a UNESCO World Heritage Site. This means that it is inviolate, inalterable. (It's worth remembering that the Buddhas of Bamiyan were also a World Heritage Site. Fat lot of good that did.) We overshoot the town and drive out to the nearby golf course across the bay in order to get a proper view of it all. It is an adorable Legoland of buildings painted whatever color the fishermen had left over from painting their boats: scarlet, buttercream, slate blue, mint green. Chris says that it can be bleak and deserted in winter, but in high summer, there are hundreds of us visitors thronging the streets and milling about in the many shops. Surely UNESCO must have some sort of intervening policing power to countervail the town's surfeit of fudge.

Lunenburg's perfection brings up the more global question of how to preserve the authenticity of the past without descending into ersatz preciousness. Peggy's Cove, on the other hand, is still a working fishing village, and the houses of its few residents do not appear to have been upgraded, but I hope they're all millionaires. It seems a lot to ask of people, that they continue to live in their photogenic privation, while the souvenir concession not thirty yards away rakes in the bucks.

There is less of a quandary when the attraction is naturally occurring. The Bay of Fundy has the highest tides in the world. Over the course of the roughly twelve-hour cycle, the water level can vary by as much as fifty-two feet. According to a pamphlet in a local tourist information center, the billion tons of seawater that flow into Minas Basin twice daily actually tilt the surrounding countryside slightly. We get to Cape Blomidon, our lookout point, while the tide is out, but it has been coming in for an hour, says a man in the parking lot. Even so, there is a vast flat of exposed ocean floor before us. We walk out on the packed red sand rilled with the pattern of the waves. We walk for a good half mile before we reach the sea.

Finally, at the water's edge, I realize that the sea has been traveling back to meet us all this time, and at a real clip, almost the speed of walking. But the water's arrival is a subtler process. First, the ground beneath our feet begins to give just a little. Then, the shade of the red sand morphs along with its softening texture, going from a matte brick to vaguely lustrous, and a few seconds later it is downright shiny. Just as you register this final transformation, the water rushes over your sneakers. Tides are not waves. Fundy is not dramatic in a *Hawaii-Five-O*-opening-credits, Hokusai-wood-block-print kind of way, but it is an astonishment just the same for the sheer size of the phenomenon. A global impact made manifest. There are a great many Mennonites visiting here as well. Fundy is a real Mennonite tourist destination, according to Chris. They are wearing ankle-length dresses in flowered cotton, their hair pinned back and adorned with small swatches of stiff black fabric—something between a bonnet and a kerchief. Their unadorned, anachronistic simplicity is the perfect comple-ment to this huge minimalist landscape, with its horizontal bands of color: blue sky, green slope, red beach, gray water. My inner art director kicks in immediately. I am not proud that I regard them as props, but I cannot stop myself from pronounc-ing, albeit silently, *These Mennonites are fabulous!*

Unable to face the heat of New York (or New Yorkers) just yet, I prolong my return by booking a sleeper on *The Ocean*, the overnight train that will take me from Halifax to Montréal. The price of my ticket includes a cunning fold-down bed in a modest private compartment and some slightly-better-than-airplane meals in the dining car. None of it is anything that could be described as plush. The finishes and surfaces are not fancy, but they are clean, if a little chipped and worn here and there. It isn't the Rovos Rail or the Orient Express, but here's what it also isn't: Amtrak! Moreover, *The Ocean* prides itself on being educational and experiential. There is even a Learning Coordinator, a friendly Francophone woman named Lyne. We can go to the globe car, a double-decker railcar at the back end of the train, and Lyne will be there if we have any ques-tions about the history of the areas we will be passing through.

It is an overcast dusk. There are no stars for the glass roof of the globe car to showcase, but it's very nice to sit on the upper deck watching the land zip by. Up in the front seat is a man, about sixty-five, wearing a polo shirt with the words RAILWAY SOCIETY OF NEWFOUNDLAND printed over the breast, having the time of his life. One of the other passengers asks in French what kind of birds we see flocked on the telephone wires as we cross over the Miramichi River. I allow as how I think they are cormorants (I guess at the word). Thus begins a long three-way conversation with Lyne in French, with me just barely keeping up. This gradual transition from English to French, the two main European cultures that make up Canada, is like the mixing of salt water with fresh in an estuary. Nova Scotia started out French, although that's now more a matter of monument than of fact. The Acadians ended up down in Louisiana, where their own dialect shortened their name to Cajuns. In the present, we almost couldn't drive by a church or a community hall that didn't have a sign out front for the local *cèilidh*, the Irish-Scottish musical gathering. Now the train is in New Brunswick, which boasts a Celtic history as well as a large Francophone population. Lyne points this out to us and also shows us how she changed her foulard when we crossed over into this province. She is wearing the New Brunswick plaid. There is no designated Québécois tartan for her to put on when we cross that border. Besides, it will be the middle of the night when we do.

[Condé Nast Traveler, *March 2008*]

A Basket Case in
North Carolina

The old Appalachian ballad "Lord Daniel" is a bracing dose of adultery and murder at seven forty-five A.M. Not that we need extra stimuli. Sleeping in is the province of the young, and the average age at John C. Campbell Folk School hovers somewhere around . . . well, to employ the equivalent of describing certain political candidates as clean and articulate, the students do seem to be a spry lot. Easily eighty of us have gathered in the community room to hear Jan Davidson, the director of the school, lead us in our first session of MorningSong, the half hour of music and stories that starts our day.

"The history of the Folk School is at least in part the history of Appalachian ballads," he tells us. When John Campbell and his wife, Olive Dame Campbell, traveled through Appalachia in the early decades of the twentieth century, Olive collected songs from the locals, collaborating on a definitive compendium in 1917. Founded eight years later in the hamlet of Brasstown, North Carolina, the Folk School is roughly two hours equidistant from Asheville, North Carolina; Atlanta; and Knoxville, Tennessee, in the far west corner of the state where it narrows to a matchbook, wedged in to stabilize Tennessee's wobbly table against the floor of Georgia.

It is here that we will spend the next six days learning crafts, some traditionally Appalachian (weaving, quilting, wood turning) and some less so (enameling, kaleidoscope making, French cooking). I have signed up for ribbed basketry for beginners. I had initially registered for blacksmithing, attracted by its Vulcan brawn, but balked when told that I would need to bring eye and ear protection and travel through the nation's airports armed with metal hand files. As the week begins, I am not a particularly big fan of baskets and their countrified bed-and-breakfast aesthetic, but in the end, I will make seven of them, ranging from a remedial little dish of a thing on the first day to a large and, if I say so myself, fairly elegant egg basket that resembles nothing so much as a pair of human buttocks in rattan. There is something you need to know about basket weaving, and that something is that basket weaving rocks.

"Make new friends, but keep the old. One is silver and the other gold." Meals at the Folk School always begin with some form of nondenominational blessing. We are encouraged to eat at a different table for each meal so that we might meet all of the roughly 125 people here. And successful group dynamics are of arguably greater value than any artistic skill we might pick up this week.

The Folk School is founded on the principles of the Danish *folkehøjskole* (literally, "folk high school") movement, a social experiment engineered by the nineteenth-century Danish philosopher Nikolaj Frederik Severin Grundtvig. The goal was to bring together adults of disparate social backgrounds and educate them in an egalitarian and democratic environment. There were to be no grades and no tests. Folk schools were emphatically not trade schools and their purpose only casually vocational. What one really learns is how to get along.

Words to the wise. Given the lack of clamor of hammer against anvil, we are graced with a lovely silence in the basketry studio. When not receiving help and instruction from Greg Filippelli, our virtuosic and endlessly patient teacher, I and my three classmates have hours in which to converse. A variety of backgrounds and viewpoints is not only inevitable, but it also speaks to the core of the folk school ethos. Happily, if the quiet of basket weaving has provided the time and space for talking, it is also the antidote to such talk. So, while one might hear things that would curl a reporter's hair if he had any left, there is the simultaneous good fortune of the moving meditation of the work to get through such moments. Vigorous defenses of the beleaguered oil companies or the flat tax are met with nothing more than the peaceful and methodical under-over-under threading of pliant, soaked reed. That old truism about this being the activity prescribed to inmates of the booby hatch seems appropriate. Blood pressure remains normal, gaskets unblown. Basket weaving (in addition to rocking) is also soothing, soothing, soothing.

So much so that I can't really speak with authority about the beauty of my surroundings or of the many things there are to do at the Folk School. I hear that there is a daily nature excursion in the early hours before MorningSong. And that the nearby town of Murphy has a limited but respectable wine selection in its gourmet coffee store. There are frequent demonstrations by some of the other instructors, and I do attend one session where the ceramics teacher creates a cunning fish. Ditto Tuesday evening's contra dancing, where I stay for a reel or two. But I do not stroll the nearby river walk, with its public art pieces; nor do I gaze meditatively out at the smoky purple mountains in the distance.

I see them, and they are beyond pretty, and I am charmed

by the rabbit that bounds across my path one evening, but for the most part, I am in the studio, weaving. All four of us are, in fact. Every night at least until nine P.M. This makes it sound like some sweatshop where we labor to meet deadlines. We are there because we want to be.

The week ends with the final show of student work on Friday evening, with each class setting up its work on tables around the main hall.

There are woven rugs, highly polished turned wooden bowls, a series of witty teapots. The dulcimer makers play "Amazing Grace" on beautiful instruments, and we all smile and clap as if we were their parents. We are all so proud of one another. It is astonishing what people have managed to accomplish in six days.

Later, a number of us walk down the road to Clay's Corner, the gas station/convenience mart of Brasstown. There is junk food, camp-stove fuel, and surprisingly good ice cream. One can rent videos, which are displayed in Clay's Possum Pit, a sunken room at the back that on Friday nights becomes a gathering place for music. A dozen or so people sit on folding chairs, listening to a blond woman sing a ballad, her voice achingly sad.

Clay's is not a photogenic place. There is none of the attractively weathered wood or relaxed cotton fashions of Walker Evans's portraits of rural American poverty. But it is authentic, to use that moving target of a word. Somewhere between reality and caricature lies the truth. Appalachia hardly has a monopoly on this ambivalent stance (*Portnoy's Complaint*, anyone?), but it is a source of near-constant joking at the Folk School. John Campbell's 1921 book, *The Southern Highlander and His Homeland*, was meant to serve in part as a comprehensive manual for the northern do-gooders who were flooding into the region at that time, armed with best intentions but laboring under the twin preconceptions of a mountain people as either noble savages full of folksy wisdom or, as Jan Davidson says, "inbred, feuding moonshiners . . . and that's just the women!"

These stereotypes endure eight decades later. David Brose, the folklorist who runs the school's history center, jokes during his MorningSong that he lives in nearby Hayesville, where "we're so poor that where my son's going to school, they're having them learn driver's and sex education in the same car." This gets a chuckle from everyone—some of whom share a similar background—but not nearly as big a laugh as when he says, "We're going to have us a hootenanny! You remember hootenannies. They were gatherings where sons and daughters of chief executive officers or Wall Street analysts would stand on auditorium stages and perform for other sons and daughters of chief executive officers or Wall Street analysts and sing with great authenticity about the terrible working conditions in Southern mill towns."

Even the Folk School's motto itself, "I Sing Behind the Plow," is replete with a similar hardscrabble, Weavers-at-Carnegie-Hall utopianism, a problematic fit with the many LIFE OR METH billboards one passes on the road from Atlanta. Still, it can be hard not to get caught up in the romance of it all. There is a certain magic to the place.

I meet a woman who has been here more than a hundred times. I hear more than a few stories about people who changed their lives radically after being here—loveless marriages ended, businesses started, etc. But the reasons given ultimately have less to do with ethnographic voyeurism so much as with the spiritual alchemy that takes place in that time out of time when one is engaged in making something. There is not sleep enough in the world that is nearly so restorative. I have never met an artist or serious craftsperson who doesn't understand and seek out this feeling. If anything, the enduring mystery of the Folk School is why it isn't the destination of choice for the emerging class of urban crafters. The week I spent there is about as close as it gets to my idea of paradise.

[The New York Times T Magazine, *May 20, 2007*]

Traveler's Tale:
A New Yorker Is Born

Forgive me in advance. Any travelogue with a six-year-old narrator necessarily leans toward the micro and juvenile, unless one was one of J. D. Salinger's super-genius Glass family prodigies, which I, in a word, wasn't. But even I understood that our New York trip over Christmas in 1970 would be different. Our annual visits were generally spent out on Long Island, at the home of our only other relatives in North America, worshipping our older cousins. But this time we were staying in Manhattan, at the Americana Hotel, now the Sheraton, on Seventh Avenue. The comparative excitement at the very center of the steam-pipe-venting, animatronic-Christmas-window winter bustle of it all was palpable. And it's an odd thing to say about New York City in 1970, but everything just worked so perfectly during that visit. There was not a portal that did not open upon approach, not a remote possibility that didn't fulfill its promise beyond all expectation.

Case in point: Back in Toronto, my neighbor Willy had a round muddy rock on his bookshelf at home; an unprepossessing half sphere whose cut side revealed a concave center carpeted with pale lavender crystals. I was uncoupled with envy. Even armed with the name of such a thing—a geode—it seemed impossible that there should be another one out there, let alone an affordable one. It was made of jewels, after all. And lo, in a mineral shop on Madison Avenue and Thirty-Fourth Street that is still in business, I was given my own, the purchase of which did not seem to bankrupt my parents. For the duration of the trip, I alternated between peering into the dark hand-held cavern of almost black amethyst, like hundreds of small animal teeth shining brilliantly—fierce, sharp, intoxicating—and inhaling the dusty geranium scent of earth and my own breath. What a remarkable city!

A preshow supper at Mamma Leone's on Forty-Eighth Street seemed theater enough in and of itself. There was a plaster chef with toque and moustache stirring a pot of spaghetti that turned around and around. Our waiter addressed my eight-year-old sister as "Beautiful" and remarked upon our table manners and the size of all three of the Rakoff siblings' goose-egg eyes, a not terribly rare occurrence when we were children. We did have big eyes and good manners, neither of which has really lasted. Our waiter was so funny. Our lasagna placed before us, it was a veritable bed quilt of layered pasta. The stars were among us, after all.

We were on our way to see Danny Kaye in *Two by Two*, the Richard Rodgers musical about Noah and the ark. And, as promised, there he was, the Court Jester, Walter Mitty himself, off the screen and in the flesh. Also in the cast, a hilarious young woman with brilliant comic timing and a roof-raising operatic voice: Madeline Kahn. It was her Broadway debut.

As we were walking up the aisle at the end, Danny Kaye broke the fourth wall to wish us all a happy New Year. I remember turning back toward the stage and waving, as if he had spoken directly to me, and thinking: Yes, yes, I will.

It wasn't my first trip to New York, and it certainly wasn't the last. But it was the trip, like one of those scenes where the gorgeous secretary whose beauty had barely been concealed behind a pair of men-don't-make-passes spectacles and a no-nonsense bun finally lets loose her stays in a cascade of perfumed hair and reveals her limpid eyes. And all of a sudden—there she is!

Indeed, there she was the whole time: ready, waiting, the only logical recipient of a love from the newly smitten hero. In the movies, he says, astonished, "How could I have been such a fool? Darling, it was you, you all along." In real life, I've essentially spent the four decades since trying to prove myself worthy of that ardor.

[The Wall Street Journal, *October 9, 2010*]

Walk This Way

State legislators were called back to Albany from their summer vacations for an emergency economic session to make ready for a lean stint that David A. Paterson, New York's governor, has promised "will get worse before it gets better." Wall Street, which accounts for 20 percent of the state's fortunes, is in decline. Tax revenues from sixteen of the state's largest banks fell to $5 million from $173 million in just one year.

In other words, New York City is about to get interesting again. Those who regret having moved here too late, having witnessed only her metastasized proliferation of glass-walled condos and cupcake purveyors, can take heart at the prospect of shuttered libraries, underfinanced schools, and grimy hospitals. Those bygone days of *Midnight Cowboy* grit might soon be upon us once more. Why, if you squint just a little bit, you can almost see Verdi Square changing back into "Needle Park."

There is one austerity measure, however, that has always been an ineluctable part of living here: walking. And it's still the very best way to get around.

Walking effectively is not unlike driving, minus the vehicle (or so I'm guessing; I've never had a driver's license in my life). There are speeders and road hogs. There is rage. And most important, there are rules. Unwritten, certainly. Unspoken (politely, at least) until now. Since there will be so many more of us taking to the streets, some checks and balances are in order to avoid complete mayhem. Herewith, just a few from the Unofficial New York City Walkers' Code. Learn them. Follow them.

Choose a lane: Yes, there are lanes. If you see something you like in a shop window, check your blind spot and, when it's safe to do so, shift over. (Happily, soon the stores will have closed, their windows boarded over, or smashed and empty from the latest blackout looting, rendering this rule as anachronistic as the requirement that men remove their hats in an elevator when a lady enters.)

No tailgating: Walking too closely behind someone for more than a block is irksome. Either pick up the pace and pass (on the left), or hang back. There should ideally be a compact car's length between you and the next person. (Disregard this rule at rush hour.) Indeed, close formations of any sort are best avoided. If you insist on walking three abreast, then listen carefully for the frustrated footfalls of those trying to get around your phalanx.

Don't even think of parking here: Running into people you know is one of the great pleasures of life in a crowded metropolis. When you see a friend, take an ambulatory hiatus and step to the side. This is doubly required in the case of strollers. Similarly, unless your dog files an individual tax return, it is inappropriate bordering on immoral to block human progress by unreeling thirty feet of retractable leash across the pavement.

We are not your mother: If you walk while texting or sending email, thereby foisting the responsibility of avoiding collision onto the rest of us, you have abrogated your rights as a walker. You, my friend, are a mere pedestrian. Whatever is on that saltine-sized screen is, I guarantee, not even fractionally as interesting as anything you might see out in the streets. Which leads to the lone daub of honey amid all this vinegar:

Look Around You! Every jaunt, every stroll, every errand brings you into contact with someone not like you. (Greetings, tinfoil-hat-wearing, manifesto-scribbling, profanity-spewing eccentric, fresh from your screening at MoMA!) Now—make sure to stand to the side while you do this next bit—look up. That old saw about neck-craning being what separates the visitors from the natives is nonsense. I've lived here for more than half of my forty-four years, and I still rubberneck like a tourist. See that thrilling array of cloud-dwelling spires, ziggurats, and temples? Monuments, every one, to the age of relative plenty in which they were erected, and then mute sentinels during the inevitable subsequent downturns, from "BROTHER, CAN YOU SPARE A DIME?" to "FORD TO CITY: DROP DEAD." They got through it. So will you. Start by putting one foot in front of the other.

[The New York Times, *Op-Ed, August 2008*]

I Like My Dog. Yours? Not So Much.

Manhattan's wealthier citizens had decamped for their summer homes, leaving the rest of us with room to breathe and stroll and enjoy summer in the greatest city in the world. Some friends and I, Italian pastries in hand, parked ourselves on the steps of a brownstone, where we observed the passing parade. A perfect New York evening until, coming through the East Village gloaming, he arrived; cunningly small, his coat an unusual, glossy dark gray, almost hematite in color. He playfully sniffed at us, treating us as no more sentient than the stoop upon which we were sitting. It was finally his probing at the wax-papered *sfogliatelle* in our hands that prompted a response from his owner.

"Milo!" she said, her voice swoopy with mock scolding. "You know you can't eat sugar."

Milo's infraction, it seems, was strictly personal, dietary, and adorable. There was no "please excuse my dog for nuzzling your food with his nose, a wet appendage that was only moments ago exploring god knows what on the sidewalk and more than likely the backside of some other dog not long before that." The thought probably never even crossed her mind. Indeed, Milo was allowed to continue to tarry, tangled among our ankles (and dessert) as unhurried as a Butoh dancer. It was only when my friend Rory pointed out—with a friendly chuckle, it should be noted—that Milo "might have found the only four New Yorkers who don't love dogs" that his owner pulled her beloved terrier away in protective haste while casting a look in Rory's direction that one might best reserve for the inappropriate slattern who shows up at the Vatican in a tube top with a pentagram Sharpie'd on her stomach.

Lest you think I'm one of those injustice-collecting urban paranoids with a tinfoil hat and a plastic bag containing a brisket and a manifesto in tiny handwriting, a New York crazy who has a problem with everybody and everything, I should mention that I grew up with—and adored—a dog of my very own. A lemon beagle named Hecuba. As channeled by my father—who kept up a running monologue of her voice throughout my childhood—she was less stalwart Queen of Troy than lovable Lucy Ricardo: unfailingly devoted, endearingly clueless (surely every family trip taken without her was nothing more than forgetfulness on our part), and charmingly flatulent. Her death was wrenching, and even now, more than three decades since her passing, when I see a beagle, I melt. I absolutely know and appreciate what it is to love a dog. But I also understand that when I say that Hecuba was the best, the sweetest dog who ever lived, it would never occur to me to expect someone else to feel that way about her. Why, then, am I continuously asked to be an ardent suitor in others' love affairs with their animals? And why does my resistance to do so put me on a continuum of sociopathy somewhere between Bernie Madoff and Hannibal Lecter?

It's the false moral component behind blind animal love that so frosts me. The faulty logic that believes that the capacity to adore a nonhuman creature is somehow a purer form of love. Just try pointing out that a relationship with a creature that cannot challenge you, that does not make you slog daily through the necessary compromise, debate, and occasional pitched battle, might be something less than deep and nuanced, and see where it gets you. By the same token, displays of evident affection on their parts and extraordinary tales of the conscience and loyalty of Balto, for example, or the miraculous intelligence of Alex the African gray notwithstanding, most nonhuman animals don't really feel the same way about us. If they did, you'd overhear a lot more "I'm really pissed off at what you said before about me getting fat and how Alice Munro writes the same book over and over. So no, I don't want to get the ball" in the nation's dog runs.

I had occasion a few years back to appear on a late-night talk show with a chimpanzee (long story, never mind). As he held my hand in his own warm, hairy dry palm, I really was overwhelmed with a rush of lovelike symptoms. The chimp seemed unbearably sweet, and his wearing a pair of diapers to prevent any on-set accidents only made him more so. Still, I demurred when the trainer asked me if I wanted to step up our level of physical contact and actually dandle him in my arms. It's not that I wasn't tempted. I was immediately taken in by those empathetic brown eyes surrounded by benevolent wrinkles. What I was feeling was the same complex firing of neurons and synapses that ascribe human emotion to the furry, the liquid eyed, the infantile. Disney and his team of animators figured this out long ago (I still can't watch the scene where Dumbo visits his incarcerated mother). But I could not rid myself of the fear (completely well-founded, as it turns out, given the recent stories of chimps in the news) that he might at that moment revert—as is his right as an animal—to his dominance-seeking nature and decide to tear my face from my skull. My desire to cradle this clingy, warm-thoraxed being

in my arms was triggered because he so reminded me of a tod-
dler. Get it? A human child. The kind of creature who might
grow up to become an oncologist, a public school teacher,
or yes, even a Grand Theft Auto–playing, Mom's-basement-
dwelling disappointment.

Not far from my apartment, within a stretch of no more
than five hundred feet, there are two doggie gyms where
Gotham's canines who aren't getting enough exercise running
through the city's parks, or are neglecting their all-important
doggie glutes and abs, can go for a workout. What can I say?
This appalls me. But do I wish these Gilded Age inanities ill?
Quite the contrary. I hope they stay open and prosper, but
only to the extent that they provide jobs for folks who need
them. It's not a contradiction. It's not even a paradox. I have
no problem with animals, I just like people more.

[O, the Oprah Magazine, *May 12, 2009*]

King of the Forest

In 1923, on holiday in the Swiss Alps, the Viennese writer Felix Salten was so taken with the natural setting and wildlife, he was inspired to write the life story of a young fawn in the woods. Salten made up the name of his protagonist from shortening the Italian word for "baby." In case you haven't read it—I certainly hadn't before writing this piece; Disney movies can eclipse their source material—*Bambi* is an astonishment. One chapter about the final moments of the last two surviving leaves on an oak tree as winter approaches is a wonder of compression and a rumination on old age and impending death as poignant as Kurt Weill's "September Song." "You're as lovely as the day you were born," says the first leaf. "Thanks," whispers the second. "You've always been so kind to me. I'm just beginning to understand how kind you are."

In another, a fox, bleeding and exhausted, "beside himself with rage and fear," stumbles into a clearing, pursued by a hunter's hound. The fox first pleads with the hound, one canine to another. Then, understanding the inevitability of his approaching end, he suddenly sits erect and speaks in a voice bitter as gall: "Aren't you ashamed, you traitor . . . You turncoat . . . You spy."

The denunciation is taken up by others in the forest. "Traitor!" screams the magpie, "Spy!" shrieks the jay.

The dog responds in kind, denouncing their benighted naïveté. Besides, he isn't the only traitor. What about the cow, the sheep, the chicken?

"They're rabble!" snarls the fox—his last defiant words as the hound sets upon him, a fine spray of blood dyeing the snow.

Salten's writing has not a trace of anthropomorphized cuteness. *Bambi*'s forest is peopled (creatured?) with characters by turns arrogant, venal, gossipy, and engaging—as flawed and varied as the cosmopolitan fauna Salten must have encountered daily in his life in Vienna.

The novel was immediately popular with both children and adults. An English-language edition followed in 1929 (translated, curiously enough, by Whittaker Chambers, who took the job to supplement the paltry salary he earned as editor of the Communist newspaper *The Daily Worker*), with a foreword by novelist and playwright John Galsworthy, who deemed it "a little masterpiece," and signed off with, "I particularly recommend it to sportsmen."

Sportsmen, however, were less enthusiastic, at least insofar as the Disney version was concerned. When the feature-length cartoon was released in 1942, the American Rifleman's Association tried to get the studio to tack a pro-hunting prologue onto the movie, something Uncle Walt declined to do. The gun lobby was justified in its worry, since entire generations of American children would go on to identify the death of Bambi's mother as among their earliest and most wrenching psychological terrors. (Disney used to have a stringent policy of withdrawing films for years at a time, so my pre-DVD childhood was *Bambi*-less. Whatever dead-cartoon-mom angst I was imprinted with was located in *Dumbo*, specifically the scene in which, chained inside a boxcar, Dumbo's mother dandles him in the cradle of her trunk, the only extremity she can get through the barred window. It is unutterably sad. I still cannot watch it.)

But as harrowing as the celluloid rendition of Bambi's maternal loss may be, it is nothing compared to Salten's original chapter, where things are bad to begin with and only become more horrible. It is winter and the once cordial animals have begun to turn on one another in the madness of hunger. The near-famine conditions have "spread bitterness and brutality." The crows kill the hare's sick young son for sport. The ferret wounds the squirrel mortally, the fox has torn the admired and stately pheasant to pieces. "It's hard to believe that it will ever be better," says Bambi's dispirited mother. Bambi himself is skittish and exhausted with hunger and cold.

Suddenly, one of the young bucks prickles with a vague presentiment of trouble. From the farthest edge of the wood, a murder of crows comes flying by, agitated. The magpies begin to screech to one another from the trees, and finally the deer can smell "that fearful scent [that] kept streaming on in a wider wave, sending terror into their hearts and uniting them all in one mad fear, in a single feverish impulse to flee, to save themselves."

The forest roars with the sound of hunters advancing from all sides, snapping twigs, beating on tree trunks to drive out the animals. A pheasant flies into the air and is killed in front of everyone. "Don't lose your head! . . . Just run, run, run!" one of his surviving compatriots panics to the others. But it is all too much for the bird and, crazed with fear, he too takes off into the air, only to be shot down.

"Then everyone lost his senses." Creatures swarm over one

another to get away. All is tumult and thunder and death. The old hare is murdered before their eyes, the sky is darkened by a rain of blood and feathers. Bambi follows behind his mother to the edge of the thicket. They are to run across the clearing, and he is to keep running, regardless of what he might see happen to her. Well, you know what happens to her. Salten and Disney share a restraint by not showing us. The chapter ends simply, "Bambi never saw his mother again."

Like many an artist, Salten first tasted prominence in death, though not his own. Born Siegmund Salzmann in 1869 in Budapest, he moved with his parents to Vienna when he was three weeks old. The city had begun granting Jews the rare privilege of full citizenship just two years prior, prompting a large Jewish migration from elsewhere in the Hapsburg Empire. Salten grew up poor in the Vienna slums, with little formal education. He labored in a series of menial clerical jobs in the insurance business while sending out his work to little or no effect until 1902, when his obituary of Emile Zola, by all accounts a moving and noteworthy piece of writing, received widespread notice and provided Salten entrée into the Jung-Wien, the Young Vienna Movement, a loose conglomeration of progressive bohemians. Artists and writers, most of them Jews, Jung-Wien counted among its members composer Franz Lehár, playwright and novelist Arthur Schnitzler, librettist Hugo von Hofmannsthal, and Stefan Zweig. Once enfolded into this rarefied klatch, Salten became a prolific novelist and a noted theater critic for various publications, shuttling back and forth between Berlin and Vienna.

Salten received only nominal Jewish instruction, it seems. He even served as an altar boy, which might account for the novel's vaguely Christian sensibility. Humans are referred to using the God-like "He" and "Him" throughout. It seems a fitting moniker for a largely unseen force that is quick to ire and possessed of awesome, arbitrary, and obliterating power. Ultimately, a grown Bambi realizes that "there is Another who is over us all, over us and over Him," A force of unquantifiable strength, but one also imbued with the attributes of mercy and lovingkindness. And yet, even if Salten hadn't known the experience directly, even the casual reader cannot fail to see in the young fawn's life of precarious freedom and probationary ease what can only be described as a deep Jewish uncertainty. The entrapment and slaughter of the scene rings with the authenticity of nothing less than a sylvan pogrom. There is other evidence to suggest that Salten's Jewish consciousness was not entirely dormant. In 1910, when Vienna's beloved mayor Karl Lueger died, Salten took some heat for an obituary he wrote in the *Presse* newspaper criticizing the encoded anti-Semitism in Lueger's falsely populist anti-intellectualism, that "disintegrates the physicians, insults the professors, jeers at learning." Salten's lingering vestigial Jewishness did not go unnoticed in *Bambi* either, at least not by one of the members of Jung Wien. The writer Karl Kraus, a Czech-born Jew who renounced his Judaism and was baptized as a Catholic at age thirty-seven, criticized Salten for muddying the purity of the German tongue by putting Yiddishisms in the mouths of his animal characters.

Bambi's religion may have been a matter of some dispute, but his gender never was. He is most assuredly a male fawn, despite his name's adoption by subsequent generations of female porn stars. It's an oddly appropriate fate, given Salten's own foray into filth. *Memoirs of Josephine Mutzenbacher,* authored by one Josephine Mutzenbacher, was a pseudonymous "autobiography" told from the point of view of an older woman looking back over her life as a courtesan. As Josephine, or "Pepi," says near the beginning, whoring "saved me from suffocating in the slums and permitted me to live like any woman of good society."

The book, a prequel to Pepi's later genteel life, documents her childhood in the destitute Ottakring district of Vienna, in a crowded tenement with her parents and two older brothers. A series of boarders who sleep in the tiny apartment's kitchen educate the juvenile Pepi in the ways of sex, although her main and most energetic instructor is her next-older brother, along with a pair of precocious siblings who live upstairs.

Salten wrote the book in 1906, seventeen years before *Bambi*, and just four years after his redemptive Zola obituary. The indignities of Pepi's youthful privation are clearly and minutely recalled by a writer whose own relief at having "gotten out" must have still been quite fresh.

There is no indication that *The Memoirs of Josephine Mutzenbacher* was a standout in its field, either critically or commercially. Salten didn't vocally claim authorship of the material and, deeply felt psychological roots notwithstanding, the book reads like pretty standard porn. There is squalor, but menace and any real hardship are largely absent from the narrative. To be sure, no one is sitting down to lavish meals or clothing themselves in finery, but one can't help wondering, why aren't these children being beaten in dingy schoolrooms by ignorant, malodorous teachers with filthy beards and long fingers? Or else having their own digits caught in the gnashing maws of early industrial factory machines? Instead of the usual Jacob Riis–style hijinks one might expect from Pepi and her ragamuffin pals—stealing from pushcarts, rolling hoops, lobbing bricks through storefront windows—they seem to spend their free time (and they have an awful lot of it) screwing around. Her days stretch out before her, with hours during which to experiment with her urchin pals, with bored housewives, with a seriously unqualified governess, a great, massy coal wagoneer in the cellar, the corrupting priest Father Mayer, an "art" photographer named Capucci, and, after the death of her mother, her own father.

It's a regular Melroseplatz. For a little girl sprung from the mind of a compatriot and contemporary of Freud, she is remarkably lacking in sexual trauma, although Salten's explanation for this has to do with class and privilege. "In my childhood, boys and girls like my brother and me were all sexually aware and eager to practice that premature knowledge," Pepi reports. "Boys did it with their sisters and girl friends as a matter of course. They had never heard of the word *incest*, or *taboo*, like the rich kids who had the opportunity to listen to the conversation of educated adults. Brothers and sisters of the poor proletarian class saw each other as males and females and would have been quite surprised if they had been told that relationships should make them see one another differently. When I could do any reading in my later years I discovered that the children in primitive societies felt and acted exactly as we did."

There is the sense from these repeated, falsely erudite primitivist fantasies from an adult Pepi that *The Memoirs of Josephine* aspires to something more than mere stroke book. We learn that, although it might have been Pepi's beauty and lack of sexual squeamishness that eventually afforded her her financial independence, it was her curious intellect that led her to a life of music and art and culture (a life not dissimilar from the one that Salten himself was delivered to once he was accepted at the tables of the Café Griensteidl). It gave her existence beauty and meaning and it gave us, the lucky readers, these pages. Yet we never get even a glimpse of this earthly reward. *The Memoirs of Josephine* ends years before the salons, the conversations, the evening musicales. It's like being invited over to someone's house for supper and being regaled with the tantalizing rigors of her Cordon Bleu training and the resultant meal she's going to cook for tomorrow night's guest. In the meantime, all we get is repetitive, consequence-free pistoning and probing. It is surpassingly dull.

And while I cannot speak to the book's authenticity—having never been Viennese, female, or sexually unbridled myself under anything but the most metaphorical circumstances, and even then only when drunk—it has the ring of falsehood about it. Salten's forest seems less idealized and idyllic than his Vienna, a city he fled at the start of World War II. He settled in Zurich and died there in 1945.

Salten and his Viennese cohort were among the first Jews raised in a largely secular milieu, allowing them to live lives and make art independent of a strictly Jewish experience. They filled the exciting new void left behind by abandoned religious traditions with an exuberant secularism, which would go on to inform painting, writing, theater, psychoanalysis, and just about every other aspect of a dynamic age hurtling into the future. A few decades later all of this would fall under the *entartete*, or "degenerate," rubric. Ironic, seeing as how there would be almost no more iconic a Nazi image than a proud stag in the forest.

[Tablet, *June 12, 2006*]

Tweenage Wasteland

It was a covert uprising in a middle school cafeteria. Like those towns that wake up one day to find their city councils overrun with candidates they have never heard of—elected on secret groundswells of support by a well-organized but clandestine network of creationists—my goddaughter Eva's school talent show was co-opted by one song. Child after child (not Eva, thank god, who was the best of the bunch and chose a Rodgers and Hammerstein classic) took the stage and performed the same pop tune, "Start of Something New." "Start of Something New"—a mirthlessly ironic title after the seventh time hearing it—is the power ballad from a Disney Channel made-for-television movie called *High School Musical*, a monster hit that has become as vital to kids as insulin, it seems.

With neither children nor cable TV of my own it's not a complete shock to find myself out of the loop. Out of the loop is my middle name; I barely know what's going on culturally with people my own age (four hundred and eight, last I checked). But it was the almost liturgical conviction with which those children sang along every single time it was (badly) performed that both was chilling and cried out for deeper investigation. These were the Tweens about whom so much has been written, almost all of it having to do with their awesome purchasing power ($50 billion annually). Television, movies, print, music, new media, all have fallen to this squeaky-voiced, writhing hydra whose tiny plastic wallets powered a cultural juggernaut that could not be ignored.

It made me wistful for the Tween product of my own youth. Primarily British, they were hard-bound comic books sent from our relatives abroad. Pilfered from my older sister, the stories involved twelve-year-old girls having adventures— foiling jewel thieves while on a seaside holiday in Brighton—or a girl who ran a ranch-cum-orphanage where she taught school and faced down nefarious land prospectors by showing what used to be called "pluck." She was aided in her daily duties by a gentle idiot man-child strongman and an ornery old coot who cooked and met all his tasks with a grudging yet endearing "hrumph." What were kids reading and seeing today, I wondered?

Tweens are variously described as ranging in age from seven anywhere up to fourteen years old. I will use twelve as my cutoff, because any dipping into the actual teen years and their attendant culture will muddy the waters of my immersion, although I fail immediately when I pick up the first volume of Gossip Girl, a series of novels by Cecily von Ziegesar. A *Liaisons Dangereuses* glimpse into prep school kids on Manhattan's Upper East Side, it is exceedingly good reading: pitch perfect, gimlet-eyed, and sexy (a little disquietingly so for this fortysomething homosexual), but in no way suitable for an eleven-year-old girl. Before he was even twenty, Roman Polanski revealed himself to be a genius by making a few short films, one of which, *The Fat and the Lean*, was the tale of a young fellow (Polanski himself) in shackles, forced to dance for the amusement and delectation of a seated, corpulent taskmaster.

Occasionally, the young boy could peer shyly through a window and see in the distance, rising over the fields and trees, the Eiffel Tower and the surrounding rooftops of Paris: beautiful and unattainable despite being so maddeningly close, it seemed to him that he could not fail to reach out and touch them. If Tween girls are reading the Gossip Girl books—or watching the forthcoming CW series of the same name, which is similarly fantastic and peopled with a gorgeous cast of very good actors, or paging through *Us Weekly*, where they can read up on the extracurricular exploits of Paris, Britney, and Lindsay—it is simply because it is illegal to tie children to radiators. These acts of transgressive aspiration are part of having free will. I was watching Ken Russell movies when I was eight. Does that make him a Tween director? No. Was that appropriate? Probably not. Did I love them? You betcha.

My foray begins in earnest with magazines: *TEENick*; *J-14*, *Just for Teens*; *High School Musical & Other Teen TV Stars*; *Tiger Beat*; *Bop*; *M*; and *Twist*. The covers are an assaultively bright citrus jumble. They are hot on the corneas; as busy as Tibetan religious murals of the cosmos, with the many faces of Tween celebrities as all the bodhisattvas and minor deities. Almost all the magazines cover the same beats: the Kids' Choice Awards, the Disney Channel Games (which I initially mistakenly think are referring to our nation's capital when I read "DC"), the upcoming Nancy Drew movie (kind of lousy; Nancy is a tone-deaf, know-it-all prig, and Emma Roberts is not a patch on her father, Eric, or aunt Julia, I'm afraid), heartthrobs like Orlando Bloom (referred to as Orly, like the French airport), and other Tween stars. Most of the periodicals have pull-out posters, horoscopes, and oddest of all, pages where readers can write in their humiliating stories. One of them is intriguingly open-ended, given both the ambiguity of the outcome and the gender malleability of the name: "I liked my best friend's older brother. I told him and he was really surprised!—Taylor, 13."

Ask almost anyone about Tweens and they will parrot the same received wisdom: that our nation's little girls (it's mostly girls) grow up far too quickly and are being taught to dress and act like whores, emulating those boozy train wrecks photographed dancing on banquettes or shown staggering out of the Chateau Marmont. Somewhere, if we are to believe local newscasts, girls spend their leisure hours by marking their territories on boys' barely mature genitals with smears of different-colored lipstick at apocryphal rainbow parties, but not here. *Twist* magazine's horoscope might warn its Leo readers to "make sure you leave time for cute boys!" and there is talk of dating and kissing, but it's all fairly chaste. I do come across one PSA from the Candie's Foundation to stop teen pregnancy, but for the rest, it's about being "flirty," having crushes, maybe stealing a kiss or two.

As for the pantheon of demigods shown on their covers, the magazines are confusing for the novice anthropologist. No one is referred to by anything but their first name. Cody, Vanessa, Devon, Ashley, Aly & AJ. "Nick wants Miley back." "Dylan has a secret gf." What does become immediately clear is that someone named Zac reigns supreme. This is Zac Efron, who plays Troy Bolton in, you guessed it, *High School Musical*, the jewel in the Disney Channel's crown and, it seems, the center of the mandala from which all Tween culture currently radiates. Efron is the classic dreamboat, with gemlike blue eyes, chestnut hair, and features still soft with youth; a boy girls can love (in all of that term's gentle, nonpenetrative meaning). Zac is everywhere, his visage shining forth on page after page.

True heartlessness is the province of the young. The window for Tween stars is incredibly narrow, which might explain the tsunami-like saturation of their images while the iron is hot. No sixteen-year-old will willingly admit to the things that sent her ten-year-old heart aflutter. The Spice Girls might as well be Jeanette MacDonald for how often they are remembered by their once-devoted fan base (which is different from those cases where Tweens have taken someone out of the slipstream of the general culture and co-opted them for their very own; it must be an unspeakably bitter pill for Avril Lavigne, for example—who cultivated her skater-boi-loving-knife-carrying-punk realness so carefully—that her primary constituency is barely five years out of wearing pull-ups to bed). There are some rare cases of longevity—Hilary Duff, for example, whose emerging adult bone structure and darker tresses have turned her into a veritable Deneuve of elegance; and Justin Timberlake, whose ascendance as a bona fide music icon has retroactively lent the Mickey Mouse Club as much credibility as a training ground of young talent as the Peking Opera School or the Bolshoi. But for the rest, a lot of the stars' appeal lies in their juvenile awkwardness. It is doubtful that *Hannah Montana* star Mitchel Musso's features will be enhanced by full-on pubescence. Still others in the pages already look too old. There is a knowingness in the features, a canny Hollywood professionalism imperfectly concealed behind the wide-eyed freckled grin and there, suddenly, is the Headshot of Dorian Gray, and one barely has to squint to see the leathery and lecherous tax exile on Ibiza three decades hence, photographed in some louche Euro nightspot, buttons straining across an ample paunch, seated at a table littered with glasses, an arm thrown over the shoulders of a too-young nymphet, while he slurs, his breath sangria-scented and hot with innuendo, "Ever been on a catamaran, angel tits?"

Or perhaps I am projecting. You would forgive me this dark view if you, too, had sat through the touchstone of them all, the very thing that started me on this misbegotten Tween haj: the Disney Channel's *High School Musical.* How to say this: *High School Musical* stinks; it is aggressively bad. It looks terrible, the choreography and direction are substandard, the songs define *forgettable*, the lip-synching is achingly obvious. The best performance comes from a jolie laide named Ashley Tisdale as an entitled princess named (hilariously) Sharpay. She chews through the proceedings like an Almodóvar heroine at full Technicolor tilt. She's Gina Gershon in *Showgirls:* the only one really in on the joke. As for the leads, Zac Efron (who is like an updated David Cassidy and really does have star quality) and Vanessa Hudgens (who doesn't), they have thin singing voices and the unthreatening faces of two Disney woodland creatures. He is the basketball star, she the math whiz ("I don't want to be the school's freaky genius girl again," she laments to her mother). Both of them have to overcome the prejudices of their respective cliques—the b-ball jocks and the mathletes—and have the courage to try out for the Big Show. The science nerds project about as much intelligence as Denise Richards in that Bond movie where she had to play a nuclear physicist, I think, and could barely pronounce the word "plutonium." And as for Troy's teammates, who deride him and shudder at the thought of musical theater and show tunes, they are the most sibilant band of meatheads I've ever seen. There's really no excuse for the cynical, proactive shittiness of *High School Musical.* Superior precedents of this very genre are thick on the ground: *Fame* and everything with Mickey and Judy spring to mind. It's just a lousy piece of product.

Taking a break from the Disney Channel, I gravitate over

to the other Tween Mecca, Nickelodeon. I start with *Ned's Declassified School Survival Guide*, starring Devon Werkheiser. It's a frenetic and slapstick view of school, with comically ogre-ish vice principals, a runaway weasel, field trips, bullies, crushes, flatulence that can blow the hinges off a bathroom door, you get the picture. A cartoon called *The Fairly Odd-Parents* is the brainchild of Butch Hartman. With an early 1960s Atomic Age look, it also takes a page from that era's brilliant Jay Ward, creator of Cold War cartoons *The Rocky and Bullwinkle Show* and *Roger Ramjet*, whose villain was named Noodles Romanoff, just one of the many gags aimed at adults. Any grown-ups watching *Fairly OddParents* will be similarly well amused. *The Naked Brothers Band*, which stars Nat and Alex Wolff, is also eminently watchable. The Wolffs are real-life brothers and the children of musician Michael Wolff and *Thirtysomething* alumna Polly Draper, who is the writer/director of this show about juvenile sibling indie-rock stars. It is very well acted, the rhythms are authentically downtown Manhattan, even with the requisite Tween frenzy of action and sets dressed in vibrant Rootie Kazootie colors. The songs, written and performed by the brothers themselves, are very good. Older brother Nat is a serious talent. And yet, I am initially troubled that the boys' characters are celebrities. Perhaps it's the redolence of the current trend of New York City juvenile-rock-bands-with-hipster-parents that creeps me out a little, but it's a larger worry that tales of ordinary children have become anathema in these fame-obsessed times. Back on Disney, *Hannah Montana* (Miley Cyrus, daughter of country star Billy Ray Cyrus) plays a girl with a double life, half regular girl, half rock star. Must everyone have an agent and an in at the Video Music Awards? On closer examination, though, I can see the importance in this imposture. Tweens shudder on the cusp of adolescence—potentially the very worst decade of life—powerless, without the vote or even housekeys in most cases. If these show-biz tots have creative lives and are seen as more than mere extensions of their parents, they are only embodying a wish-fulfillment of exactly the same kind that powers the multimillion-dollar Chick Lit industry, with its tales of recently divorced women, invisible and unloved at home but somehow absolute catnip for the marble-torsoed-hugely-wealthy-sensitive-and-searingly-intellectual groundskeepers of Tuscany and Provence. With that in mind, it's easy to see how impressive *The Naked Brothers Band*—a show about an actual family made by an actual family—really is. It is almost better than it needs to be (unlike *High School Musical*, which, it bears repeating, sucks the big moose cock, as we used to say in Canada).

I'm probably just hewing to my sex, gravitating toward the boy programming, a bit of a surprise, given what a little homo I was and remain. But the girl stuff is just too girly, even for me. There are Tween laws of thermodynamics. If Tween girls are targeted with a junior high school–based world of budding romance with floppy-haired, beryl-eyed boys like Zac Efron (pant, pant), then Tween boys are courted with its equal and opposing force: not the hyper-violent postapocalyptic dystopia of video games but that self-same academic environment suffused with bodily humor that, it doesn't take a psychiatrist to see, is in large part born of the sexual anxiety of the disparity between the sexes at that age. For time immemorial, it has never escaped the notice of Tween boys that, as their female cohort starts their blossoming lurch toward womanhood, the boys, by contrast, are nowhere near beginning to change, either emotionally or corporeally. The Disney Channel vs. Nickelodeon. The schism is unmistakable: Threshold to Love for the girls, Body and Its Dangers for the boys; the peaceable but decidedly separate Kingdoms of Rainbows and Farts. The boys will grow into men and graduate to the vastly more mature diversions of, uh, *Jackass* and Adam Sandler movies. But what of the girls? What can I hope for that crowd that I saw devotedly mouthing "Zac Efron"? (Actually, given half the chance, I'd devotedly mouth Zac Efron myself. He's twenty, okay? I checked.)

It's clearly a developmental phase that must be gotten through. All the CDs, magazines, and TV programs seem, at first blush, to be nothing more than a training program for an adulthood of *Cosmo* reading and cosmo drinking. A dispiriting notion, that. Except when one remembers that in a few years, these girls will have moved on to Young Adult books. Gossip Girl might concern itself with the overprivileged and shallow, but it's skillful writing, a suitable precursor to the pleasures of Edith Wharton. Other titles will provide healthy doses of a darker reality, books epitomized by Francesca Lia Block's now decade-old Weetzie Bat series. There is the forthcoming *The Plain Janes*, a fantastically good graphic novel for teen girls by Cecil Castellucci and Jim Rugg. Set in a post-terrorist-attack world, it is about the lifesaving powers of making art.

It is inevitable. The same girls who are now drunk on the helium-voiced singers will migrate within two years or so, the time it takes most New Yorkers to get around to washing their windows.

[Radar, *October, 2007*]

Unaccustomed as I Am . . . : How to Give a Wedding Toast

In this modern age of divorce, death, remarriage, and recrimination, the strict code of wedding etiquette collapses like a soufflé, at least it ought to. At a wedding I attended recently, the best man rose to make a speech to the bride and groom. Nice tradition, I thought, hoping for a certain degree of wit and emotion, despite the fact that he was a rather thick-necked fellow with a crew cut and a rented tuxedo; one of the groom's frat brothers from college. After yelling "Dude!" to the groom and repeatedly high-fiving and punching him, he then proceeded to imitate (I was told) the Pee-wee Herman dance to the song "Tequila."

I was furious at being held hostage by this lunkhead (precisely the type of lunkhead I spent my time assiduously avoiding in college), all in service to some outmoded tradition. So what if he was the best man? Did this give him license to inflict this moronic torture upon us? Why, I wondered, couldn't the one giving the wedding toast be the maid of honor, or the mother of the bride, or the groom's ex-girlfriend, or the bride's ex-girlfriend, for that matter? A quick survey of the experts, both past and present, offered almost no guidance:

"The first toast is always a toast to the bride, proposed by the best man," Millicent Fenwick states in her 1948 edition of

Vogue's Book of Etiquette (Simon & Schuster). It is, she continues, "even more than a custom, a rule." She also shows, incidentally, a table-setting diagram with no fewer than four forks, and complimentary cigarettes (!) at each place. (In a similar vein, a cookbook from the same period lists step one of making chicken salad as "Have your girl prepare a chicken.") Elizabeth Post (Emily's granddaughter-in-law), in her *Complete Book of Wedding Etiquette* (HarperCollins, 1991), proposes the following for the "extroverted" groom: "My debt to the Adamses is two fold—first for having brought Kate into the world, and second for entrusting her to me."

Somewhere in there, we're supposed to find guidance for those type Bs among us who are neither the best man, nor marrying women named Kate Adams.

Let's dispense immediately with the flawed notion that if what you say is from the heart, then that's all that counts. No one with half a brain in their head would ever confuse honesty with eloquence. You will receive no compliments from the assembled guests if you throw up or burst into tears, no matter how genuine or heartfelt.

So, in the true spirit of stealing the show, here are some pointers, reminders, and caveats:

Make it short. My friend Margaret tells the following story: "My father-in-law had unearthed an old tape of Gideon at age three. He hadn't cued it up and, after talking already for twenty minutes, he sat there trying to find the place on the tape. People got restless, and he looked up and yelled, 'Don't make me compete! I'm competing here!' and I thought, 'Yeah! 'Cause your act stinks!' He's such a sweet man, but at that length, I found myself judging his performance, not his sentiment. And I was really angry." Nothing can turn an audience against you more than overstaying your welcome. Remember, this is not your day; it is the bride and groom's. The trick is to get on and off as charmingly and quickly as possible, leaving the other guests intrigued and secretly wanting to date you.

Make it nice. "Everyone was making jokes about how bald my husband, Rick, was," relates Suzanne. "It was all pretty good-natured. But then my best friend got up and said, looking directly into Rick's face, 'Well, I just have to say, you've always had enough hair for me.' There were whoops from the other tables, and Rick laughed, but I thought, 'What, should I leave now? Am I, like, in the way?' I'll be honest, I don't see her as much as I used to. I thought it was a very weird thing to say."

It seems so perfect, you've had a drink or two, so has everyone else, why not get up there and tell the bride that you've always been in love with her husband? Or that you hate her dress? Guffaw, guffaw, right? Wrong! There's something about weddings that turns everyone into those birds they take down mine shafts to sniff out noxious gases. People are just itching to bestow the Miss Havisham Award for Most Bitter Person. It gives them something memorable to latch on to during the inevitable post mortem of the party, and the verdict is invariably pity for the poor sap who let her anger or inappropriateness show. Additionally, the bride and groom will never forgive you, nor should they. Moreover, they will never forget. *Every single time* they ever use the gift you got them (and you'd better pray, after that display, that they like it), they—and their children after them—will recall with derisive laughter, your drunken, hostile, pathetic blunder.

Make it personal. "I basically got up there and let the guests know that the groom was the luckiest man in the world to be getting my best friend as his wife, and told him, in the nicest way imaginable, that if he ever hurt her, I'd tear his tongue out with my bare hands," says Amy. "Everyone was talking about *him* and *his* MBA and *his* business and there was nobody bearing witness to my fabulous, fabulous friend, who, although she might not be exactly what his narrow-minded parents had in mind, blows him out of the proverbial water and they should all collectively be on their knees kissing the ground she walked on. So that's what I did." It's important to remember why you, and not someone else, are standing up there with drink in hand. It's because you know the wedding couple, or at least one of them. Nobody really wants to hear your general take on marriage as a ritual, unless of course you're Margaret Mead. What they want is your insight into the people getting married. Talk about the first time you met them, or how pleased you are with their choice of mate, and why. You've been given the microphone because of your privileged relationship with the couple. Let the audience sense this. Let the bride and groom be so overcome with the strength of your bond that they ask you along on the honeymoon. Decline their invitation, ever so sweetly.

The world has changed since the age of the stogie and brandy snifter and the after-dinner badinage of men. You're no longer expected, or even allowed, to sit there demurely listening, a half-smile playing over your lips as they expound on the virtue and beauty of the bride and the stalwart, manly qualities of the groom. Even Millicent Fenwick broadened her horizons from the strict world of etiquette to run for Congress—and win. Like Ann Richards said, Ginger did everything Fred did, only backward and in high heels. The rules that dictate what to say and how to say it are the same ones you use in your daily life with the people you love. In fact, that's precisely it: These are people you love. Speak to them, and about them, accordingly. The rest is just so much silverware.

There you are, palms sweating, stomach churning. And the wedding isn't for a month. Calm down, start slow, AND GET A PENCIL!

Some things to talk about:

· Who are you? Be exceptionally brief here, unless you really know nobody at the wedding. Like a book report for school, try to find the happy medium between treating your teacher as if she arrived from Mars yesterday and assuming she's already read *Great Expectations*.

· Where did you first meet the bride or groom?
　– If she/he is your sister/brother, how did you get along as children?
　– If she/he is your friend, when was the first time you remember them talking about this person they thought they were falling in love with?

· Why specifically do you like their choice of spouse? Be nice. If you can't be nice, be specific; it often reads as nice.

· How are *you* feeling on this day of your best friend's marriage? (Hint: you feel good).

Okay, let's try it:

"Hello. My name is _____ and I'm _____'s best _____. I've known _____ for _____ years, ever since we first met at _____. I seem to remember, I was having some trouble with the _____ and how exactly to do it. She/He looked directly at me and said (in a way I found immediately charming and which I was soon to recognize as her/his inimitable _____, which I'm sure you all know):

"_____." [*Pause here for audience laughter.*]

Well, that was a long time ago, and now _____ is marrying _____, and I, for one, couldn't be happier. Why, I remember the first day she/he came back to the small studio we were renting in _____—I was working on a small still life in oils, I believe—and talked about this great guy/girl she/he'd just met. I knew then that this was the one. And when I finally met _____, why, I loved everything about him/her. Particularly his/her _____, not to mention unfailing _____.

So all I can say to you two is, best of luck. I'm so pleased I could be here. Won't you all join me in raising your glasses? To _____ and _____.

You'll all find my home phone number conveniently printed on the small cards underneath your bread plates. Thank you."

[*Discovered on David Rakoff's hard drive, Beinecke Library, Yale University. Written circa September 2008.*]

David Rakoff's *Half Empty* Worldview Is Full of Wit

TERRY GROSS, HOST: This is *Fresh Air*. I'm Terry Gross.

The title of David Rakoff's new book, *Half Empty*, gives you some sense of his predisposition towards life: Prepare for the worst. *Half Empty* seems like a good follow-up to his other book titles: *Don't Get Too Comfortable* and *Fraud*.

Rakoff is best known for his humorous magazine essays and his stories on *This American Life*. He's had several small acting roles and wrote and starred in the film that won an Oscar this year for Best Dramatic Short.

His new book starts with an essay about negative thinking called "The Bleak Shall Inherit the Earth" and moves on to tell the story of the small role he got in a movie with Bette Midler and Diane Keaton and why he didn't make it to the end of the film.

Another chapter describes reporting on New York City's first exotic-erotic ball and expo. But the last chapter is about his recurrence of cancer, which is currently being treated. He was told at one point that he'd have to have his arm and shoulder amputated. His first bout with cancer was when he was twenty-two. He's in his mid-forties now.

David Rakoff, welcome back to *Fresh Air*.

MR. DAVID RAKOFF (AUTHOR, *HALF EMPTY*): Thank you so much for having me.

TERRY: I really enjoy your writing. And when I got to the last chapter of your book, I just let out this real oh-no kind of gasp, because it talks about a recurrence of your cancer, and I wasn't happy to read about that. But it's an awfully well-written chapter.

[*Laughter*]

DAVID: Well, thank you hugely because that's the big—that was the big problem for me in terms of this book, which is somewhat more personal than the previous books. You know, I've always bridled at the term "memoirist" because I've wanted to be known for the quality of my writing as opposed to the particulars of my biography. So that's a huge worry for me. So thank you very much for that.

TERRY: So in this chapter, you describe a recurrence of cancer. You'd had lymphoma in your twenties. And this time it was in, like, your collarbone, near your neck.

DAVID: It's in the soft tissue. It's a sarcoma. And it was caused by the radiation I received for the previous cancer.

TERRY: That kills me.

DAVID: It's pretty rare.

TERRY: I have to say, that kills me.

DAVID: Oh, I know. I know, but you know, it's like living near a bad industrial site or something. And the science has advanced so much, and yeah, it's rare but becoming less rare as a population who got radiation ages ago, you know.

So it's a few things to be thankful for. I mean, it's you know, I sound like a Pollyanna, like that girl from *Bleak House* that I even describe, in Dickens, where she gets smallpox and virtually dances across the room because of how much less vain she'll become or something, and you just want to punch her in the face.

But a few good things. One is that as much time elapsed as it did, which made me a candidate for more treatment. You know, I could withstand more treatment because enough decades had passed. And also, if I had gotten my radiation two years earlier, I would also have to be worried about heart disease because they changed the protocol in '87. So there are reasons within that crappy news to be thankful.

TERRY: So because of the location of the tumor, you were at risk of having your arm cut off, actually more than your arm.

DAVID: Yeah, the shoulder from neck to armpit because everything's so crowded there with, like, arteries and stuff. It was certainly a danger.

TERRY: Yeah, and are you still in danger?

DAVID: I'm in a little bit of danger because the tumor has been very tenacious. And right now, there's another recurrence. But I'm currently in chemo for that, and the hope is that the chemo will shrink it the necessary few millimeters that it's no longer touching quite so many vital cables that go down your arm and that my wonderful surgeon might be able to go in and get the tumor without taking the arm.

But, again, as they keep on telling me, no one dies from the arm. You know, so there's a lot of stuff you can do with one arm, you know, like continue living.

[*Laughter*]

So—you know what I mean. So my arm is in danger, but for now, knock on the wood trim on my nice desk, I'm not in danger, which is a distinction worth making.

TERRY: Absolutely, and that's great news. So now you need to do a reading from the book.

DAVID: Okay.

TERRY: And I want you to read from page 212, and this is after you, you've gotten, you know, mixed diagnoses in a period of time since the tumor was diagnosed. So first you were told that they had to take the arm, and then you were told that they didn't. So where does this reading come in? What were you told?

DAVID: This reading comes in right when, you know, the first person who told me he was going to take the arm, I sort of checked up on him, and it turned out that he was—I don't want to say dangerous quack—but I did manage within the course of, say, ninety minutes to find three oncologists who knew exactly who he was, one of whom said he gets great results that can't be replicated, which is essentially calling someone a fraud, and another fellow who simply screamed no—upon hearing mention of his name.

So I wrote him off, you know, and went to see another doctor, who was not a dangerous quack. But the nondangerous quack said, well, we've got to take the arm. So it seemed when someone with credibility tells you, you know, it was more of a fait accompli, and it was a lot less rosy a scenario, and I couldn't quite write him off. And this is from that moment, I guess.

TERRY: Would you read it?

DAVID: Sure.

[*Reading*] "And down the rough hill we slid. I am back trying to be unsentimental about a non-dominant limb, doing the trade-off in my mind: An arm for continued existence.

"It's an exchange I can live with, although I am fixated on how radical the cut, from neck to armpit, leaving me without even a shoulder to balance things out.

"I imagine that the rest of my life, I will see the tiniest, involuntary flinch on the faces of people as they react with an immediate and pre-conscious disgust at the asymmetry of my silhouette.

"Nevertheless, I become defensive pessimism in action, puncturing my fear by learning to go without something before it's officially discontinued, weaning myself off of saffron or Iranian caviar before it becomes no longer available and trying to ascribe a similar luxurious dispensability to my left arm.

"I begin to type with one hand—one finger is more like it. Considering what I do for a living, it's appalling that I'm still hunt-and-peck. I accomplish a host of tasks: putting on my shoes, new slip-ons purchased without even looking at the price tag. I remember this kind of heedless spending in the face of illness; buttoning my fly; showering; dressing; shaving.

"I manage to cut an avocado in half by wedging the leathery black pear against the counter with my stomach and, thus steadied, go at it with a knife. In the evenings, with my bloodstream a sticky river of Ativan, wine, and codeine, it all feels eminently doable.

"In the cold light of day, however, unable to carry a chair to move it into a corner, for example, what I'm about to embark on feels a little bigger and harder."

TERRY: That's David Rakoff, reading from his new book, *Half Empty.*

You know, part of your book *Half Empty* is about the power of negative thinking. Like, when you're sick, people tell you, like, doctors tell you, and also people into integrative medicine tell you: Try to think positively.

But that's hard for many of us to do. And you write a lot in the book about the power of negative thinking. You even interview somebody who wrote a book by that title. And you refer to negative thinking in that passage that you just read. What is the power of negative thinking in your mind?

DAVID: Well, the power of negative thinking, it's a very specific kind of negative thinking. And it's a kind of negative thinking called defensive pessimism, which I think was a term coined by, or if not coined by, certainly adopted by, a psychologist called, named Julie Norem.

And Julie Norem wrote a book called *The Positive Power of Negative Thinking*, which was about defensive pessimism. What defensive pessimism is is a kind of anxiety-management technique.

The defensive pessimist sort of looks at something and says this is going to be a disaster. And because of that, they lower their expectations, and they think this is going to be a disaster because of such and such.

And they go through all of the negative capacities, the negative capabilities of a given event. You know, you imagine the worst-case scenario you can, and you go through it step by step, and you dismantle those things, and you manage your anxiety about it.

So you think, oh, god, I can't believe that I'm going to have to give a speech. I always trip on the microphone cord. So I'm going to make sure to look and see where the cord is. Or my fly is always undone, so I'm going to make sure about my fly, or I'm going to have my notes ready, or I'm going to rehearse an extra time. And in so doing, you do manage to conquer your fear of something.

TERRY: You were diagnosed with cancer in your twenties. Now you're in your forties and have a cancer diagnosis again. Are you dealing with it emotionally differently now in your forties than you did in your twenties?

DAVID: Yes, I think I am. I think—well, first of all, the cancer that I had in my twenties was, I even referred to it as the dilettante cancer. You know, it was Hodgkin's lymphoma, eminently curable and just a whole different ballgame from what I've got now.

And I was a little less interested in knowing about the cancer back then in my twenties. I was sort of like, well, do whatever you need to do. I'm just going to sit here and lie back and think of England.

[*Laughter*]

And whatever you guys want to do to me, it's perfectly fine.

And this time, necessarily, I have to be more engaged. It's different because I am the only person running my life. I suppose that was true certainly in my twenties, but now I'm a good few decades into adult life.

TERRY: My guest is David Rakoff. He's best known for his humorous essays and his stories on *This American Life*. His new book is called *Half Empty*. We'll talk more after a break. This is *Fresh Air*.

[*Sound bite of music*]

My guest is the writer David Rakoff. He's a contributor to *This American Life*. He has a new book, which is called *Half Empty*.

You write: "They say there are no atheists in foxholes. I am still not moved to either pray or ask why me." Why not?

DAVID: Because—writer Melissa Bank said it best: The only proper answer to "Why me?" is, "Well, why not you?" You know, the universe is anarchic and doesn't care about us and unfortunately, it—there's no greater rhyme or reason as to why it would be me.

And since there is no actual answer as to why me, it's not a question I feel really entitled to ask. And in so many other ways, I'm so far ahead of the game.

I have access to great medical care. My general baseline health, aside from the late unpleasantness of the cancer, is great. And it's great because I'm privileged to have great health, you know, and I live in a country where I'm not making sneakers for a living, and I don't live near a toxic waste dump.

And, you know, so you can't win all the contests and then lose at one contest and say why am I not winning this contest as well. It's random, you know. So truthfully, again, do I wish it weren't me? Absolutely. But I still can't then make that logistical jump to thinking there's a reason why it shouldn't be me.

TERRY: Right after you were diagnosed with your recurrence of cancer, you performed in a short film that won an Oscar this year for Best Dramatic Short Film.

DAVID: Yeah.

TERRY: You wrote the adaptation. It was adapted from a story or a play?

DAVID: From a script, from a short script.

TERRY: That somebody else had written?

DAVID: Yeah, Anders Thomas Jensen, I think his name was, a Danish fellow. I never met him. He lives in Denmark. I think that's his name.

TERRY: Okay, so we're going to play a clip from the film, from the very beginning. So I want you to explain what the film is about.

DAVID: The film is essentially about the worst moving day ever. Two gentlemen are in their new apartment, and the history of the apartment that preceded them catches up with them in a series of absolutely grisly and violent ways. Does that make . . .

TERRY: Yes.

DAVID: Oh, okay, cool.

TERRY: And the film is called *The New Tenants.* So in this scene, you are sitting across the table in your new apartment with your boyfriend, who you have moved in with. And he's trying to eat dinner and is very annoyed by your cigarette smoke because you're just, like, chain-smoking and delivering this monologue as you smoke.

DAVID: Yes.

   [*Sound bite of film short,* The New Tenants]
   [*Sound bite of music*]

DAVID: (*as Frank*) No one gets out alive. Everybody buys the farm at some point and usually in the most hideous, least-photogenic manner. I mean, every second, in every country, in every city, in every hospital, someone is just giving up the ghost in some vile farting, shitting, vomiting display, just every orifice discharging at the exact same moment.

Literally every second, someone is having their one final thought, which ought to be some sort of profound, Oh, so that's what it's all about kind of revelation but is more often than not, I guarantee you, something like, No, I have so many regrets.

Say a bomb goes off in a marketplace, you know, detonated by some suicidal zealot who hates I don't know—you know, fruit or vegetables or local handicrafts—viscera and gobbets of flesh and wet hanks of hair and teeth and splinters of bone are just shooting through airborne sprays of blood like on those soft drink commercials where the lemon slices splash through the arc of soda in some slow-motion orgasm of what it means to be refreshing.

And every time it happens, it gets less tragic, not more. They just push it further and further in the newspaper. Or say the reactor down the river a piece one day extrudes a plume of god knows what into the atmosphere. And, you know, it's eight seconds before anybody notices, but what do you know, the townspeople, they start to bleed from the eyes and their hair falls out, and the cancer wards just fill up. And nobody takes responsibility, nobody even apologizes.

And children are getting caught in factory machinery, and everybody's all like, No, not the children. The children are our future. The future of my next three-pack of undershirts, maybe.

China's burning enough coal to choke us all to death. Oh, and their food supply, which frankly now is our food supply, is just one toxic surprise after another. I mean, no one has a fucking [*beeped for radio broadcast*—ed.] clue. I mean, the water supply is drying up. All of Africa has AIDS.

Privacy is gone. Europe is all hamburger-eating fatsos

and loose nukes. I mean, we're just, we're just fucked [*beeped for radio broadcast*—ed.] beyond all measure. And you tell me not to smoke while you're eating?

UNIDENTIFIED MAN #1 (ACTOR): (*as character*) Are you done?

DAVID: (*as Frank*) Yes.

TERRY: Okay, so that's David Rakoff in the short film *The New Tenants*. That is, by the way, on the Internet, and on iTunes, if you want to see it.

So what a festival of negativity.

[*Laughter*]

All designed, I think, to justify that you're smoking while your boyfriend is eating, even though he, like, hates cigarette smoke. But if the world is, like, in such bad shape, then why shouldn't you smoke?

So how did it feel to do that monologue so soon after getting this, like, horrible diagnosis?

DAVID: No, this is the thing. My character wears a scarf in the film because my neck had been excavated a week before. I had not received my diagnosis. It was during the two weeks that I was waiting for my diagnosis that I delivered that monologue.

And even as I was delivering the monologue, which I have to say was both, as they used to say on the commercials, fun to make and fun to eat, easy to write and easy to deliver because it was so I-can-access-that-character-quite-easily.

But even as I was delivering it, I thought, you know something? This is going to bite you on the ass. You know, this kind of unearned, undergraduate darkness that you're spewing with such ease and such adolescent pride, just you wait, mister. You're going to get your little comeuppance.

And lo and behold, a week later, I did. I got my diagnosis. Yeah, it was a fascinating two weeks, I must say.

TERRY: You had a lot of friends in the early nineties who you lost to the AIDS epidemic.

DAVID: Yes.

TERRY: And I'm wondering if seeing so many friends die young affected at all how you dealt with a diagnosis that is not life-threatening, thank goodness, but is still, like, you know, a scary diagnosis?

DAVID: Oh, well, I mean, I should clarify. The diagnosis is life-threatening if it goes to my lungs in a certain way, you know. And, in fact, the surgery that I had around the time of the Oscars I think was to take out a little bit of spread in my lung. And luckily enough, it was localized and could be cut out, and I was out of the hospital within twenty-four hours.

But it is a life-threatening diagnosis if it goes to my lungs in a sort of a more Jackson Pollocky kind of way, god forbid. I hope it doesn't.

But yes, you're absolutely right. Seeing so many friends who were truly young and friends of friends, and you know, it was you know, I'm a gay guy, and living in New York City during the eighties and nineties, during the height of the pandemic, it was like living in wartime, but a very specific kind of war, which was that it was a very limited sector of the population was engaged in it.

And there were other people beside you everywhere who simply weren't fighting it. You know, they weren't even conscious of it. And it was very strange to be—to feel so in the trenches and to be going from hospital to hospital, you know, more than one a day sometimes, visiting people who were dying, you know.

It did help me, or not help me, but it did cross my mind that my fervent will to live—and it is fervent, and it is still in operation, and is in fact the area of my life of which I'm most optimistic, and I think that people really do tend to be hugely optimistic about their own chances of survival just, you know, going from day to day.

But it did cross my mind, and it remains in my mind, that all of the people that I know who did die, they didn't die because they wanted to live less than I do. You know, they didn't die before some because their desire to continue existing was found wanting in ways that my own is somehow better. And that was and that is tremendously instructive to me.

TERRY: David Rakoff will be back in the second half of the show. His new collection of essays is called *Half Empty*. I'm Terry Gross, and this is *Fresh Air*.

[*Sound bite of music*]

This is *Fresh Air*. I'm Terry Gross back with David Rakoff. He's best known for his humorous magazine essays and his stories on *This American Life*. His new collection of essays is called *Half Empty*. The book starts with an essay on the power of negative thinking and ends with a story of his recurrence of cancer, for which he's currently being treated.

Another chapter I really liked in your book is about visiting your therapist when he's dying of colon cancer in a hospice. And I think when you have a therapist, you imagine how much easier they deal with anxiety and with the problems of life than you do.

[*Laughter*]

Just like . . .

DAVID: Yeah. Exactly.

TERRY: . . . because they seem to know what they're doing and they're, you know, a good therapist is very good at guiding their patient.

DAVID: Mm-hmm.

TERRY: So I guess I wonder what it was like to watch a very good therapist, your therapist, or your former therapist, handle death.

DAVID: Well, you know, I'm a child of therapists, so the bloom is off the rose for me. I mean I respect therapy a lot, but I'm—I perhaps don't see therapists and those who administer therapy as being quite as invincible, perhaps.

TERRY: Mm-hmm.

DAVID: Do you know what I mean?

TERRY: Yeah.

DAVID: So it's not like I don't—I'm pretty clear-eyed about what therapists can and cannot achieve on their own in their own lives. But watching him die—in the process of dying—was very sad. I mean he was young. I don't think he was even fifty-five years old. And it was—it was very strange, given how intimately I felt towards him, but at the same time knowing very little about him. It's a very one-sided relationship, you know, the therapist-patient relationship. You talk about yourself for, you know, in my case a decade with this man and I really didn't have the details of his life. So it was very sad, but I also had to really be very careful that what I was sad about wasn't simply the cancellation of "The David Show." You know what I mean?

TERRY: Yes. I love when you say that in the book, but explain what you mean.

DAVID: Well, you know, I wanted to make sure that I was very sad about this fellow who I really—who really saved my life. You know, he really did save my life. I had gone into therapy after my first bout with cancer because I really hadn't dealt with it and I was, you know, classic post-traumatic stress. I was just barely functional, and he really helped me through that. And then he just—the reason I managed to become a writer and leave my day job is almost entirely up to him. I really owed him everything. And so I felt incredibly grateful for that. But I also, I didn't know the man very well. I didn't have the details of his life. It's a one-sided relationship. And so I had to make sure that what I was mourning or feeling bad about was the unjust—and I'll say it, unjust—a really good egg was dying before his time . . . the unjust death of a man who was . . . who seemed good and that I wasn't mourning the death of the reliquary of my best observations, my best bons mots of ten years' duration. Do you know what I mean? I didn't want it to be sort of like, Oh, no, that's a great archive of David Rakoffiana.

TERRY: Yeah.

DAVID: You know what I mean?

TERRY: Yeah, I do.

DAVID: And so that's what I mean by the cancellation of "The David Show." I wanted to be very judicious and clear what I was being sad about.

TERRY: In your chapter about your therapist, you have a great description of yourself when describing your thoughts after telling the therapist that you're going to stop seeing him. And I'd like you to read that for us.

DAVID: Yes. This is when he, he—I'm not talking about terminating. I seem to be avoiding the topic, and finally he stops me one day. I'm ranting about, I think, human rights in China or something like that. And he finally says, you know, look, we've got to talk about you terminating. This is a big thing.

[*Reading*] "Turning things around, I asked him what his feelings were about our ending things. 'I'm incredibly angry,' he responded fondly. 'How dare you? You should at least have to come and have coffee with me once a week.' I asked if he felt this way about most of his patients. 'Not really,' he responded.

"Sigh. Should you happen to be possessed of a certain verbal acuity coupled with a relentless, hair-trigger humor and surface cheer spackling over a chronic melancholia and loneliness—a grotesquely caricatured version of your deepest self, which you trot out at the slightest provocation to endearing and glib comic effect, thus rendering you the kind of fellow who is beloved by all yet loved by none, all of it to distract, however fleetingly, from the cold and dead-faced truth that with each passing year you face the unavoidable certainty of a solitary future in which you will perish one day while vainly attempting the Heimlich maneuver on yourself over the back of a kitchen chair— then this confirmation that you have triumphed again and managed to gull yet another mark, except this time it was the one person you'd hoped might be immune to your ever-creakier, puddle-shallow, sideshow-barker variation on adorable, even though you'd been launching this campaign weekly with a single-minded concentration from day one—well, it conjures up feelings that are best described as mixed, to say the least."

TERRY: I just want to point out, since our listeners don't have a copy of your book in front of them, that most of that reading was one sentence.

[*Laughter*]

That one very well-balanced juggling act there. So I just want to ask you, did you consciously intend to keep that one sentence?

DAVID: Yeah. Yeah. It felt—I like, well, I like a little ranty sandwich of a sentence or a lasagna of a sentence or, you know, or a mille-feuille of a sentence, to be perfectly homosexual about the metaphor.

[*Laughter*]

I like things that, you know, build in that way with semicolons and em dashes and things like that.

TERRY: Do you think of yourself as somebody who is the kind of fellow who is beloved by all, yet loved by none?

DAVID: We are verging into territory that's a little too personal.

TERRY: That's fine.

DAVID: So let me just say . . .

TERRY: Okay.

DAVID: . . . yes, I do.

[*Laughter*]

TERRY: Okay. We'll leave it there, I suppose.

DAVID: Yes. I guess so.

TERRY: So you have a very funny section in your book about, about your childhood. And . . .

DAVID: Yes.

[*Laughter*]

TERRY: And fun—I mean you say you had a very happy childhood. You know, you had a very happy childhood, even though you'd never ever want to go back to being a child. Why wouldn't you want to go back to that era, even though you had a happy childhood?

DAVID: I had—well, I had what, I had a beautiful childhood and a lovely childhood. I just didn't like being a child. I didn't like the rank injustice of not being listened to. I didn't like the lack of autonomy. I didn't like my chubby little hands that couldn't manipulate the world of objects in the way that I wanted them to. Being a child for me was an exercise in impotent powerlessness. I just wasn't—and I was never terribly good at that kind of no-holds-barred fun. I mean, you know, I've essentially made a career on not being good at no-holds-barred fun. But, you know, I just never sort of, like, hey, yes, let's go play.

[*Laughter*]

I was always more sort of, like, does everybody know where the fire exit is and let's make sure there's enough oxygen in this elevator. You know, it's just—there was always, you know, and as a grown-up it's much easier to work—to navigate the world with that, because then you can just go home to your own apartment. And so I just never really loved being a child, even though all of the attributes and perquisites were so in place. I had a gorgeous, gorgeous childhood, and yet I just didn't like being there. You know, just not for me.

TERRY: You write that you feel like you were mentally calibrated to be—what was the age? It was thirty-seven or forty-two or . . .

DAVID: It was something like forty-seven to fifty-three or something like that.

TERRY: Forty-seven to fifty-three. Yeah. So are you in that zone now?

DAVID: I'm about to. I'm essentially forty-six, so very soon I'll be my perfect age.

[*Laughter*]

With a ruin of a body, but you know, a perfect age.

TERRY: Why is that a perfect age for you—you hope?

[*Laughter*]

DAVID: Yes. Exactly. Because certain things—one no longer has to worry about certain things. You no longer have to quite—you can be sort of comfortable in your skin even as your skin is rattled and ravaged and sun damaged and you no longer have to sort of explain things about yourself and you no longer have to make excuses for yourself. And I think a certain kind of wisdom has kicked in for everybody, and people I think are a lot more accepting of the world and their place in it.

TERRY: So now I have to get you to read a passage about your home when you were growing up.

DAVID: The physical attributes of the home?

TERRY: Yes.

DAVID: [*Reading*] "No, indeed. I freely admit to having had all the accoutrements that make for a lovely childhood, one replete with the perquisites of great creature comfort in a bustling and cultured metropolis, in a home decorated in typical late twentieth-century secular humanist Jewish psychiatrist. African masks, paintings both abstract and figurative, framed museum posters, Marimekko bedspreads. And listen, on the hi-fi—why, it's *The Weavers at Carnegie Hall* or *Jacques Brel Is Alive and Well and Living in Paris*, or is that Miriam Makeba clicking her way through a Xhosa lullaby? And on the bookshelf, among the art monographs, the Saul Bellow and Philip Roth novels, the Günter Grass first editions, collected *New Yorkers*, Time-Life Great Books, *National Geographics*, and *Horizon* magazines—there, tucked in behind the *Encyclopedia Judaica*, you might just find that old illustrated copy of *The Joy of Oral Sex*, a gag gift never thrown out."

TERRY: Did you find that copy?

[*Laughter*]

DAVID: Oh, yes. I remember it—I remember when it was unwrapped at the birthday party. I remember who gave it, and you know, the disinhibited psychiatrist who gave it as the gift and the sheepish oohs and ahs and chuckles when it was unwrapped.

[*Laughter*]

I remember it all.

TERRY: Okay. So with all that great stuff on the bookshelves and the Weavers on the turntable, it must've really helped you fall in love with books.

DAVID: It helped me fall in love with the whole world, except for sports. . . .

[*Laughter*]

But do you know what I mean? It's just—the world was all there. I loved books, but I loved art, I loved— you know, and it was all there for the taking. And you know, children are sponges, and I was incredibly lucky to have such extraordinary stuff to soak up. Yeah, it really did.

TERRY: My guest is David Rakoff. He's best known for his humorous essays and his stories on *This American Life*. His new book is called *Half Empty*.

We'll talk more after a break.

This is *Fresh Air*.

[*Sound bite of music*]

TERRY: If you're just joining us, my guest is David Rakoff. He's a contributor to *This American Life*. He has a new book, which is called *Half Empty*.

Before you started writing books you were writing in the publishing industry as a publicist. You were writing press releases. You were writing speeches for a publisher who you worked with. And I was wondering if you wrote your own press release for your new book.

DAVID: No, I didn't. For this particular book?

TERRY: Mm-hmm.

DAVID: I didn't. I had a hand in flap copy and jacket copy in the past, but no, I did not. I don't know why. I think I might've tried my hand at it and it was a disaster and we, you know, the publisher and my editor were very sweet in even sort of listening to what I had to say. But I think they went back to the version that they had on hand. I think this book was a little closer to home than the other books, so I don't think that I was quite on my game. But I used to write—before my first book came out I wrote the negative review for it. Before I even wrote the book I wrote the mean review about myself. That helped.

TERRY: A mean review of yourself?

DAVID: Yeah, which was basically every essay by David Rakoff takes the same form, which is: I was stylishly dismissive of X until I did X and then I realized that people are decent and I feel lonely-slash-sad-slash-fat.

[*Laughter*]

You know, and I kept that. That's always a good watch word for, you know, a good sentence for me to stay hip to myself, I think.

TERRY: Was that also an example of negative thinking, that if you write the bad review . . .

DAVID: Precisely.

TERRY: . . . then you won't be disappointed when somebody else writes it?

DAVID: Exactly.

TERRY: And you wrote a more perceptively negative review than anyone else can do, right?

DAVID: Exactly. You disarm your detractors and then you leave them without arrows. But of course even that doesn't work, because people still have oh so many arrows that they can fling.

[*Laughter*]

TERRY: You can't even think of all of them in advance.

DAVID: And now we have World Wide Web, where they can do so immediately and in hoards.

TERRY: You are obviously somebody who is very attuned to beauty in the world—beauty in literature, in music and art. So if, god forbid, you had to have the surgery where your arm was removed—and I know one of your fears is that you won't be beautiful—that your body will be disfigured.

DAVID: Mm-hmm.

TERRY: And, I mean, for those of us who aren't beautiful to begin with, do you know what I mean, that it's always a question of, like, what does it mean for somebody to be beautiful? Is it different than, like, beautiful art? I mean you're born the way you're born. If you have a big nose, you have a big nose. So, like, that aesthetic—the aesthetic that you have when it's about art, is that aesthetic still appropriately applied when it's about people and—do you know what I'm saying?

DAVID: I do. Well, here's the thing, I'm not beautiful. I mean, I'm a perfectly normal-looking Jewish guy. My face has never been my fortune nor has my body. I mean, truly, you know, which is why I developed conversation. So physical beauty has never been part of my equation. It's just not on my shopping list. With the arm, I'm not talking about beauty so much as I'm actually talking about symmetry. And it's not even the arm, it's the shoulder. Do you know what I mean?

TERRY: Mm-hmm.

DAVID: What I'm talking about is literally a preconscious kind of primate's response to a lack of symmetry that would lead to that inevitable tiny micro-gesture, but that would be a flinch of asymmetry. You can make up for it in many ways if you have a shoulder, but it's the lack of the shoulder that I was fixated on and remain a tiny bit fixated on.

But also, I'm fortunate in that I am forty-six years old and I do have a nifty little career so that the comma, noun after my name is David Rakoff comma writer, that I'm very fortunate in that that's kind of established. So even if I do lose my arm, I mean, it'll invariably come up, you know, for the rest of my life if it happens, but I have managed to establish an identity that is based on my internal self and for that I feel tremendously lucky. I'm not in my twenties, and I, you know, and luckily enough I'm here in this particular position. Does that make sense?

TERRY: Yes.

DAVID: I don't think it'll define me as much as it might have twenty years ago.

TERRY: No. I think that makes perfect sense. So, you say that when you have to get an MRI that . . .

DAVID: Woo.

TERRY: . . . claustrophobia of the MRI.

DAVID: Oy vey iz mir!

TERRY: . . . requires a little anti-anxiety medication.

DAVID: Yeah.

TERRY: But you have an Elizabeth Bishop poem that you've memorized that you recite to yourself. What's the poem?

DAVID: It's "Letter to N.Y." Shall I try and see if I can do it?

TERRY: Yeah. I was hoping.

DAVID: Okay. Let me think of the order.

TERRY: N.Y. being New York.

DAVID: I think so. I think so.

In your next letter I wish you would say
where you were going and what you were doing.
How are the plays and after the plays,
what other pleasures you are pursuing:
Taking taxis in the middle of the night,
driving as if to save your soul,
where the road goes round and round the park
and the meter glares like a moral owl,
and all of the trees look so queer and green
standing alone in big black caves.
And suddenly you're in a different place,
where everything seems to happen in waves,
and all of the jokes you just can't catch,
like dirty words rubbed off a slate,
and the music is loud but also dim
and it gets so terribly late.
And coming home to the brownstone house,
to the gray sidewalk, the watered street,
one side of the buildings rises with the sun,
like a glistening field of wheat.
Wheat, not oats, dear.
And if it is wheat, I'm afraid it's none of your sowing,

nevertheless, I would like to hear
what you are doing and where you were going.*

TERRY: Wow, that's a great . . .

DAVID: In my life I will never achieve anything that beautiful.

TERRY: . . . that's a great poem. I really like the way you
read it.

DAVID: Isn't it lovely?

TERRY: Sure. Yeah. And I'm not sure, I said N.Y. is New York. I
mean I don't really know if that's New York, so.

DAVID: I don't know, either. I think it is New York.

TERRY: Mm-hmm.

DAVID: But it's a lovely thing to recite. And it certainly beats,
Oh, my god, I'm in a coffin. Get me out, get me out,
you know.

[*Laughter*]

So it helps a little bit.

TERRY: Isn't that a great thing about memorizing poetry,
though, that, like, there is . . .

* This transcript of Elizabeth Bishop's "Letter to N.Y." as David Rakoff
recited it is reproduced with kind permission of Farrar, Straus and Giroux.
For the original text of the poem, please see p. 338.

DAVID: Yes.

TERRY: It takes you—if you recite it, it gets you into—it changes your thought pattern into . . .

DAVID: Yes.

TERRY: . . . into the poem and into something, like, beautiful or funny or whatever poem you've chosen.

Well, David Rakoff, it's really been great to talk with you. Thank you so much, and I wish you, you know, good health and all the best.

DAVID: It is just an honor and a pleasure, and thank you.

TERRY: David Rakoff is a contributor to *This American Life*. His new collection of essays is called *Half Empty*. You can read an excerpt on our website, freshair.npr.org.

[Fresh Air *interview, WHYY Radio, September 21, 2010.*
Translation copyright © 2010 NPR.]

The Craft That Consumed Me

It's rare that I'm not at work on some sort of craft project. I've often enthused about the need to make things; how it employs a unique set of muscles—physical, intellectual, spiritual—that I can attain a state of flow when making something that I almost never can when writing. Much like those of an athletic bent who are constantly succumbing to, or having to resist, the impulse to turn everything into a ball (or so I assume—I have never been moved to use a ball even as a ball), if you make things, all objects house the potential to be turned into something else. They fairly beg to be turned into something else.

The eggs were something of a departure, given their utter uselessness. Actually, strike that. That insistence on functionality over aesthetics is something of a lie I tell myself, possibly homophobic in nature, or else it's a penitential inoculation against my getting too big for my britches. If I stress utility, I will be less tempted to think of the visual stuff I make as "art," and consequently of myself as a you-know-what, a label really only rightly conferred by others. I've certainly lost myself in making purely ornamental things before—lino cuts, paper cuts, snow globes, etc.—but I do get an extra lift if the finished product is practical to boot.

The most recent obsession just prior to the egg project was duct-tape wallets, a perfect storm of pretty and pragmatic that lasted for a good few years. Virtually everyone I know received a duct-tape wallet (or in a few rare cases—three to be exact—a duct-tape evening clutch), rendered in multi-colored Paul Smith–style stripes. (Check out TapeBrothers .com, which features an extraordinary selection, even my most-loathed pattern of all time after perhaps animal-print anything: camouflage. But brace yourself for the hatred of your UPS guy; good duct tape is very heavy.)

The wallets got nicer and nicer, the craftsmanship ever more deft, and often there is sufficient gratification in that, but with each new billfold, I felt the pleasure of creation ebbing ever farther out. Until one day, like Chris Cooper's orchid thief character in the movie *Adaptation*, who, having exhausted his ichthyological jones to such an extent that it was expunged from his system with a final pescaphobic verdict of "fuck fish," I knew that I could not, for the time being, bear to hear that whining protest from the sticky roll as I tore off another length of tape, no matter how pretty the color. So, no more wallets. They would take their place alongside the miniature Japanese folding screens, slide-top wooden boxes, and countless other crafting jags, never to be returned to, for the moment at least.

The fallow period never lasts long, though. I have let half decades elapse between books, because books have to be written and writing is awful, but if you are the type of person who makes things, there is no profit in worrying about how or why or when the next project will come into being beyond simply acknowledging that it is inevitable that it will be very soon. In this particular instance, I was cooking something and thought, Why don't I blow these eggs out instead of cracking them and then I can mount them on those golf tees? (Wooden golf tees, easily five hundred in number, a failed promotion for a sports book at a day job I left over twelve years ago. I took them out of the publisher's garbage and brought them home, where they sat in a cupboard all these years, just waiting for the moment they would be needed. Needed for what? I never knew, only that their day would come and that I should resist the occasional desire to make some order in the apartment by throwing out a tin of five hundred golf tees.) It really was as simple as that.

There was at least something gratifying in how, if they couldn't be useful, they evidenced thrift; kitchen and office waste, both repurposed, coming together as a unified object. The eggs sank—their downward slide slowed by a bead of glue—and settled upon their small wooden pedestals with a satisfying stability, the way an arch actually derives strength from downward pressure. But the putty-brown eggshell and colored wooden tees were ugly. Happily, other corporate pilferings over the years meant I have a drawerful of good old-fashioned Sharpies. Now matte black, the egg sculptures' chromatic sins were hidden, leaving behind the pristine and almost Brancusi-like elegance of their form.

After describing them to a sculptor friend, she showed up the next day with a small plastic container of powdered graphite and two solid Koh-I-Noor graphite sticks. "I thought it might make the surfaces more interesting." She was right. Graphite is a marvelous material to work with; slippery and fine and deeply insinuating. The hematite-black powder worked its way into the pores of the shells, deepening and silvering the shell; the light and the dark occupying the same space like a photographic negative.

Now they looked forged, as heavy as iron doorstops. Another friend misjudged the weight of one—it is an empty egg—her hand ready for the heft of at least five pounds of metal against her palm. The thing went flying, breaking in pieces.

I was surprised by two things: One, that the inner membrane of the egg was still moist, and even warm, fully weeks after being emptied. Such enduring evidence of its animal past despite its mineral-looking present. Second, it was incredibly easy to repair. Actually, let's make that three things: I was unprepared for the repaired egg, with its dings and divots and fissures, to be not just lovelier and more interesting-looking than its whole counterpart, but to evoke feelings of almost parental protectiveness and affection in me. My friend left, apologizing profusely. I impressed upon her repeatedly how little I minded, how truly okay it was.

When she was a safe distance from the apartment, I broke all the eggs.

The reassembly is slapdash, employing all manner of adhesives: Elmer's, a stronger wood glue found in the cupboard, nail polish (the cheapest clear varnish purchased from a clearance bowl at the Duane Reade). There was one specimen I feared was irreparable, so uniquely smithereened was he in his table drop (despite their undeniable femalehood—they are ova, after all—I think of them as male, probably something to do with the gunmetal masculinity of their finish and the scrimmaging jostle required in their creation). He had to be triaged, reassembled shard by shard with tweezers and a fine-webbed ligature of hospital gauze, making him resemble one of the evil neighbor boy Sid's chimerical monsters from the original *Toy Story* movie. He's found a good home and is doing quite well by all accounts.

Calamity might be central to their creation, but the fact that I settled on the graphite eggs only proves that there are no accidents. These wounded soldiers are really the only logical things I could be making right now. In the last year and a half, I have been in surgery four times, with more likely still to come. What choice do I have, really, than to mend, resurface, and buff these marred specimens back to some sort of life, and to hope to see in their patched and valiant surfaces something like beauty?

[Salon, *August 2010*]

The Waiting

I am nothing if not compliant. I held still as I was shuttled back and forth through the wondrous high-tech donut, inhaling and holding my breath when instructed. Less than three minutes later, I hopped off the narrow table and put my sweater back on.

"Have a fantastic day," the technician said as I left.

"Fantastic"? Fantastic days are what you wish upon those who have so few sunrises left, those whose lungs are so lesion-spangled with new cancer, that they should be embracing as much life as they can. Time's a-wasting, go out and have yourself a fantastic day!

Fantastic days are for goners. Was I fated to take some final vacation to see Venice for the first and last time? Or should I corral some long-cherished idol (I'm talkin' to you, Meryl Streep) into posing for a photograph with me, both of us giving a thumbs-up to the camera before she beats a hasty retreat back to the Land of the Living? That kind of fantastic day?

In truth, after close to three years into my current illness—a rather tenacious sarcoma around the area of my left collarbone—I try not to invest too much importance in the casual words of others, mostly to let them off the hook. With the exception of the wildly unprofessional X-ray technician in

1988 who, spying my radiation-strafed lungs (a result of the primitive treatment for my first bout of cancer, and the likely cause of my present sarcoma), asked how long I'd had AIDS, caregivers seem trained to keep their language and voices neutral for just this reason: It's an unfair burden on them when so many of us who are sick are looking for signs or unstated reasons to hope during the waiting.

And there will always be waiting. It begins immediately. Unless your presenting problem is a headache and you show up at the hospital with a knife sticking out of your skull, tests will always have to be done and then results will have to be delivered. Biopsies must be frozen, sliced, dyed, and analyzed. If a culture has to be grown, then you have to bide your time while cell division takes its course. Disparate hospital departments, if not entirely disparate hospitals, cities, or states will have to find and speak to one another, leaving you with nothing but a lump, inexplicable bruising, months of unexplained fatigue, your own imagination, or heaven forbid, the Internet to occupy your mind. Those weeks before diagnosis can be among the most torturous times. There is a reason you're called a patient once the plastic bracelet goes on.

It has taken years for me to learn not to analyze the voices and vocabularies of those taking care of me. For the most part, I've been very lucky even as I've been less than fortunate. The doctors and nurses in my life don't prolong the anticipation with pleasantries. We joke around a lot, but that's the second order of business. With a long illness, there are stretches of triumph that feel like cosmic rewards for good behavior followed by inexplicable setbacks that seem like indictments of your character. With so much muddy logic crowding out reason, it's best when news, good or bad, is delivered quickly and clearly. I will forever be grateful to my oncologist for opening

the door and saying, "Damn it, the tumor's ten percent bigger," before he even said hello.

I would never be able to do their jobs. In the same boat,
I would probably mimic my first surgeon, who was so flus-
tered and out of his depth—he'd seen the mass, taken out only
part of it, thereby spreading cancer cells through the area, and
closed me back up—that he engaged me in banter about the
modern-dance scene and a ubiquitous no-knead-bread recipe
before telling me that I had a malignancy. I felt hoodwinked
and unsafe: the blood-soaked prom queen minus her vengeful
power of telekinesis.

We like to think that the empathy broadcast with the swoop-
ing, downward intonation of the "awwww" is an evolutionary
comfort, something we are programmed to welcome and offer
freely ourselves. As a comment on something that has already
happened, it probably works. But as an anticipatory tool, it
does not soften the blow, indeed it does the opposite. It leaves
you exposed, like grabbing on to the trunk of a tree for support
in a storm only to find the wood soaked through and punky
and coming apart in your hands. The sweetest bedtime-story
delivery is no help when the words it delivers are a version of
". . . and behind this door is a tiger. Brace yourself."

Have a fantastic day.

[The New York Times Magazine, *April 15, 2011*]

When Bad Things Happen to Do-Good People

I've not read *Three Cups of Tea*, Greg Mortenson's bestselling book about his life building schools for Afghan girls, nor *Three Cups of Deceit*, Jon Krakauer's powder keg of a takedown, which accused Mr. Mortenson of malfeasance and appeared on the website Byliner. What interests me is not the details of what happened but that implicit in the lack of sympathetic hand-wringing over Mr. Mortenson's exposure is a kind of righteous vindication.

This isn't due to any added outrage that money meant to help impoverished girls might have gone astray, nor to a collective devotion to the idea that we are, all of us—Wall Street robber baron, selfless do-gooder—equal under the law. It is because we knew all along that *nobody* could be that good. How did we know? Because *we're* not that good. Mr. Mortenson's altruism is an indictment of our own sloth, and so some punishment—of him—might be in order.

True, some of us might be galvanized to join whatever struggle is at hand, or at the very least donate. But most of us will not. Eventually, one's day goes on and one's petty concerns take over again. The discomfort passes. But before that happens, for a few moments, lingering in the air like a bad smell, is that unspoken challenge innate in public acts of courage and altruism: "What are *you* doing?"

Speaking for myself, the answer is usually a highly uncomfortable "Nothing."

In channeling energy and resources into something other than, say, branded vodka and pumping up one's reality television ratings with a bogus presidential campaign, Mr. Mortenson is acknowledging our collective humanity, and the so-many-fewer-than-six degrees that separate us from the needy. Like it or not, we are implicated, and this can lead to some deep philosophical musing: One's faith in humanity is restored even while we feel a little bit bad about ourselves. (By contrast, the antics of Donald Trump leave us feeling precisely the opposite.)

It is a heady mixture of emotions that Mr. Mortenson's possible downfall stirs up. A combination of envy over his altruism—the initial goodness and courage he displayed that so few of us have or act upon—and its cousin, schadenfreude, that multivalent and exquisite feeling of pleasure taken in someone else's pain.

In a study in the journal *Science* in 2009, a team of Japanese researchers set out to examine the possible connections and differences between the two. When subjects felt envy, their brain scans showed increased activity in their anterior cingulate cortex, a region associated with aversive emotion, pain, and conflict. When schadenfreude was invoked, the reward circuits of their brains lighted up, the ventral striatum and medial orbitofrontal cortex, the same parts of our brains that hum when we're enjoying good food or winning contests.

Perhaps the particularly poisonous draught of gall that is envy—one of the seven deadly sins, we've been told—isn't all bad. The brooding funk brought on by someone else's possessing what we lack gives us the competitive boost to try harder: an evolutionary leg up. But schadenfreude's comfortable vantage is the reverse. The food has already been hunted, gathered, and cooked, the contest has been won. Torpor reigns.

If Mr. Mortenson's apparent fall from grace stems from a failure of character, it also has the ancillary benefit of showing us that the world is indeed a good deal more complicated than merely taking tea with our enemies. That global realities of entrenched money and power, diametrically opposed ideologies, religious conflict, and centuries-long geopolitical animosities can render change nigh on impossible, so why try? It confirms the good judgment inherent in our own inaction. It certainly allows me to live another day without getting off the couch.

They say that schoolyard tune of "Nya nya nya nya nya!" is universal; the same melody and intonation the world over. One likes to think that as one gets older, the impulse to stand over another and sing it while pointing like some scornful and victorious Marvelette diminishes. Maybe we just find other ways to do so.

[The New York Times, *Op-Ed, April 30, 2011*]

Author David Rakoff Calms Himself by Keeping a Full Pantry

Friday, April 13, 2012

The day begins, as every day of the year does, winter and summer, with black iced coffee. There is always a pot of it in the fridge. I really can't bear hot coffee unless it's essentially turned into a dessert with milk and sugar, and I'll just say it: I get really judgey, and tinged with a mild despair, about folks paying upwards of four dollars a cup for something that is literally easier to make at home than it is to shower. This is the only beverage I will mention. I'm a nondrinker, and the many glasses of club soda downed daily, thanks to my Sodastream machine, hardly seemed worth the cyber-ink. Except to say I might love that machine more than anybody or anything.

I met my friend Jackie for breakfast out at Tarallucci e Vino. It's nice and quiet in the mornings. I had the salmon quiche. I could eat salmon in any form every day of my life (this can also be said about potato chips, avocado, anything fried). The fish was a little overcooked. Did I therefore leave any on my plate? Don't be ridiculous.

I foraged lunch from the fridge, two Persian cucumbers, some kiwi fruit. (Quiche, kiwi fruit, it's nouvelle 1979 at my house; everything but the Jean-Pierre Rampal playing.) With more laziness than virtue, I'm now at a point in my life where I eat whatever I like, whenever I like.

In the evening, to my friends Kent and Deborah's for supper. She made a particularly good, silky chicken curry with raisins over Israeli couscous. For dessert there was cut pineapple, and I ate a chocolate turtle that I still kind of regret. The thing wasn't much bigger than an ice cube or a chocolate from a Whitman's Sampler, but it packed the heft of a thousand suns. Even five days later, I'm still feeling it.

Saturday, April 14

Iced black coffee, natch. Tinned and tubed fish is part of my colonial heritage, so a whole-grain English muffin with avocado, salmon paste from a tube from the absolutely kick-ass food department at Ikea (the cheapest smoked salmon in the city, and everything feels super-clean and beautifully packaged, which led me to buy a pretty bottle of elderberry syrup, which is so off-puttingly floral, it's like drinking someone's grandmother), and smoked cod liver from a tin.

Lunch was more cucumber and kiwi. It was the first truly hot day. I stayed in and worked, only emerging at dark to meet my friends Stephen and Cate at Sakagura, an *izakaya* in the basement of an office building on Forty-Third Street. During a brief time I lived in Tokyo, back in 1987, I was frequently taken to, say, the third floor of an unprepossessing building full of dental practices, and there would be a restaurant specializing in eel, for example. Sakagura has a similarly hidden, Japanese Brigadoon feel. The standouts were *yaki onigiri*, triangular hockey pucks of rice, roasted and topped with sweet miso and a fine shred of *shiso* leaf. Weirdly good; so much more than the sum of its parts.

Sunday, April 15

My friend Kristin is a relatively new New Yorker, so we went for breakfast at the restaurant at the top of the Beekman Tower Hotel in the East Fifties. I had a perfectly acceptable eggs Benedict with smoked salmon and hot coffee, for a change. The views are really terrific. The city is truly at its loveliest, but a riot of pollen. I returned home, wheezing like Chris Christie vetoing marriage equality, in time to pop an antihistamine and receive my order from FreshDirect.

My local grocer is Gristedes. It's both grubbily down-at-heel and shockingly expensive. Moreover, I'm not super jazzed on John Catsimatidis's politics, so I try to avoid it. And truly, I love FreshDirect. I've never received anything that isn't as good as or better than if I'd picked it out myself. Having food in the fridge, freezer, and pantry calms me right down. It also makes me eat a ton, like a dog with no satiety mechanism.

I immediately ate a handful of ridiculously good strawberries, and poured myself a bowl of Kettle salt-and-pepper potato chips, and promptly stowed the bag out of sight (also like a dog, if I can't see the food, I'm less prone to eat a week's worth of groceries in one sitting).

Up to Ninety-Sixth Street to rent a movie with my friend Abigail and her kids, Daniel and Susanna, whom I adore. Abby made very good pan-sautéed chicken thighs with lots of herbs over Arborio rice and cooked spinach finished with butter and salt and pepper. I made oatmeal-raisin-ginger cookies—crisp, not soft—and bought strawberries for dessert.

Monday, April 16

Black iced coffee and Grape-Nuts with soy milk. That ninth-grade science classification of milk as being a colloidal dispersion has stuck with, and disgusted me. Aside from cooking or coffee-as-dessert, I almost never drink milk.

One of the many privileges of being freelance is that I can take five steps from my desk and be in the kitchen. I had bought chicken thighs (I kind of loathe white meat), which I cooked up with cremini mushrooms, some preserved lemons I made back in February, herbes de Provence, mustard, and powdered clementine peel, one of my most prized ingredients, which I make by air-drying the rind and pulverizing it in a coffee grinder. It's fragrant and pretty; bright-orange dust that packs a great citrus punch. Makes truly great vinaigrette.

For supper, I stayed in and ate the chicken over whole-wheat Israeli couscous, which I first fried in some of the schmaltz, and a green salad with orange-y dressing. I was given a bag of chocolate Kisses for Purim. I've been keeping them in the freezer, so I had a few of those. I like letting the frozen pebble melt slowly in my mouth. Three of them take fully twenty minutes to eat.

Tuesday, April 17

Tax day. Perhaps a sense of relief made me eat more, but I'd have gorged just as much had I been facing an audit. Black iced coffee, and a Bosc pear eaten on the hoof.

I was in SoHo. Over Christmas, I had been given a ridiculously generous gift card to one of the original Temples of Food, a violatingly expensive emporium. One would kind of have to be a dunderhead to shop there with anything but a gift card, although in truth, they're not as cynically overpriced as that Eli Zabar. I bought a brown-rice tuna-and-avocado roll (which, in truth, was totally reasonable at $7.50). Still hungry, I went to the bread counter and bought a steno-pad-thin slice of Sullivan Street mushroom pizza. Jim Lahey's no-knead bread was as much of a life-changer for me as my Sodastream, but the pizza was oddly lacking in flavor, a double injustice at close to five bucks, although free for me, which I try to bear in mind in that "and such small portions!" punch line kind of way. It was a day in which I couldn't get full. Twenty minutes later, I bought a ham-and-cheese croissant at the Grand Central Market and ate it on the way home.

In the evening, I went to my friend Roy's apartment for excellent pan-fried hamburgers, which we ate with Israeli couscous. (Three times in one week. I regret nothing.) A green salad, and for dessert, some dates and two chocolate truffles. The hint of booze in one of them briefly knocks me on my teetotal ass.

Wednesday, April 18

Black iced coffee, whole-grain English muffin with smoked-whitefish salad and avocado.

For lunch, some of the chicken I cooked—almost better cold than hot—an Asian pear, and a Persian cucumber.

In the evening, I went with my friend Paul to see Kenneth Lonergan's *Margaret* at the Elinor Bunin Munroe Film Center at Lincoln Center, the new cinematheque built underneath Diller & Scofidio's cunning lawn that torques like a Pringle. *Margaret* was an astonishment! I don't know why it didn't win every Oscar and why it isn't spoken of as a masterpiece. It is.

Beforehand, we grabbed a bite at Indie, the very good café on the ground floor. We shared a bowl of eggplant parmigiana, along with some crostini, thin, oil-brushed chips of baguette with three small bowls: a bright emerald pesto, a spicy-orange Romesco, and something braised and green with ricotta salata (Chard? Kale?). Neither Paul nor I could remember what it was once it arrived.

Dessert of some artisanal caramel corn from the concession stand, artisanally long in the transaction. A little too tooth-sticky, I'm afraid. But *Margaret* made me forget all of that. It was all I could do not to finish the bag within the first ten minutes of the film.

[Grub Street, *April 20, 2012*]

Oh! The Places You Will Not Go!

(Co-written with Jonathan Goldstein)

IRA GLASS: It's *This American Life*. I'm Ira Glass. Each week on our program, of course, we choose a theme, bring you different kinds of stories on that theme. Today's program, "Show Me the Way," stories of what happens when you turn to unusual people or maybe even the wrong person for advice. We've arrived at Act Two of our program. Act Two, "Oh, the Places You Won't Go" [*sic*].

In this act, like in the first act, somebody needs help. And instead of turning to those nearby, he writes a letter. The correspondence is read by Jonathan Goldstein and David Rakoff.

GREGOR SAMSA (READ BY JONATHAN GOLDSTEIN): Herr Doctor, I find myself, for reasons inexplicable to me or my loving family, to have woken up this morning transformed into a cockroach. I am reasonably certain this is not a dream. Can you help?

I am usually in very fine fettle in the morning. But as a result of my new condition, I find myself unable to go into work. And while my life has never been what you might call a bed of roses, this unfortunate turn of events has certainly made it worse.

By way of example, this letter has been composed by painstakingly mashing my antennae into the keys of my father's typewriter. It has taken me close to four hours and has left me with a horrendous migraine. I write to you because I have heard of your brilliance and your keen appreciation for the absurdity of this world. Please help. Yours, Gregor Samsa, Prague.

DR. SEUSS (READ BY DAVID RAKOFF): Samsa, I've only just opened your letter. Fear not, worry neither. We'll soon have you better. You might feel like a freak, but I'll make you quite well. Your problem's unique, yet your name rings a bell. A silkworm I knew used to live in a trillium. I think his name was Samsa. Or was it Fitzwilliam?

Oh, well. Please forgive me. My mind is a haze. One really meets so many faces nowadays.

If you ooze like a slug or you prick like a cactus, every ill-feeling bug finds his way to my practice. Whether dozens of styes mar your one-hundred-eyed face, whatever your ailment, you're in the right place. Not to brag, but I've never yet failed to determine whatever root causes were vexing a vermin.

Rest assured, I'll endeavor to glean and deduce. You'll be better than ever or my name isn't Seuss.

GREGOR SAMSA: Dear Dr. Seuss, perhaps you do not understand. And for this, I am probably to blame for not having made this point more clear. While I am now a cockroach, I was not always one. I was born a man and am now a bug.

Do you see? Is this even pertinent to my case? I mention it only in the interest of aiding your diagnosis. I hope

I have not offended you with my quibbling. If I have, the only defense I can offer is that I have not been myself.

I feel that time is of the essence in this matter because without my being able to go into the office, I fear my whole family will all too soon wind up in the poor house. To my great embarrassment, my father has already taken to eating his meals with lesser employees of the bank. Very sincerely, Gregor Samsa.

P.S., Pardon me if this is a rude question, but I must ask. Is metrical rhyme an American mode of correspondence? If so, I apologize for not responding in kind. Were circumstances different—that is, were I not a bug—I would have very much enjoyed the challenge. As it is, though, typing even the simplest of prose taxes me for hours.

DR. SEUSS: The way that I speak gets a comment each time. Some people have accents, while I like to rhyme. Just as those who I treat might have thorax or a stinger, but nothing that ever resembled a finger, it's simply my way. I mean nothing by it. If you'd digits to type with, I'd tell you to try it.

But still, this attempt to be merely convivial can backfire sometimes and make me seem trivial. And then I am forced to make mollifications by dryly reciting my qualifications.

See, I'm a doctor who chiefly helps insects particular, a recap just briefly of my vitae curricular. One patient of mine, a tubercular chigger, was referred by a june bug who'd shrunk, then got bigger. I made the arrangements and booked him a trip to a mulberry thicket for that flea with the grippe.

And there did he rest and sip syllabub tea. But the thicket's the ticket for curing a flea. A potato bug who would eat nothing but onions, a millipede suffering from two thousand bunions. A night crawler who could crawl only by day, a mantis who lost the volition to pray. A fruit fly whose flying resisted fruition are just a short list of the kinds of conditions I've treated. And all were made well double-quick. I'm the one who they call when a crawly is sick.

But cockroach to human, or vice or verse? What a mystery, a new one confounding. What's worse is I've leafed through the pages of yellowing journals. Through thoughts from the sages I've sifted for kernels. And no one, it seems, has devised an approach for how to return to a man from a roach. For the nonce, I'd advise some geranium juice. But stop if it turns your extremities puce. And I will consult with my college chum Bruce. Till then, stay strong, Samsa. Your loyal friend, Seuss.

GREGOR SAMSA: Dear Doctor, please forgive me for my presumption. But I fear you may not appreciate the gravity of my situation. I am a hideous monster, and I'm only getting worse. Earlier today, my own father lobbed a basket of apples at me, one of which is still embedded in the soft flesh of my back. Our charwoman, too, has grown weary of my grotesque physical appearance.

And whereas once she entered my room with good-natured shouts of "Come out, you old cockroach!" when I hid beneath the couch, now she threatens to crack me on the crown with a chair when I crawl too close. At your word, I am prepared to have my dear sister, the only one who seems to be able to stomach me, pack me into a wooden crate with air holes and ship me to your office.

My fate rests in your hands. Please, doctor, you are my only hope. Yours, G. Samsa.

DR. SEUSS: Oh, Samsa, descriptions like that are invidious. It's human and callous to call yourself hideous. I reckon among those of similar breed, you're actually handsome, quite handsome indeed. Remember when tempted to heap self-reproach that he who formed lilies created the roach.

But now to this new factor with which I must grapple. You say you've been wounded, that now there's an apple that's currently making its home in your back? Is it in the soft tissue? Did your carapace crack?

I've questioned my colleagues and asked my attorney about your perhaps maybe making the journey to see me and thereby see your problems ended. Alas, the consensus is: not recommended.

The trip is too long, and they would not allow a cockroach through customs. Plus, I don't see how it would any way help ease your suffering and pain. The cost of the postage alone is insane.

But do not lose hope. Disregard the above. I have news. I've engaged the services of a carrier jubjub bird flying to you and in his beak berries, one green and one blue. Chew the blue thirty times, and the green thirty, too. In a week's time, you'll see that you'll be good as new.

Now, rest and eat lots of magnolia custard and rosehip soufflé and some dewdrops with mustard. And pay special mind if you're starting to blister. Wash the area daily. You mentioned a sister? Is she the one there who might broker a truce? Samsa, please take good care. Concernedly, Seuss.

GREGOR SAMSA: Dear doctor, I feared at the beginning of this ordeal that I was no longer me. And now, I know this certainly to be the case. At first, I thought my change had to do merely with the physical, with this horrifying metamorphosis. But now I see that it is much deeper than that.

I used to wonder in my idle moments in a train carriage or an unfamiliar hotel bedroom when I was still traveling for my work, what might I do if ever my scant good fortune ran out? Well, Gregor, I used to think to myself, that would be easy. If I ever became a burden to the family, I would simply walk out the front door and throw myself in front of a team of carriage horses.

You have told me to stay strong, not to give up, as if the two were opposite things. But I'm afraid you are mistaken. We both are. Sometimes, to give oneself up one must be strong.

In thanks for your friendship, I have composed for you a rhyme. It's the first one I've written since my boyhood. And you'll have to pardon me if it isn't very good.

You shall be remembered as the doctor who tried to determine what turned Gregor Samsa to vermin. Forgive me. I was not able to get any further. Goodbye, dear Dr. Seuss. Samsa, I am-sa.

DR. SEUSS: I read your last letter with no small alarm. It sounds like you're fixing to do yourself harm. I know that you feel like you've got nothing left, like your time has run out, you're abandoned, bereft of all hope, that you've been forced to bear it in silence, your family's scorn, their indifference, their violence.

I take it the jubjub bird failed to arrive. So how, my dear friend, will we keep you alive? I'd recommend exercise, plenty of fruit, but finally cede that such bromides are moot. Samsa, I need you to martial your will. There isn't a purgative, poultice, or pill or anything else on the pharmacy shelf that will make you so healthy as much as yourself.

You think your new body has made you a bother. You hold yourself guilty while blameless your father. Gregor, we'd all die if physical beauty was needed for others to render their duty.

Ever since our first letter, I've had this strange notion that I'd make you better, ignoring the ocean that makes up the distance that renders you Seussless. But despite my persistence, I've been worse than useless. I'm astonished at times when I think of the past, of my thousands of rhymes, of how life is so vast. I'm left, then, to wonder how anyone gleans a purpose or sense of what anything means.

It's not ours for the knowing. Its meaning abstruse. We both best be going. Your loving friend, Seuss.

GRETE SAMSA (READ BY JULIE SNYDER): Dear doctor, I found your letters among my brother's things when my parents and I were cleaning out our flat in preparation of moving. It is my sad duty to inform you that Gregor died some three weeks ago, perhaps from his injury, an act for which my father blamed himself for days on end, although I doubt it.

I think Gregor may well have starved himself to death. When the charwoman found him, she pushed at his body with the handle of her broom, and he slid across the floor with no more weight than a dried leaf. Before our charwoman disposed of him, I took one last look and saw that Gregor's shell had cracked open. And just underneath were little wings. He was a beetle, not a cockroach as we had feared. A beetle, nothing more. Even the word is lovely.

I know that ever since his childhood, Gregor had always had very vivid dreams of flight that left him happy in the morning. If only he himself had known, I kept thinking. At any rate, dear doctor, I thought you should know what befell my poor brother and to thank you for all your efforts in his behalf. If you should find yourself ever in Prague, please consider yourself most welcome in our home. Sincerely, Grete Samsa.

[This American Life, *Episode 470:*
"Show Me the Way," July 27, 2012]

Stiff as a Board,
Light as a Feather

IRA GLASS: We have arrived at Act Three of our program. Act Three: "Stiff as a Board, Light as a Feather."

In our bodies, blood moves, cells appear and cells die off, proteins form and are consumed, all invisibly to us. Until the moment that something goes wrong. And then we have no choice but to see the effects. The next story, from our live show, is from David Rakoff.

DAVID RAKOFF: It hardly merits the term "dream," it's such a throwaway moment. But I've had it three times now. The dream, or dreamlet, goes like this. I say to an unidentified companion, "Hey, watch this."

It's the punch line to that old joke, what are an idiot's last words? Except in my case, it is already too late. The idiot has already acted upon his idiot brag, the shallow part of the quarry has been dived into, the electric fence down by the rail yards unsuccessfully scaled, and my Trans Am has already failed to make it around Dead Man's Curve or down Killers Hill or off of, I don't know, Prom Night Suicide Cliff.

I had surgery last December—my fourth in as many years—to remove a tenacious and nasty tumor behind my left collarbone. I've also had radiation and about a year and a half's worth of chemo and counting. This last operation severed the nerves of my left arm, which relieved me of a great deal of pain. I'd spent three years prior to that popping enough OxyContin to satisfy every man, woman, and child in Wasilla.

But the surgery also left me with what's known as a flail limb. It is attached, but aside from being able to shrug Talmudically, I can neither move nor feel my left arm. It now hangs from my side heavy and insensate as a bag of oranges.

But this is a dream after all. So "Hey, watch this," I say. And up goes the left arm. The resurrection of the dead limb feels both utterly logical and completely magical. But it is precisely that magical feeling that lets me know immediately that I have moved in error, and the jig, as it always is, is soon to be up.

I either literally pinch myself or snap my fingers in my ears trying to establish some reality. Or I ask someone "Is this real?" But I already know.

There are some questions in life, the very speaking of which are their own undoing. Am I fired? Is this a date? Are you breaking up with me? Yes. No. Yes.

The voice, my voice, that is asking "Is this real?" is the sound that is waking me up to the world where—alas— the dream's a total cliché. Anyone with one working limb would dream it, which frankly, yawn.

The one difference I might point to is how I move in the dream. The limb floats up like a table at a séance. I am one of those empty windsock men outside of used-car lots who suddenly billows up into three-dimensional life. The arm rises, and there at the top of my gesture, my fingers frill like a sea anemone caught by an unseen current.

There is no functionality to it. I am not reaching for something, pulling the pin from a fire extinguisher, or hailing a cab. Mine is an extremely graceful and, I'll just say it, faggy gesture. Unmistakably, a gesture from ballet class, a gesture of someone who danced. Which is very different from having been a dancer.

I danced a lot, all through my childhood bedroom. It's an incredibly generic trait for a certain type of boy. Like a straight boy being obsessed with baseball, except it's better.

And after that, I danced fairly seriously in university. But I was never really that great. And it's close to three decades ago now.

I took classes across the street at the women's college, not the most rigorous of places. And as a boy, one of at most three males in any of the classes, the standards were even laxer. Any illusions I might have had about my scant abilities were blown to smithereens by the occasional class I took at a proper dance studio down on Fifty-Fifth Street in the real world, where actual New York City dancers came.

It was an exercise in humiliation and trying to make myself as invisible as possible. The only saving grace, indeed, the only reason I really went at all, were the twenty minutes in the men's changing room before and after. There's almost no way to explain it to a younger person, but you cannot imagine the rare thrill it was to see beautiful naked people in those pre-Internet days of the early 1980s. I would walk slowly to the subway undone, clinging to the sides of buildings like someone who'd just come from the eye doctor.

If I retained anything from dancing, it's a physical precision that certainly helps in my new daily one-armed tasks. They're the same as my old two-armed chores. They're not epic or horrifying. Some of them don't even take much longer, but they're all, to one degree or another, more annoying than they used to be, requiring planning, strategy, and a certain enhanced gracefulness.

Oral hygiene: Hold the handle of the toothbrush between your teeth the way FDR or Burgess Meredith playing the Penguin bit down on their cigarette holders. Put the toothpaste on the brush, recap the tube, put it away. You really have to keep things tidy, because if they pile up, you'll just be in the soup. Then reverse the brush and put the bristles in your mouth, proceed.

Washing your right arm: Soap up your right thigh in the shower, put your foot up on the edge of the tub, and then move your arm over your soapy lower limb back and forth like an old-timey barbershop razor strop.

Grating cheese: Get a pot with a looped handle, the heavier the better. This will anchor the bowl that you want the cheese to go into. Put the bowl into the pot. Now take a wooden spoon and feed it through the handle of the grater and the loop of the pot, and then tuck the end down into the waistband of your jeans. Clean underpants are a good idea. Jam yourself up against the kitchen counter and go to town.

Special kitchen note: Always, always, always have your bum hand safely out of the way, preferably in a sling since you now have a limb that you could literally—no joke—cook on the stove without even knowing it. Which makes me feel not like a freak, exactly, but well, actually, like a freak.

At dinner with friends recently, the conversation turned to what about yourself was still in need of change? They all seem to feel that they were living half lives.

One fellow hoped that he could be more like the god Pan, unabashedly lusty and embracing experience with gusto. Another wanted to feel less disengaged at key moments, able to feel more fully, committedly human, and less like that old science-fiction B-movie trope: "What is this wetness on Triton 3000's face plate?" "Why, space robot, you're crying!"

We were going around the table, so the natural progression of things demanded that I eventually get a turn to weigh in as well. Suppose you're out to dinner with a group of triathletes, all discussing their training regimens. And you have no legs.

They can't flat-out ignore you, and they also can't say words to the effect of, Well, we all know what your event is—getting all that marvelous wonderful parking, you lucky thing!

It was uncomfortable, and I suspect more for me than for them. I have no idea. But thanks to my rapidly dividing cells, I no longer have that feeling—although I remember it very well—that if I just buckled down to the great work at hand, lived more authentically, stopped procrastinating, cut out sugar, then my best self was just there right around the corner.

Yeah, no. I'm done with all that. I'm done with so many things.

Like dancing. I've no idea if I can do it anymore. I've been, frankly, too frightened and too embarrassed to try it, even alone in my apartment.

There was a time, however—as recently as about a

couple of years ago, when I was already one course of radiation and two surgeries into all this nonsense—when doing simple barre exercises while holding on to a kitchen chair achieved what they always used to do. What they're supposed to do.

As best as I can describe it, it's the gestures themselves, their repetition, their slowness. It all hollows one out. One becomes a reed or a pipe, and the movement and the air pass through and you become this altered, humming, dare I say, beautiful working instrument of placement and form and concentration. But like I said, that's a long time ago. And a version of myself that has long since ceased to exist. Before I became such an observer—I'm sorry.

[IRA: *So at this point, David Rakoff walks away from the microphone. And just when it seems like he might walk off stage, like he quit, he turns, and turns again. And then raises his right knee, and then places that foot down again, and then traces a half circle on the ground with his left foot. And then he lunges, he arches his back, swings his right arm in an arc from low to high, all totally graceful. And then, he dances.* (Music: "What'll I Do," performed by Nat King Cole; choreography by Monica Bill Barnes—*ed.*)]

DAVID: Look, mine is not a unique situation. Everybody loses ability—everybody loses ability as they age. If you're lucky, this happens over the course of a few decades. If you're not . . .

But the story is essentially the same. You go along the road as time and the elements lay waste to your luggage, scattering the contents into the bushes. Until there you are, standing with a battered and empty suitcase that, frankly, no one wants to look at anymore. It's just the way it is. But how lovely those moments were, gone now except occasionally in dreams, when one could still turn to someone and promise them something truly worth their while, just by saying "Hey, watch this."

[This American Life, *Episode 464:*
"Invisible Made Visible," May 18, 2012]

Love, Dishonor, Marry, Die, Cherish, Perish

The infant, named Margaret, had hair on her head
Thick and wild as a fire, and three times as red.
The midwife, a brawny and capable whelper,
Gave one look and crossed herself. "God above help
    her,"
She whispered, but gave the new mother a smile,
"A big, healthy girl. Now you rest for a while . . ."

But later that night, with her husband in bed
The midwife gave free and full voice to her dread:
"I tell you that girl's in the grip of dark forces.
This August her husband died, trampled by horses.
She herself works on the packaging floor
But she'll be on her back for a fortnight or more.
And as for the plant, they will take her back, *maybe*
A fat lot of good is a girl with a baby,
Her story's too sad, sure, I almost can't bear it,
Nineteen-year-old widow, no family of merit.
Her mother's an *eejit*, the father a souse
Who drank away all of their money, their house.
You've seen girls like that who must go it alone,
By age twenty-five, she's a withered old crone.

Even now, she's as pale as a thing stuck with leeches,
And thin! Her dugs ought to be ripe, swelling peaches
Her milk may not come, and what comes will be gall
(She gets some food from the St. Vincent de Paul).
But true, if you ask me, I don't know what's worse:
A life full of want or a babe that's a curse.

You know me, *I* think that most infants are fair
But I've never seen so much Lucifer's Hair.
She'll grow to a strumpet, or else a virago."
Outside, thunder tore through the clouds of Chicago
And sundered the air that was needled with sleet
Although it washed clean the aroma of meat
That clung to the neighborhood's mortar and bricks,
And puddled up into the greasy, wet slicks
That, once dry, would once again smell of old blood.
To truly be clean would require Noah's flood.
Otherwise, always the smell of old carrion,
Deep as a well and as loud as a clarion.
The stockyards were too big. Each day brought a fresh
Onslaught of slaughter, and smell of dead flesh.

"You hear that?" the midwife continued. "This birth
Is bad news, proclaimed both by heaven and earth."

Margaret grew quickly, a biddable child,
Not overly sickly, her temperament mild.
As a baby, her mother would sneak her to work.
The foremen thought brats caused the women to shirk.
And so she'd stayed hidden, quite comfortably
    swaddled
In a nest of their overcoats. All the girls coddled

Her, stealing a kiss 'til they had to go back
To their place at the table, where daily they'd pack
Up the loins and the roasts, all the parts of the cattle
And pigs who'd been carved up, like corpses at battle.

Frankie, dubbed "Finn McCool" after the giant
Of myth, had his size, and was just as defiant;
Big as a draught horse and strong as a steer
Frank had his enemies quaking in fear.
The tales of his strength and his temper abounded,
And God help the soul who might think them
    unfounded.
If Frank said that one time, in Wichita, Kansas,
He'd killed a man who had addressed him as Francis,
Or how, at the Somme, he had taken a bullet
And with his bare hands, he had managed to pull it
Straight out of his flesh . . . more's the pity for you
If you dared to venture, "But Frank, that's not true."
Even the foremen were slow to upbraid him
Though he did far less work than for what they paid
    him.
"Frankie will do it because Frankie can,
A law to hisself is that wall of a man!"

They'd met on the streetcar en route to the slaughter-
house, she the young widow, a six-year-old daughter,
And soon they were three, and ere long, for her sins
They'd grown now to five, with a pair of boy twins.

At school, Margaret learned basic reading and sums—
But mostly developed a hatred of nuns,
Who seemed to delight in a disciplinary

Code just as ruthless as 'twas arbitrary;
They meted out lashings and thrashings despotic
(With a thrill she would later construe as erotic):
Constance, who'd routinely knock Margaret's slate
To the floor, was monstrous and brimming with hate;
The sinister grin of old Sister Loretta
Who seemed to be driven by some old vendetta
That Margaret tried hard to appease and to fix
Although it perplexed her since she was just six.
She hoped perfect conduct might act as her savior,
But truly, no matter what Margaret's behavior,
They singled her out for particular violence,
And so she perfected a stoical silence.
"You! Red-headed terror, you want fifteen more?"
She'd shake her head slowly, her eyes on the floor.
So, when she left school at the age of eleven
To work at the factory, it seemed to her heaven.

The girls on the line who had hidden and kissed her
Welcomed her back and told her they'd missed her.
Each day she would bathe in a sea of their chatter,
Twelve-hour shifts—*standing!*—and it didn't matter;
A kerchief concealing her culpable hair,
Her mother's old shirtwaist, which thrilled her to wear.
The great roll of paper they pulled from the wall,
The huge spool of butcher's twine . . . she loved it all.
Everything seemed bathed in a heavenly light,
Perhaps, it was just as a contrast to night.
Supper, the same every day of the week:
Some contraband meat; a spleen or a cheek;
An accordion of tripe or a great, lolling tongue,
Occasional marrow bones, rare (thank god!) lung.

Both meat and the light at the close of the day
Fried wearily down to a dead, bloodless gray.
Some bread soaked in drippings. Then toilet, then
    prayers,
Then waiting for Frank's boots to batter the stairs.

Drink, in some men, is a beautiful thing.
Sweet Eamon Dolan finds courage to sing,
Shy William Thomas will realize he's handsome,
But Frank holds them prisoner without any ransom.
Who were you talking to? What was his name?
D'you take me for daft? Every night was the same:
Her mother would wash, while she'd dry the dishes,
Frankie would pace the room, angry, suspicious,
Occasionally some glass or plate would be broken
(Those were the lucky nights. Crockery as token).
Some mornings her mother used powder for masking
A shiner, but soon all the girls just stopped asking.

The threats go for hours. At long last he ceases
And stumbling, half-blind in his boozy paresis,
He crosses the room and falls into the bed.
Nearby, Margaret prays, "Dear God, please make
    Frank dead."

At twelve, Margaret grew quite suddenly bigger,
And showed the beginnings of womanly figure.
The old shirtwaists that had once fit her just right,
Had, in the wrong places, become just too tight,
Clinging and gaping where once they had hung.
Her mother was frightened, *Sure, Peg's just too young.*
The garments' constriction confirming her fears—

Though younger than Juliet's fourteen by two years—
The Romeos, pomaded, would soon come a-knocking,
Cockaded, parading. Too true, though still shocking,
Her Margaret gave off a narcotic allure,
Just how might she manage to keep her girl pure?
She tried as she could to conceal Margaret when
They had to walk past all the slaughter-floor men.

Each walk 'cross the floor was a dance of avoiding
The puddles of blood and the catcalls of "Hoyden!"
"Why all o'yer rushing? Stay back, you've got time.
My meat's not a rib, but it's certainly prime."
Each insult occasioned a new gale of laughs
They toasted each other by knocking their gaffes
Together like musketeers crossing their swords
Knee-deep in carrion but feeling like lords.
That red hair, that figure, had adult men sputtering
A wordless desire, or else they'd be muttering
Dark boasts, which a harsh glance could usually halt,
But the theme of it all was that *Peg* was at fault.
That *she* had invited, incited the wolfish
Responses, this siren, so stuck-up and selfish
Who had no right acting so shy and so prim
"You'd think she had diamonds all up in that quim!"
"I'll have you remember the girl is my daughter!"
Her mother would yell, but the men of the slaughter-
house would only be goaded to further chest-
    poundings,
Barbaric, in keeping with their vile surroundings:
The drain in the floor, a near-useless feature
Meant to dispatch all the blood of the creatures,
But gobbets of scarlet-black visceral scraps

Routinely stopped them up, clogging the traps.
Above them, hog carcasses, splayed open, red,
Like empty, ribbed, meat overcoats, overhead.

Margaret employed what she'd learned from the nuns,
Deaf to the crude innuendo and puns.
Her eyes she kept focused upon the far door,
Through which she could exit the abattoir floor.
She also employed something else the nuns taught
Her by accident: namely to fly in her thoughts
To a place close yet distant, both here and not here;
Present, but untouched by doubt or by fear.
For instance, she mused on the linguistic feat
That gave creatures names quite apart from their meat.
One didn't eat "pig," as one didn't "count muttons"
When going to sleep. Margaret thought of the buttons
From bone on her shirtwaists, her boots' good strong
    laces
Of rawhide, and then, Margaret pictured the faces
That daily she saw on the thousands of creatures
Their snouts notwithstanding, how human the
    features.
And, thinking about the brown eyes of the cattle,
She got through the door. She had skirted the battle.
Deep February, a bone-cracking freeze.
The ice, like a scythe, felled the boughs from the trees;
The blood of the stockyards froze into pink ponds
And etched the glass panes with its crystalline fronds.
"Margaret, go home," said her mother, "the group
will cover your absence. Take scraps for some soup.
Francis has fever and maybe the croup,
And Patrick this morning was all drowsy droop.

I asked Mrs. Kovacs to take the odd look . . ."
Margaret cleaned up, took her coat from the hook.
The wind was belligerent, brazen, and bold.
The tram's iron tracks fairly sang in the cold.

The twins, half asleep, were reluctantly fed,
She wash-clothed their faces and put them to bed,
Before she had finished verse two of her lullaby,
They'd gone off to sleep. And now, spouting some
    alibi,
Frankie was there, "I come home, I was worried . . ."
He *did* seem quite nervous; more sweaty and hurried
Than his norm. "Where's yer Maw," he was able to
    say.
"At work, Frank. You know, as she is *every day.*"
Frankie seemed off somehow, almost confused
In his very own home. She was almost amused
Until she remembered that one would be wrong
To find any amusement in Frank for too long.

Sure enough, the change came, an invisible lever
Was pulled and a new resolve—"it's now or never"—
Put steel in his eyes and a set to his jaw,
He gripped at the jamb with a great, meaty paw.
Somehow he had managed to shake off his fright
And back was the Frank who tormented each night.
Nervousness gone, his Gibraltar-like bulk
Barring her exit, a light-blocking hulk.
"Let me pass, Frank," she whispered at almost a purr,
The way that one tries not to jangle a cur.
But Frank took ahold of her slender right wrist
And, pulling her close with a threatening twist:

"You puttin' on airs. It's always been *your* way."
He stood breathing heavily, blocking the doorway.
He twisted some more, and she screamed, "Frankie,
    don't."
"This is *my* house, *my* castle. Enough with 'you *won't*.'
I seen how you look at me. Thrills me to bits.
Tease me by tossing your hair, and those tits . . .
Surely this won't be the worst of your sins."
"Frankie," she wept, and implored him, "the twins!"
"You'd have me believe . . ." Frankie laughingly
    haggled,
His smile a dark cave of teeth, rotting and snaggled,
". . . A fast girl like you when you tell me 'it hurts!' "
While his steak of a hand bothered up Margaret's
    skirts.

———

Mrs. Kovacs was sitting on Margaret's bed,
In her lap cradling the fevered girl's head.
Her mother, on seeing the petticoats, red
And torn up, thought at first that Margaret was dead.
"What happened?" she asked, dowsing a rag at the
    sink.
Kovacs, fed up, spat out, "What do you think?"
She drew herself up, "I'm sure I've no idea . . ."
She made herself haughty when things weren't clear—
She dabbed with the rag at her daughter's hot brow,
But still couldn't figure the Why or the How.
Faced with the evidence, things still never sank
In. Or wouldn't. Until Mrs. Kovacs said, "Why not ask
    Frank?"

And *still* then she chose not to see what was true,
Instead, she grabbed Peg and shrieked, "What did
      you do?"
"The poor girl did nothing. Your Fancy-Man Hero's
The one who was doin'. The coward. The zero."

But Kovacs should better have screamed at the wall.
Margaret's mother was lost in the thrall
Of an anger, white-hot, she had no tools to parse—
If it weren't so tragic, it could have been farce—
Her daughter no longer her charge, now her captor,
She screamed in her face, then she shook her, she
      slapped her.
"Don't dare close your eyes, Miss. We're nowhere near
      through.
I asked you, now tell me. Just. What. Did. You. DO?"

"Enough!" Kovacs cried. "The poor girl is senseless.
What kind of monster would beat a defenseless . . .
I come . . . as you asked me . . . to see to the boys.
I heard what I thought was a fight over toys,
But clearly, I come upon Frank unawares,
Who quickly shoved past, nearly pushed me
      downstairs."
"Where was Frank going?" her mother began,
But Kovacs just stopped her, "Believe me, yer man
Won't be back no time soon. And I tell you myself
If he does, I will call the cops. Look at her . . . Twelve!"

But to look at her daughter she now was unable.
Everywhere else—be it cupboard or table—
Seemed fine, as before, neither sullied nor tainted

But one look at Margaret, she knew she'd have fainted.
She sighed, "Filthy water will seek its own level,
What *did* I expect, with that hair o' the devil . . ."
She turned from her child, shook her head with a
    mutter,
"And so, as I feared, I've a girl from the gutter."

It took seven days until Frankie came back.
He'd drunk that whole week, and he'd gotten the sack.
Mrs. Kovacs never did end up calling the law
Since Margaret was five days gone, burrowed in straw
Of a western-bound boxcar, past Denver by then.
And nobody ever saw Margaret again.

Well, speaking quite strictly, not technically true.
But no one back home, no one whom she once knew.
The Margaret of Now left the Margaret Before
On a train hugging close to Lake Michigan's shore
Before peeling off on its way to the coast
Margaret, alone, with two dollars at most
Scrounged up by Mrs. Kovacs; a rye loaf with seeds,
Some sausage, a knife which, "Please God, you won't
    need."
About two hours out, in her iron-wheeled home,
And Margaret found out that she wasn't alone.
A man, dark and thin and about twenty-two-ish,
She pegged him as either a Bohunk or Jewish.
Too weak to feel fear (she was halfway to dead),
He stayed where he was, though he bowed down his
    head
In a gesture of most polite, courtliest greeting
As though in the dining car's first-class, first seating.

The only thing he did with any persistence
Was offer her food. Otherwise the short distance
Between them might have been the deepest of moats,
They kept to their sides, bundled up in their coats.

Until one night, rolling across the white flats
Of a snowy Dakota, the barely there slats
Of the car were no match for the blizzard outside.
Margaret was simply unable to hide
From the cold so severe she feared she might die
And there was the man now beside her. "Let I . . ."
He said, stuffing straw into all of the cracks,
He lay down, pulling Margaret in, molding her back
To his front, then enfolding her, so that she'd feel
His warmth while he whispered, repeated, "*Sha,
    Schtil . . .*"
And soon Margaret slept in the train's gentle quaking,
But warm and relaxed and no longer shaking.
His song was a comfort, a womb she could bundle in.
But no meaning at all: "*Rozhinkes . . . Mandlen . . .*"
She woke the next morning, the train briefly parked
To take on supplies. Her friend had disembarked.
From then on until Margaret reached her destination
The cold didn't manage the same penetration.

If in '28, you had chanced by the water
Of Seattle's harbor, you might spy three daughters
Working alongside two sons and a mother
And dad, you would see something lovely and other:
The father, a raven-haired man, Japanese,
The mother, with hair like the autumnal trees,
And children just Western enough so's to pass

With tresses the color of bright polished brass.
The wife wraps your fish, gives you one of her smiles,
But her eyes tell a journey of thousands of miles.
And in the Midwest, a babe pulled from the loins
Has a head full of curls shining like copper coins,
And the midwife is twigged to a child from years back
But there've been so many babies, by now she's lost
    track.

———

"To pay for what crime, what malfeasance, what sin?"
Clifford's mother mused, picking her blouse from her
    skin.
"Malibu's breezy, Hollywood's shady
But Burbank? He might as well've brought us to
    Hades!
I could just yip when I think of the crime it
Was moving me out here *'because of the climate.'* "
The fan in her hand the scene's sole, languid motion,
"I once heard it said that there was an ocean
Not terribly distant from where we sit here,
But, I suppose that was just a bum steer.
Escaping me now are the details specific,
But could it be named something like 'The Pacific'?"
Her voice was dramatic, befitting her role
Of a truth-telling wag: witty, gin-dry, and droll.

She reasoned it thus: that it surely beat weeping
And couldn't help smiling with how out of keeping
It was with the truth of her fate-handed cards
Her down-at-heel block with its sun-roasted yards

She found it amusing and helped pass the day
To speak like a guest at a fancy soiree,
She battled the hours without end with a heightened
Insouciance, like whistling when, truly, one's
     frightened.
With steely resolve she kept up this appearance
Her husband no more than a mild interference
The way one might greet less than optimal weather.
His half-palsied body? As light as a feather!
Diminishing powers of speech, what a scream!
Feeding and grooming (hours each), *such* a dream.
It might take all morning to just get him showered
And yet one might think she had married Noël
     Coward
Such *teddibly* juicy, just-so bits of news
With witty, urbane, *comme il faut aperçus*.
Even though it was usually just she and her son
Who, though six, proved a rapt audience of one.

She sat on the porch with her thousand-yard stare
And spent each day parked in her old wicker chair.
The yard a brown painting of motionless calm
The packed, ochre dirt and the lone, scraggly palm.
No sway to its fronds nor the measly dry grasses,
Immobile and baking in air like molasses.
Nearby was the car, having one was a must,
A '38 Packard, near silver with dust.
Her husband had needed it when he was traveling
But that, too, was part of the wholesale unraveling
Of what had once been a not-horrible life,
But now here she was, neither widow nor wife
Like flies trapped in amber, the three of them stuck
Like so many others dealt cards of rough luck.

Clifford, attempting to shake off her blues,
Might draw her a hat or a new pair of shoes:
A bonnet fantastic, bombastic, and huge, he
Appended three veils and a tiny Mount Fuji.
Pumps clasped with diamonds and marabou trimming
And thick soles of glass, housing live goldfish,
    swimming!
His mother surveyed his designs with a laugh,
"If I wore these both, I would be a giraffe."

He lived for her laughter and after that how
She might rustle the fine hair that fell 'cross his brow.
"You have scads more talent, beyond any other
Kid I've ever seen, and I'm not just your mother.
I'm a good judge of art." With her fingers she gaveled
The armrest. "I've seen things. Remember, I've
    traveled."

Remember she'd traveled? As if he'd forget.
Her life before him was the thing that beget
His voracious desire and unquenchable fond-
ness for all the world's beauty that lay just beyond
Their veranda enclosed in its old fly-flecked screen.
Cliff sometimes felt like the one who had been.

The Great War concluded a scant two years prior.
They'd sailed to a Europe no longer on fire,
"Our trunks bore initials with golden embossing
A French tutor booked for each day of the crossing
And Father tipped porters with whole silver dollars!
I had a wool coat with a beaver-fur collar,
And *dresses*! A new one for each day at sea
Not counting the outfits we'd change after tea

And for each ensemble, a different purse!"
(Clifford had memorized chapter and verse.)

"He was so profligate, heedless, and rash.
It's quite a feat how, with no help from the Crash
How easily parted our gold from that fool
By '26 Sally and I had to leave school."
As with all else, she would choose to be funny
About how her father had squandered his money:
"And all of us crammed in that one narrow row house.
If not for our wages, there would have been no house.
Last I heard, Father was down on the Bowery,
A whole mess of bother and woe was my dowry.
Your grandfather, Clifford, could sure make a mess
Of a perfectly good situa— I digress.

Fish knives and cake forks, and gleaming tureens!
Truly, your aunt and I ate like young queens.
New Year's on board was all revel and roister-
ing. Crackers with prizes, and champagne with
    oysters."
Each knot from the shore, she could feel adolescence
Depart in the wake's churning, green
    phosphorescence,
And churning in *her* was, as if by duress,
An appetite—bone deep—a need to transgress.
The evenings were worse, once the supper bell rang,
The darkness, the wine, well, her blood fairly sang.
"A dark Turkish ensign gave me my first kiss,"
And then she paused, "Should I be telling you this?
Ah, might as well learn," she went on with a shrug,
"His tongue in my mouth was a slimy, fat slug.

I remember I thought to myself, 'Holy Jesus,
This will *not* be worth it unless Father sees us.' "

With deepest conviction she found near hilarious
Clifford stopped viewing the trip as vicarious.
Studying programs, the postcards, the scraps,
He fingered the flyers and mangled the maps
An El Greco folio she'd kept from the Prado
A stub from the D'Oyly Carte's thrilling *Mikado*
She'd tied to a Soho-bought gilt ivory fan,
(He counted the two as a stop in Japan).
Above all, the thing that had captured his heart,
And opened his world: reproductions of art.
Bernini and Rubens, Poussin and David
They filled Clifford with a near-physical need
To render as best as he could all he saw
The only desire Clifford had was to draw,
To master the methods the artist commands
That translate a thing from the eye to the hands.
There might be a hint in the dry introductions
He'd flip back between them and the reproductions.
Clifford consumed them as if they were food;
He studied how color might render a mood
Skin tone and placement, drapery and flowers
Moonlight on lovers asleep beneath bowers
Torments endured with a saint's skyward smile
Nuance, technique, composition, and style.
Landscapes with dream-like blue hills in the
    distance,
The Sabine's dramatic, up-reaching resistance
Of strong Roman arms that were trying to rape her,
His greasy young fingers had yellowed the paper.

The jam smears and markings and smudges and rips
All left in the scrapbooks she'd kept of her trips.
Souvenirs treasured like they were his own,
He swore that he'd go there as well once he'd grown.
"Make sure to say yes, then, if anyone offers,
Since there's not a *sou* in the family coffers."

She gave up entirely the impulse to say,
"It's lovely out, Cliffie, why don't you go play?"
And play where, exactly? The yard was an eyesore
(They'd seen in a newsreel, a famine in Mysore,
Identical dirt turned to similar mud,
A sacred cow chewing its sad, holy cud
Flies crawling over a child's thin, dry face,
She heard Clifford whisper, "That's just like my
    place!").
He liked it indoors where, dark as a séance,
Hunched over his sketchbook with pencil and
    crayons
And sprawled on the carpet in front of the wireless
He filled up the pages, his output was tireless.

Amethyst asters on brown banks of peat,
Aloes with leaves thick and fleshy as meat.
Beryl-eyed lions and gray monkeys who so
Resembled the creatures of *Le Douanier Rousseau*.
Succulents' paddles and dew-heavy fronds,
Tourmaline fish swam through indigo ponds,
Ivies that twined with a grip near prehensile . . .
All sprang alive from the tip of Cliff's pencil.
Inspired by his *Child's Book of Fauna and Flora*
And broadcasts of *Rex Bond, Inveterate Explorer!*

O Rex! Weekly captured or worse, left for dead
In faraway places that filled Clifford's head
Rex could escape from the direst of rotten spots
Bloodthirsty tigers or cannibal Hottentots,
Meeting his end in the desert, the drink,
Tsetse flies, quicksand, or thrown in the clink
Left on a newly calved iceberg, adrift
But lately the perils had made a slight shift.
Fictional savages, strange voodoo mystics
Supplanted by dangers far more realistic.
Now Japs with their cunning, or Jerries with Mausers
Tried, but could not muss the crease of his trousers.
"For boys, just remember, the fieriest blitz
Is no match against our American wits!
Stay alert and stay wise to all foreign-born knavery.
Show grit and resolve and mimic the bravery
Of all of our men on the land, air, and sea
Who continue to fight so that we may be free!
When a threat rears its head, don't shrink and don't
    cower
Just rise to the challenge, like Amber Wave Flour!
Takes recipes meager and renders them rich,
If eager for tender cakes, Mother should switch!
And remember, the dawn comes when things seem
    most bleak,
Good night, boy and girls, and please tune in next
    week!"

There's little as scalding as juvenile ardor.
It's quickening as hatred or anger, but harder
To parse, 'specially when one must feign not to covet
One's heart's one desire, one's secret beloved

Since others might feel it was somehow unsuitable
So you become guarded, sphinx-like, inscrutable.
But sleep—free of judgment—knits care's raveled
    sleeve.
In slumber, without so much as "by your leave,"
Was Clifford allowed certain muscles to flex
And truly be all that he could to dear Rex.
A Rex, needing rescue, who'd sent an alert
To Clifford, uniquely equipped to avert
A numinous, formless, Rex-threat'ning disaster
Conspiring to injure his muscular master.
He'd find Rex bound up in some old, empty warehouse
And carry him home (in the dream it was their
    house)
He'd bathe him and generally salve the abuses
By pressing his lips to incipient bruises.
Until, the repletion near up to the hilt, he
Would waken quite shaken and sweaty (and guilty),
To find that his mother was calling his name . . .
So back to the world of his clandestine shame.

———

"I may well be shrewd, but not 'shrewish,'" she'd
    titter,
By which she meant not irretrievably bitter;
Twelve years and counting, still able to joke
Despite her sick husband, quite corkscrewed with
    stroke.
And truly she was shrewd, had practical knowledge
And worked in the local community college
Keeping the books, a quite valuable service

The dean told her numbers had made him quite
  nervous.
And thanks to her privileged employee's status
She put Cliff in Life Drawing, totally gratis.
"It's each Monday night for three hours," she told
Him, "it's serious, no joking, your classmates are old.
And though you're fifteen, you will *still* be the best.
Just wait, they'll be bug-eyed, bedazzled, impressed.
And soon you'll draw bodies just like as you see 'em,
It's this class today and tomorrow, museum!
But Cliffie," she said—yes she really was shrewd—
"The models you draw you will draw in the nude."
And paying close heed to her dear son's reflexes,
She added "Nude men and women, it is both sexes."
And there it was! An almost invisible thing
Like seeing a breeze or a hummingbird's wing,
The mention of men had gone straight to his heart
And her son gave an almost electrical start
Which caused within *her* some invisible flower
To bloom, because dear ones, all knowledge is
  power.

Of course she was right, Cliff drew circles around
All the others, and what's more, he happily found
His *talent* his most pronounced characteristic,
Not "longhair" or "pansy" or other sadistic
Abuse, instead he was now deemed "The Professor."
And his youth made him safe, he was also confessor:
Marie, whose red thermos contains scotch and
  water,
Barbara who hates that she hates her own daughter,
Dan's sorrow masked by the face of a bon vivant,

Clifford stayed silent like any good confidant.
Grown-ups, it seemed, were quite blithely un-curious,
A silence and safety Cliff found quite luxurious
Their secrets would never expand to a chat.
He would listen, was young, he could draw, that was
    that.

And as for the drawing, he loved the deep rigor
Demanded of him, he attacked with new vigor
The honing of skill, lines were finer, less crude
It registered barely that subjects were nude.
The occasional breast, due to space, time, and gravity
Might give a brief shock, but there was no depravity
Nor any great interest about what was there
He was frankly relieved for the chevron of hair
Concealing some deeper and unwanted knowledge,
Until one day Paul, on the track team at college,
Posed and put Cliff through the sufferings of Job
The instant he untied and took off his robe.

His limbs like the *David*'s, impossibly fine,
And lacing just under like flesh-covered twine
The veins that gave life to this ambulant art,
Shunting blood from his (sure to be beautiful) heart
'Cross the shoulders and down to the backside's deep
    cleft,
To his manhood that hung with imperious heft,
To the ribs, blue with shade 'neath his chest's
    cantilever,
Cliff was undone as if he'd caught a fever.
His charcoal went wide in an anarchic scrawl
Clifford felt hot, cold, then started to fall

He heard someone laugh, as though this was a game
Then he blacked out as everyone shouted his name.

Infirmary couch, with its cool, oxblood Naugahyde
Clifford felt boneless and battered and raw inside.
A verdict passed down that could not be revoked,
Something was loosed that felt formerly choked;
A process, unstoppable, once it began
Like trying to put shaving cream back in its can.
A vaguely elating but frightening bubble,
He felt buoyant and free and yet somehow in trouble.
In excess of caution, they'd summoned his mother
And asked her, concerned, had there been any
      other
Such fevers of late, whether he had been sick,
"His head hit the floor like a cloth-covered brick."
They told her that it had been Paul who had carried
      him
(Cliff, dimly conscious, thought they'd said married
      him).
Surveying this savior, she said with a stealthy
Murmur that no one could hear, "*He* seems healthy."
Clifford seemed fine, all were happy, relieved.
He was no worse for wear, and the others believed
That the culprit was likely the heat of the room
To which Clifford's mother responded with
      "Hmmm . . ."

————

Children's illogic can be an exquisitely
structured mistake. Take Aunt Sally's visit:

Each May Clifford's mother took two weeks off work
For her sister and niece who would come from New
    York.
They'd go meet their train (Cliff inspecting their
    berth)
Then back to the house for a fortnight of mirth.
Albums to leaf through, plus meals to eat. After
They'd sit on the porch, both exploding with laughter
From nonsense, like asking "How big were his feet?"
About a man Sally had seen on the street.
Everything lilted or swooped with their joking,
Baby talk always accompanied smoking:
"Weach fow a Wucky inthtead of a thweet!"
Eyes bugged and lips smacked. Oh, what a rare treat!
His mother's delivery, so usually brusque
Would, during those visits—especially near dusk—
Ooze sultry and slower and wooze on the brink
Of the "'D'-to-'J' journey" (where "drink" becomes
    "jrink").
The change wasn't only confined to their speech:
Everything that came within Sally's reach
Seemed somehow transformed, and largely because
Of just her, like when the house landed in Oz.
Prior and post, life could hardly be duller
But during! The world buzzed in bright Technicolor.
An adverb of joy, to his six-year-old thinking,
To "do it 'Auntsally'" meant action plus drinking,
Ice cream for breakfast and socks never matching!
Bark like a dog for a fierce tummy-scratching.
There was none of the darkness that can come with
    alcohol.
Just a delightful ignoring of protocol.

As he grew older, he realized the frivolous
Nature hid goodness that bordered on chivalrous.
Sally was truly the bestest of eggs,
She'd spend hours massaging the chicken-bone legs
Of Cliff's unresponsive but darting-eyed father,
She'd keep up the chatter, like it was no bother
"There you are, Hiram. As handsome as ever."
Her kindness encased in a varnish of clever,
She'd talcum his feet, or bring in fresh flowers,
Read him a *Photoplay* for what seemed like hours.

———

"For what seemed like hours," while always subjective
Was now so unknowable, flimsy, selective,
In thrall to the twists of his brain's involutions
The cranial mists and synaptic occlusions
He'd had to contend with since he'd had his stroke,
Like trying to sculpt something solid from smoke.
Everything now: liquid Space, rubber Time,
Tenuous grasps of both reason or rhyme
Could now trap his words in a Mobius loop,
He'd spent a whole day thinking "Elegant Soup"
(Despite that no broth was remotely forthcoming
And how could it be that his knees would be humming?
Or buzzing? Bees' Knees? [Be Sneeze!]). So confusing
Hours might go by in such meaningless musing.

Hiram was Hirschl, of that he was certain—
Though other details were obscured by a curtain
Of knowledge he no longer knew if he knew,
So, Hiram was Hirschl, and Hirschl is . . . you?

Hirschl came more than three decades before,
A lead to some landsman outside Baltimore
Had failed to achieve a reliable connection,
And so in the *Forverts*'s classified section,
From Bozeman, Montana, a dry goods concern:
"Be ready to work and be willing to learn."

And so with no warning and no indication,
The years concertina'd; expansion, deflation . . .
Images atomized, sudden dispersals
Time barreled forward, loped back through reversals,
And now, from some darkest recess of his brain
A vision—long-lost—of The Girl on the Train.

He'd come upon others while riding the rails
But no one that young, nor as haunted or frail.
And hair! Surely reddest hair he ever saw
He'd briefly thought there was a fire in the straw.
Out there alone, barely thirteen years old
Such shaking! And not only due to the cold.

She knew, in some way, that he meant her no harm
And silently slid herself into his arms.
To try to allay any feelings of skittish-
ness, he rocked her to sleep with an old song in Yiddish.
"Raisins and almonds," "A little white goat,"
She burrowed herself in the depths of his coat.

Clifford is here now, his good, gentle child,
He'd love nothing more than to be able to smile,
To look at the drawings Cliff spread 'cross the bed,
Be anything but unresponsive, half dead

Perhaps the return of this strange, red-haired flower
Is simple nostalgia for when he had power.

"Let's let him sleep, Cliff." Sally turns out the light.
Hirschl stares forward at nothing all night.

———

The only plant Sally's bright light failed to nourish
Was Helen, her daughter, too timid to flourish.
And Sally's attempts were, quite frankly, misguided,
Always a cut-up, she joshed and she chided
And went on and on at uncomfortable length
Thinking (in error) that Helen had strength
To be able to laugh, or at least grasp the gist
That the jests were at scars whose wounds did not exist.
In this regard, Helen was tone-deaf. Fantastic
Untruths sounded real, not the least bit sarcastic.
Ah, but tone deafness shuttles in any direction;
To Sally, the japing was naught but affection.
She had no idea that her joking fell flat,
That calling her slender girl "Porky" and "fat"
Or just outright fictions like, "*Try* not to limp,"
Made Helen curl inward: a cowed, sheepish shrimp.
Constantly braced for harsh words or cold looks,
Perpetually hunched, as if carrying books
With titles like *Helen, the Girl No One Wanted.*
Cliff felt the bond of the outcast, the taunted.

Where he had been strengthened almost to
    unbreakable
(By sketching his tormentors' torments unspeakable)

She was contrite, too polite, over-dutiful
Never aware that, in truth, she was beautiful.
Taller, it's true, than a girl ought to be,
Boys, when they looked, called her "Flagpole" or
　　"Tree,"
But Clifford could see with an eye almost clinical—
Yet open, affectionate, not at all cynical—
The classic proportions informing her shape.
It was all he could do not to grab her and drape
Her in bedsheets as toga, and once he had made
That, he'd ringlet her hair with a daub of pomade.
And Helen would let him, though she, two years older,
Felt Clifford was wiser than she, he was bolder,
With deeply held views on all manner of things:
Mustard (No!), Claude Monet (Yes!), cabbages, kings.
When they were young, they'd begun each trip shyly—
Regarding the other suspiciously, slyly—
Until, not unlike the way both of their mothers
Resumed their old bond, quite impervious to others,
By Day Two, to see them, it would have seemed
　　quibbling
To call them just cousins. They acted like siblings.
And though his allegiance was chief to his art
She felt he had only her interests at heart.
She never felt his deep absorption neglect, nor
Ever stopped feeling he was her protector.
If Clifford proposed it, she'd echo with "Me, too!"
To things she'd have otherwise never agreed to.

To wit: behind privets and glinting like jewels
Lay largely unguarded cerulean pools.
All maintained perfectly, pristine as new,

Temptingly empty, impossibly blue.
The owners, at country homes up in the mountains,
Cared little, it seemed, for the frothing of fountains
Nor for the colonnades, marble, mosaic
(A rectangle would have been far too prosaic),
The plaster Poseidons on acanthus plinths,
Friezes aswirl with young mermaids and nymphs
All lay unnoticed, unloved, un-enjoyed,
How could they not but dive into this void?
Daily—when either was seized by the whim—
They'd slip through the hedges and go for a swim.
Make free with the towels in poolside cabanas,
And eat from the trees: mangoes, loquats, bananas.
One time they'd both scrambled up into trees
And stayed well concealed 'til the old Japanese
Man who tended the grounds had passed by out of
     sight.
Helen had never felt such thrilling fright.
She'd all but stopped breathing, so's not to arouse
The gardener's gaze up into the green boughs.
The coast clear, she clambered to earth and then
     joined
Clifford, his arms full of fruit he'd purloined.

"Take these," he said, filling her arms with the loot
That he'd pulled from the branches. Now laden with
     fruit,
Clutching them all to her rubberized bodice
Clifford regarded her, whispering "Goddess."
The bright orange globes did their best to defeat her,
And fall from the grasp of their poolside Demeter.
"Cliffie, they're dropping, there must be a dozen . . ."

She started to say, but was stopped by her cousin
With a quietly stern admonition, "Don't talk, I
Just need to compose you." His black Brownie
    Hawkeye
The charm, like a mesmerist's watch on a chain
Helen fell silent and wondered again
How Clifford could somehow just know how to take
    light
And coax magic into a box of black Bakelite.
Moving her under an arch of white flowers
Artist and muse worked together for hours.
Dismissing some poses as "striving for cute,"
Clifford said softly, "Now roll down your suit."
He gave her a couple of oranges, "Here."
And showed her just how she should hold up each
    sphere.
His voice held no sneer nor a trace of a jest.
She trusted him fully that baring her chest
Would make the best pictures. She laughed when she
    saw
The inside-out breasts of the cups of the bra.
"Keep laughing," he said, didn't need to ask twice;
She felt so secure and the breeze felt so nice.
They worked thirty minutes or so, 'til the sun
Started to set, at which Clifford said, "Done."
Back through the hedge to the house where they let
Sally juice the "breasts" for crêpes suzette.

———

Ten A.M. in December in midtown Manhattan,
Helen sits at her desk in a dress of blue satin.
A pearl among swine, so at odds with the bustling

Of mid-morning business, her taffeta's rustling.
A vision of cocktails in coffee-break light.
She is garbed for the company party that night.
It is too far a trek out to Avenue J,
Just to go home to change at the end of the day,
So she sits, doing work, ignoring the mounting
Whispers and jokes, led by Kay in Accounting.
She's aware that her dress makes the other girls laugh
As they congregate over the mimeograph.
Helen gamely endures not the kindest of stares,
With aplomb, for you see, Helen no longer cares.
Well, that's mostly the truth. Though some doubts still
        impinge
Each year 'round Thanksgiving, an unwelcome twinge
Starts to niggle and rankle and by mid-December
She wonders anew, *Do they all still remember?*
Helen turns a blind eye to the smirks and the winks.
Surely it's not still about that, she thinks.

Time's gone by since that silly, regrettable business
When she became known as The Girl Who Ruined
        Christmas.
Helen harbors the hope that the passing five years
Have made folks forget both the vomit and tears
And throwing of glassware and drunken oration,
That half-hour tirade of recrimination
Where, feeling misused, she had got pretty plastered,
And named His name publicly, called him a bastard.
The details are fuzzy, though others have told her
She insulted this one and cried on that shoulder,
Then lurched 'round the ballroom, all pitching and
        weaving
And ended the night in the ladies' lounge, heaving.

How had it begun, before things all turned rotten?
She can pinpoint the day, she has never forgotten
How he came to her desk and leaned over her chair
To look at some papers, and then smelled her hair.
"Gardenias," he'd said, his voice sultry and lazy
And hot on her ear, Helen felt she'd gone crazy.
"A fragrance so heady it borders on sickly,"
He'd purred at her neck and then just as quickly
Was back to all business, demanding she call
Some client, as if he'd said nothing at all.

She was certainly never an expert at men,
But an inkling was twinkling, especially when
The next day he all but confirmed Helen's hunch.
When he leaned from his office and asked her to
      lunch.
Their talk was all awkward and formal to start
He said that he found her efficient and smart.
She thanked him, then stopped, she was quite at a loss.
She'd never before really talked to her boss.
They each had martinis, which helped turn things
      mellow,
He asked where she lived, and if she had a fellow.
He reached for her hand and asked, "Will you allow
An old man to wonder who's kissing you now?"

It was close and convenient, his spare midtown rental.
And after, *more* drinks at a bar near Grand Central
To sit once again in uncomfortable silence
Like two guilty parties to some kind of violence.
They sipped among other oblivion seekers,
While June Christy sang from the bar's tinny speakers.

He settled the bill and they got to their feet,
And emerged from the afternoon hush to the street.

They walked arm in arm in some crude imitation
Of other real couples en route to the station.
Such leisurely strolling, although it's grown late
Against her best judgment it feels like a date.
His booze-cloud blown over, now happy, near beaming
He stops at a window of cutlery, gleaming,
He points out the wares, taking note of a set that
He likes best of all, then he says, "*We* should get that."
She knows it's a joke, all this idle house-playing
But briefly she hopes that he means what he's saying.
Her presence, she thinks, is what's rendered him
    gladder
But really it's just that he aimed for, and had her.
The hideous reason behind his new glow is
What Helen—and many just like her—don't know is
That men's moods turn light and their spirits expand,
The moment they sense an escape is at hand.
He patted her cheek as he said, "I'm replenished,"
Then off through the crowd for the next train to
    Greenwich.

Helen pictured his house with its broad flagstone path.
The windows lit up, a child fresh from the bath,
And wondered if *she* might just smell on his skin,
The coppery scent of their afternoon sin.

At her desk the next Monday it was business as always.
There were no words exchanged, not a glance in the
    hallways.

With relief, Helen thought, *Well that's that. Nevermore.*
'Til Friday (again) at his pied-à-terre door.

And Friday thereafter, and each after that
For close to two years, 'til their actions begat
What such actions are wont to when caution's ignored.
The cure was a thing she could scarcely afford.
They talked in his office behind the closed door.
(She could tell from his face that he'd been there
    before.)
In the envelope left the next day on her desk,
Was two hundred cash and a downtown address.

She'd never had visions of roses or cupids,
From the beginning she wasn't that stupid.
What you don't hope for can't turn 'round to hurt you.
Besides, she had long before given her virtue.
There hadn't been untoward coaxing or urging
This wasn't The Ogre Defiling The Virgin
He's older than she, but they'd both played the game
Of never once speaking the other one's name.
Their mutual distance a plan jointly hatched
To keep things unserious, flip, and detached.
It was—truth be told, when she coolly reflected—
Not all that much different from what she'd expected.
Expected, she thought, and it sounded absurd.
How long had it been since she'd uttered that word?

And yet there were moments—unbarred,
    undefended—
When Helen concocted, cooked up, and pretended
She had all the trappings that go with the life of

The thoroughly satisfied, *marrified* wife of
A man who might keep her, despite the new battle
That said wives were really no better than chattel,
The difference too scant between "bridal" and "bridle"
And girls who'd had everything, now suicidal,
Finally finding their voices to speak
Of their feminine fetters, this loathsome mystique;
This problem that theretofore hadn't a name
And still, Helen couldn't resist, just the same,
To wonder, how might such a cared-for existence
Feel after decades of hard-won subsistence.
A mistress of manor, so calm, so serene
To know that there nowhere was any vitrine
Whose silvery wares would be ever denied her.
She tamped such a rampant desire deep inside her
And hoped if she kept the dream hidden and frozen
She soon would forget that she'd never been chosen.

But dreams scream as loud, whether thriving or dying
And Helen despite herself never stopped trying
With boxes of candy to New England camps,
And weekly, she cut and saved all foreign stamps
"I thought that your son . . ." and she'd leave it at that.
He would pocket the packet while donning his hat
And give her a friendly yet cursory nod
In thanks for the postage that came from abroad
With turrets and toucans, or archdukes, and antelope
Carefully trimmed and then slipped in an envelope.
She gave it her all not to trawl for his gaze
And used just those words, thus ensuring the phrase
Stayed tossed off, lest he find her maternal gesture
Too avid, or larded with over-investure.

A strategy subtler than some store-bought toy,
The covert seduction of man through his boy.
And as for less hidden campaigning, that too
Reared its head. Only once, with a "This is for you . . ."
When Helen presented a square of manila,
The contents so personal she thought it might kill her.
And if he suspected her ardor, he'd mock it,
So she was relieved when it joined in the pocket
The stamps. Her relief was compounded still when
He'd never brought up Helen's token again.

————

The doctor's door must have had five or more locks,
With a sixth to secure Helen's cash in a box.
He lowered the blinds to block out the sun
(Helen felt guilty before they'd begun).
Just a knife-blade of rays now bisected the room,
A useless divider twixt Sorrow and Gloom.
His first words—as though not already quite clear—
Were, "If anyone asks, you have *never* been here."
Helen, to show there would be no such slips,
Turned a key at her mouth as she locked up her lips.
She'd done it to combat the scent of despair
That pervaded the shaded, funereal air,
That she understood and could always be trusted,
But he curled his lip and seemed almost disgusted.
As if she was flirting or being beguiling,
He muttered, "I thought that *by now* you'd stop
      smiling."
She slackened her face, said "I'm sorry" and hastened
Undressing and feeling quite thoroughly chastened.

She lay back and placed her feet in the cold stirrups
And faced toward the window, all birdsong and
    chirrups.

A gauzy pad moist with some drops to sedate her,
A red rubber bulb, and a plain kitchen grater
He used on what looked like a brick of pink soap
The color of dawn, the exact shade of hope.
Waxy rose strands fell down into the water
(To flush out a son or incipient daughter?)
Woozy now, Helen regarded the basin
And angled herself so she might put her face in,
and leaned near the surface and took in a breath
Of almonds and ether, of freedom and death.

To help with the nausea, he gave her some pills—
'Though woefully few; she felt green at the gills.
The trip back to Brooklyn, she stood on the train.
She seriously thought she'd pass out from the pain.

———

There were stories of girls, all summarily sacked, who
Found out they no longer had jobs to come back to,
At least she had that, but she started to feel
That it hardly seemed worth it to work for a heel.
For each passing day found her feeling less grateful
Primarily 'cause he was hurtful and hateful.
Some minimal kindness was not a tall order.
Instead he was rude or he outright ignored her.
Until she decided that this wasn't right.
And stood in the door of his office one night.

She asked if he'd ever again say Hello,
Fedora'd and coated and ready to go
He took a step backward as if sensing danger
And fixed her with eyes of a cold-blooded stranger.
"I don't know what your game is, and frankly don't
    care,
But don't threaten me, Helen. I warn you, beware."
The very next Monday, from others she heard
That, without her knowledge, he'd had her transferred.
At least (tiny comfort) they didn't demote her
But Helen became what is known as a "floater."
Doing steno for this one, or helping with filing
And through it all Helen made sure to keep smiling.
The salt in the wound was the sight that then faced
    her,
Those looks he exchanged with the girl who'd replaced
    her.
She made herself steely, was ever the stoic
She held back her tears with an effort heroic.
But something was growing with each passing day,
'Til it burst forth the night of her shameful display.
She'd figured they'd fire her within the New Year
But Helen soon realized she'd nothing to fear.
(What she didn't know was the company's bosses
Viewed Helen as one of those typical crosses
A company's role it is—sadly—to bear
A lazy one here, or a crazy one there
And so no one made any move to relieve her
But mostly because they just didn't believe her.)

Perhaps there are those who consider it shameful
That Helen comes yearly, all dressed up and gameful.

Just showing herself in the very same setting
Cannot be a help to ensure folks' forgetting.
But she won't stay home or remain out of sight.
To do so, she thinks, *would just prove that they're right.*
She might have been drunk and too forward, uncouth
But each word she'd spoken had been but the truth.
Miss one or two parties and then, before long
The general consensus would be, "She was wrong."
A version to which she refused to be pliant,
So each year, she stands there, alone and defiant
While others quaff cocktails and gradually lose
The strictures that slowly dissolve with the booze.
There's tippling and coupling, embracing with brio.
And all being scored by the hired jazz trio.
Helen just stands there, observing it all,
Sipping her gimlet against the far wall.

The evening progresses, the room now quite loud
And here's Kay from Accounting! She weaves through
    the crowd.
A man on her left arm, a drink in her right.
"All alone are we, Helen? No fella tonight?"
Kay wears on her face an expression of utter
Concern, like her mouth couldn't even melt butter.

And here is the truth Helen long had resisted
In most of their eyes, she just barely existed,
Except as a source of some acid-tinged mirth,
A punch line, it seems, is the source of her worth.
They don't think of that time, indeed, they don't
    care.
She has always, to them, barely even been there.

The time when this might have been painful is past.
Nothing hurts Helen now, her heart has been cast
In bronze or in iron, or chiseled from lime,
Or some other substance as adamantine.
Her biggest regret is the five wasted years
That she's chided herself over shedding those tears.
Instead of her wishing for eyes that stayed dry
She should cherish that Helen, so able to cry,
That Helen who felt things and then wasn't scared
To air them in public. That Helen who cared
Enough about things she could speak them aloud,
That Helen of whom she might ever be proud.
Taking both of Kay's hands with no rancor, no bile,
Helen looks in her eyes and breaks into a smile.
"You're right," Helen says, "I should call it a day."
Helen smiles one more time, and then adds, "Fuck off,
  Kay."

———

Helen takes off her dress and gets ready for bed.
There is peace deep within her, where once only
  dread.
And there, in the comforting nocturnal gloom
An image took form in the air of her room:
Was it really as distant as sixteen long years
Since Clifford had handed her two golden spheres
He'd plucked from a fruit-laden tangerine tree
And holding his camera had said, "Look at me."
He posed her, half naked, like some Aphrodite.
Helen felt marvelous, brilliant, and mighty
The picture he'd taken was her at her best

The oranges, one each to cover a breast.
She'd never felt better than she did that day
And rued that she'd given the picture away,
She shook her head, pained, for this hardly
     distinguished
Itself from her many gifts she had relinquished.

She watches the window for most of the night,
Turn from deep black as it gathers up light.
And as the panes bloom to a beautiful blue
She lights on a theory, although it feels true:
Babylonian, Aztec, Gregorian, or Julian
All calendars *must* know those hours when cerulean
Skies seem so pure and to go on forever,
That one feels each dream and one's every endeavor's
Success is as sure as the coming of dawn.

She gulped in the air with a satisfied yawn.
A calm had descended around five A.M.,
Which made her immune to the power of Them.
Gets up, quite refreshed, sets the coffee to perk.
For once looking forward to going to work.
She pours out a cup, adds a stream of cold milk
And smiles as it swirls just like taffeta silk.

———

O, just like the song says, my heart's San Francisco's!
(Suck on that dear, while I work out where this
     goes . . .)
From the very first day, Clifford couldn't conceive
Why anyone ever decided to leave.

Hills, Bay, and art, ineluctably bound
To make Clifford feel, *I was lost, now am found.*
And crowning it all was the chief among joys:
The liquid, ubiquitous river of boys.
Fuckable, kissable, dateable, rentable,
Faeries and rough trade, or highly presentable,
Stupid as livestock or literate in Firbank,
All of it galaxies distant from Burbank.

O, San Francisco, I've left you my heart!
(Tug those two down while you rub on that part . . .)
A boy on a stoop who was palming his crotch,
It seemed impolite, Clifford thought, not to watch
Then up to his flat where they diddled for hours,
Another one's rump had near-magical powers;
Clifford the bull and that ass the torero
That led him for blocks the wrong way on Guerrero
A mouth like a summer-ripe plum, or a calf
Fuzzed with gold hair, or a neck, or a laugh
Could make Clifford fall (and might leave him with
    pubic lice),
And still he felt like he had landed in paradise.

In you, San Francisco, my heart's what I left
(Make your tongue rigid and poke at that cleft . . .)
Smoke a fat spliff and then off to the Castro
Where, blissed-out and bonelessly slumped in the last
    row
They felt simultaneously boneless and vital
And jazzed by the Wurlitzer's pre-show recital.
Just one more trip taken en masse to the washroom
To have a quick pee and ingest primo mushrooms,

Look at that queen, that unbearable phony
Wearing full leather to Antonioni.
Their thinking was agile, imbued with bravura
Though logic was fragile, so *L'avventura*
Might start out a brilliantly dark meditation
On anomie in the post-war generation
Sick with the bourgeoisie's morals-free habits . . .
Who thinks that the aisles are now crawling with
     rabbits?
This décor resembles a palace, a mosque, or . . .
How could they deny Judy Garland that Oscar?
It's over with Jimmy, he's petty, aggressive
And frankly, that much *toile* gets pretty oppressive.
Seen *Cabaret*? Liza's three-fourths mascara!
Hey, what was that poem by dear Frank O'Hara?
"Lana Turner get up and . . . shoot John Stompanato!"
My *god*, Kathryn Grayson had killer vibrato.
Wait, Cheryl Whatever was Lana T's daughter
And . . . how have we ended up here at the water?

A quiet walk home, maybe rent a blue video
The velvet-black woods of the nighttime Presidio
Tempered the high's non-contextual mirth
And slowly returned them to heaven on earth.
The wee small hours always concluded with this
A feeling of grateful repletion and bliss.
He thought to himself, "How pear-shaped could this go
Anywhere *other* than my San Francisco."
An insight that always cut keen as a knife
Whose wound was pure pleasure; Clifford loved, *loved*
     his life.
And credited most of that to his dear city,

He lived the reverse of what plagued Walter Mitty
No secrets, no longing, no desperate hoping
Just reach out and grab from a world cracked wide
    open.

———

Clifford once hoped that each Bay Area Brahmin
Would, aside from their wealth, have one more thing
    in common:
A portrait by him, rich with painterly skill,
He'd soon be the Sargent—nowadays—of Nob Hill
But that dream was forced through a major revision
The instant he'd gone out to drum up commissions.
Fresh out of art school, and more than proficient
He'd thought, like a dope, that his gifts were sufficient.
Not understanding his role was a mixture
Of lapdog and popinjay, servant and fixture.
Cliff lacked the fawning gene, just couldn't glom
Onto dowagers ignorant of Vietnam,
Or husbands who thought it was his first time hearing
The usual jokes about "guys who have earrings."
"I thought you were some chick, with all that long
    hair."
(Although a true passion of his, somehow the ratio
Was off; Clifford just could not give that much
    fellatio.)
The only regret was one of economics
When he quit for a life in the underground comics.
But the joy of it outshone his bank account's lack,
He climbed down from Nob Hill and never looked
    back.

———

Who left their heart in San Fran? It was me!
(It's so good with two, dear. Shall we try three?)
Body surf over the ocean's green swells,
Truffle for dick or go forage morels.
Sun-washed and fog-bound, electric with sex
Challenging, easy, naïve, and complex
It still filled him with a near-supplicant awe
That even grown up, they allowed him to draw
And then—here's the part that was screamingly
    funny—
They'd then say "Good job, Cliff," and then give him
    money!
Be a go-getter or bonelessly languid,
Laid out, displayed like a groaning-board banquet.
The square and the dyke and the faggot, the freak
Could easily find and then get what they seek
Unlike, say, New York where, regardless of hope
Or desire, lay a point where a red velvet rope
Stood between you and the goals of your dreams
(At least when he visits, that's just how it seems).

"Cap'n Cocksure and Throbbin'," his randy young pal
In tales like "The Shoot-out at KY Corral."
Regardless of each issue's sticky predicaments
They'd end in a blending of muscles and ligaments.
He brought to bear all from his life-drawing class
(Plus, given the Cap'n his ex's Pete's ass).
Tights of carnelian, a jock blue as lapis
And filled to a size as befitting Priapus.
In truth, he was Bruce Wang, a wealthy civilian

(The jokes were all similarly crude and vaudevillian).
Monthly, he'd battle some muscular villain
Who turned almost instantly horny and willing,
And ended with Cap'n who'd then throw his
    massive . . .
Err . . . *weight* behind Throbbin', posed Grecian (and
    passive).
Thrusting and pumping, reliably nude,
Cliff's magnum opus was thrillingly lewd.
The work of an overgrown, over-sexed kid
Rex Bond unfiltered, by way of Cliff's id.
Blanche Tilley believed in true Heaven, real Hell
Her hair an immovable nautilus shell,
Was galvanized with a conviction near feral
When she sensed that children were somehow in
    peril.
Unburdened by much intellectual heft
She battled the evil she saw on the Left
"A mere servant to all concerned wives and mothers."
(A woman who, truthfully, given her druthers,
Would see all the Libbers, the Hippies, the Gays
Hounded and rounded up and locked away.)
"I look at the state of this country today
And see such depravity, moral decay
That, truly, it makes me just weep for the nation
These crimes in the name of their 'Gay Liberation.'
Just how do the First Amendment's full rights
Extend to this sodomite rapist in tights?"
She called the strip filthy, overt, immature.
All charges to which Cliff responded with "Sure!
Cocksure is vulgar, he's dirty and loud
Excessive and horny, and makes me so proud.

I draw him for those who might like it or need it,
But if you don't want to, Blanche, well, then don't
     read it!

"In some ways we two are a heaven-made match
But like much in life, there's a deal-breaking catch:
We both love our lives, our convictions are strong
You'd think we'd be fast friends, but you would think
     wrong.
We think we're the ones who are open, convivial
While others are hateful if not downright trivial.
We each fill the other with loathing and fear
We'd each like the other to just disappear.
To you, I'm a sinner, sprung full-formed from Sodom
Of lowliest creatures, I dwell at the bottom
I know it won't sway you the smallest scintilla
To point out the sex is quite firmly vanilla,
The hatred you harbor's divorced from reality
I draw a sweet blow job, you see bestiality.
How I wish you would stop up that bile-spewing
     spigot
You use when you speak, you rebarbative bigot.
You're through and through Dixie and I, San
     Francisco.
Despite a shared fondness we both have for Crisco,
Try as I might, I simply can't see
A way or a day when we two might agree.
So pack up your sideshow and go back down South
Where I won't come knock the dick out of *your*
     mouth."

———

Susan had never donned quite so bourgeois
A garment as Thursday night's Christian Lacroix.
In college—just five years gone—she'd have abhorred it
But now, being honest, she fucking adored it.
The shoulders, the bodice, *insane* retro pouf,
Where once an indictment, now good, calming proof;
She'd no longer be tarred by the words "shame" or
    "greed,"
Tossed about by the weak. No, now Susan was freed!
If she wanted to spend half the whole day adorning
Herself, well what of it? The American Morning
Had dawned! At Oberlin stuff she'd feigned being
    above,
Had turned into all that she most dearly loved.
And conversely, stuff she might actively seek
Now repelled her as sub-par, too lenient, and weak.
Out was group therapy (adieu agoraphobics!),
In was massage, Silver Palate, aerobics.
Innermost was a Susan Improved and Untrammeled
Sleeker and diamond-bright, sharp and enameled!
She happily ate "poisonous" white-flour pasta
Whereas all those Ultimate Frisbee white Rastas
Didn't seem sexy and free anymore,
And frankly, the U.S. in El Salvador
(Or out of it? Truly, she'd largely lost track
And hadn't the patience to find her way back),
Among frailer aspects of the human condition
Now just turned her stomach. Once-hated ambition
Awakened her senses like rarest perfume;
It could render her weak-kneed across a large room.

It was all large rooms lately, all beautifully appointed
And Susan had somehow been specially anointed

To stand in them prettily, playing her part:
Girl at the nexus of commerce and art.
Her father was glad to augment the small salary
She made as factotum at the Nonnie Cash Gallery.
Nonnie was in the news seven months back
When she'd ended a group show by handing out crack.
"Let's turn this new vice into something convivial!"
(The chief of police called her "clueless and trivial.")
Susan adored her and worshipped her style,
Loved her pronouncements of "perfect" and "vile,"
Loved the sheer whim, the madcap willy-nillyness
And how deeply seriously Nonnie took her own
      silliness
(Though she'd have loved Hitler, if forced to confess,
If he had seen fit to have bought her that dress).

"The opening demands it!" Nonnie said on their
      spree,
"And Spraycan can bloody well pay, thanks to me."
There was bourbon in hypos, doled out by chic
      nurses—
in truth white-clad models—Osetra beggars' purses.
The waiters were done up like Jean Genet felons:
Brush cuts, fake shiners, with asses like melons.
And serving as Boswells to Nonnie's new caper,
Scribes from *East Village Eye*, *FMR*, *Paper*.
Nonnie barked orders in Urdu and Xhosa,
And with a *"Ragazzi, servite qualcosa!"*
Came the blush that rose when her blood started to
      sing
From a room where the energy gets into swing.
Look at this shit, she thought, *pure onanism!*
Ransom-note lettering, sequins, and jism,

Neiman impasto with touches of Basquiat,
Smoke, sizzle, bells, whistles . . . all of it diddly-squat!
Nonnie'd built him a name by dint of sheer will.
A bluff that distracted from his lack of skill.
Despite what collectors seemed willing to pay,
Spraycan 3000 had nothing to say.

Nathan was due as the evening wound down.
They'd rented a car for a week out of town.
Josh was in Chappaqua seeing his mom
They'd stop, pick him up, then continue right on
With luck they would reach the Cape not long past one,
A week on the ocean had sounded like fun.
But then the foreboding that started to loom
When Susan saw Nate standing there 'cross the room,
Clad in the uniform he'd worn since Ohio:
Birkenstocks, drawstring pants (think Putumayo).
With no small remorse, she thought, *He and his mess*
Better not come near this fabulous dress.

———

Ah, whither love's ardor whose heat used to scorch
    her?
Now his mere face can assail her like torture
And being alone with him renders her frantic
It makes her a hectoring shrew, a pedantic
Wet blanket, although it is also true, in her defense
That Nate can be maddeningly oafish and dense.
Who chips a mug without knowing it, or
Doesn't see that they've just spilt some milk on the
    floor?

And once pointed out, he goes all Lotus
Position-y, saying mildly, "Wow. I didn't notice."
She didn't want some belching, farting, or toga-
Clad frat boy, but frankly, the wheat germ, the yoga
Seemed ersatz, some also-ran version of "mellow,"
This go-with-the-flow, unassailable fellow,
She just didn't buy Nathan's pressure-wrought grace,
And wanted sometimes just to slap that sweet face.

Now Day Three in Wellfleet, they've lost all their
    power
Which means no hot water, no lights, and cold
    showers.
And all Nathan does is repeat "This is cozy."
She thinks that perhaps she'll just get up and mosey
To where he is sitting to give him a smack.
Maybe the blow would do something to crack
This passive-aggressive façade for his shirking
Just going downstairs to get things back to working.
Or maybe, she thinks, *I'll just fuck your best friend.*
Now, something like that might just bring to an end
This constant pretending that everything's fine.
Maybe then you might evidence some sort of spine.
A thunderstorm could be heard off in the distance.
Susan had offered Josh any assistance.
"Sure," Josh replied, "you can come hold the ladder."
Nathan kept reading, which just made her madder,
And then madder *still* when he hadn't detected
Her tone, which was heavily sarcasm-inflected:
"Need anything up here, Nate, before we're done?"
"No, that's okay," Nate replied, "you guys have fun."
"We will." Her smile had a slight rodentine tightness.

Nathan went back to his *Unbearable Lightness*
Of Being, that summer's one de rigueur book,
And, lost in the story, did not even look
Up from the page for an hour or more
When the others came through the basement stairs
    door.
"You were gone for a while. Must have got a lot done."
"Oh, we did," Susan said, squinting, as the lights all
    surged on.

———

Take Posner's of Great Neck, the Falls at Niagara
And throw in that white marble tomb that's in
    Agra—
Now if you compared the three places, you might
Think the Taj and Niagara were hiding their light.
At Posner's, the subtle, subdued, and hermetic
Had no part to play. The rococo aesthetic—
An Empire, Art Deco, Chinoiserie garble
Of crystal and frescoes and gilt and (yes) marble;
A maximal, turbo-charged, top-drawer milieu—
Appealed to a moneyed crowd of locals who
Insisted on only the toppest of drawers,
Weddings befitting a Louis Quatorze.
Venetian palazzo floors pounded by horas
Cut-velvet drapes framing chopped-liver Torahs.
Ceilings adorned with Tiepolo clouds
Vaulted above the dressed-to-the-nines crowds
Who gave off their *own* light with such glinting
    frequency
(good thing one need not kill creatures for sequins).

Nathan, from one of the outlying tables,
His feet tangled up in the disc jockey's cables,
Surveyed the room as unseen as a ghost
While he mulled over what he might say for his toast.
That the couple had asked him for this benediction
Seemed at odds with them parking him here by the
    kitchen.
His invite was late—a forgotten addendum—
For Nate, there could be no more clear referendum
That he need but endure through this evening and then
He would likely not see Josh and Susan again.

That he had said yes was still a surprise,
And not just to him, it was there in the eyes
Of the guests who had seen a mirage and drew near
And then covered their shock with a "Nathan, you're
    here!"
And then silence, they'd nothing to say beyond that.
A few of the braver souls lingered to chat
They all knew, it was neither a secret nor mystery
That he and the couple had quite an odd history
Their bonds were a tangle of friendship and sex.
Josh his best pal once, and Susan his ex.
For a while he could hardly go out in the city
Without being a punch line or object of pity.
"Poor Nathan" had virtually become his real name
And so he showed up just to show he was game.
His shirt had been ironed, his belt brightly buckled,
A shine on his shoes, a well-turned-out cuckold.

Susan's sister was speaking, a princess in peach.
"Hello, I am Mindy, and this is my speech.

*Susan, you are the best sister plus you've always had
     great comic timing,
So I know you won't hold it against me when I do my
     specialty and*

make my toast in rhyming.
*You've always been a terrific runner, even though it
     made your shoes damp*
*Especially when you were impersonating Mrs. Zolteck
     from Talmud Torah*

when we were at camp.
*Josh, we have become the best of friends and I'm so
     happy now I'm your sister,*
*But when we go out together let's try not to get
     blisters . . ."*

Nathan's mind wandered as Mindy meandered.
The effort he'd squandered, if this was the standard,
Seemed hours badly wasted, until he recalled
That, time notwithstanding, he'd nothing at all.
He'd pored over *Bartlett's* for couplets to filch
He'd stayed up 'til three and still came up with zilch
Except for instructions he'd underscored twice
Just two words in length, and those words were, "Be
     Nice!"
Too often, he'd noticed, emotions betray us
And reason departs once we're up on the dais.
He'd witnessed uncomfortable moments where others
Had lost their way quickly, where sisters and brothers
Had gotten too prickly and peppered their babbling
With stories of benders or lesbian dabbling,
Or spot-on impressions of mothers-in-law,
Which, true, Nathan thought, always garnered guffaws

But the price seemed too high with the laughs seldom
    cloaking
Hostility masquerading as joking.

No, he'd swallow his rage and bank all his fire
He knew that in his case the bar was set higher.
He'd have to be careful and hide what his heart meant
(Disingenuous malice was Susan's department).
They'd be hungry for blood even though they had
    supped,
Folks were just waiting for him to erupt
In tears or some other unsightly reaction,
And Nathan would not give them that satisfaction.
Though Susan's a slattern, and Josh was a lout
At least Nathan knew what he'd not talk about:

I won't wish them divorce, that they wither and sicken,
Or tonight that they choke on their salmon (or
    chicken).
I'll stay mum on that time when the cottage lost power
In that storm on the Cape, and they left for an hour
And they thought it was just the cleverest ruse
To pretend it took that long to switch out the fuse.
Or that time you advised me, with so much insistence,
That I should be granting poor Susan more distance.
That the worst I could do was to hamper and crowd
    her,
That if she felt stifled she'd just take a powder.
That a plant needs its space just as much as its water
And above all, not give her the ring that I'd bought her.
Which in retrospect only elicits a "Gosh!
I hardly deserved a friend like you, Josh."

No, I won't air that laundry, or make myself foolish
To satisfy appetites venal and ghoulish.
I will *not* be the blot on this hellish affair.
And with that Nathan pushed out, and rose from his
　　chair.
And just by the tapping of knife against crystal,
All eyes turned his way, like he'd fired off a pistol.

"Joshua, Susan, dear family and friends,
A few words, if you will, before everything ends
And you skip out of here to begin your new life
As happily married husband and wife.
You've promised to honor, to love and obey,
We've sipped our champagne and been cleansed with
　　sorbet
All in endorsement of your Hers and His-dom.
So, let me add my two cents' worth of wisdom.
Herewith, as a coda to this evening historical
I just thought I'd tell you this tale allegorical.

I was racking my brains sitting here at this table
Until I remembered this suitable fable.
Each reptilian hero, each animal squeal
Serves a purpose, you see, because they reveal
A truth about life, even as they distort us
So here is 'The Tale of the Scorpion and Tortoise.'
The scorpion was hamstrung, his tail all aquiver.
Just how would he manage to get 'cross the river?
'The water's so deep,' he observed with a sigh,
Which pricked at the ears of the tortoise nearby.
'Well, why don't you swim?' asked the slow-moving
　　fellow.

'Unless you're afraid. Is that it, you are yellow?'
'That's rude,' said the scorpion, 'and I'm not afraid
So much as unable. It's not how I'm made.'

'Forgive me, I didn't mean to be glib when
I said that, I figured you were an amphibian.
The error was one of misclassification
I mistakenly figured you for a crustacean.'

'No offense taken,' the scorpion replied.
'But how 'bout you help me to reach the far side?
You swim like a dream, and you have what I lack.
What say you take me across on your back?'

'I'm really not sure that's the best thing to do,'
Said the tortoise, 'Now that I see that it's you.
You're the scorpion and—how can I say this?—just . . .
     well . . .
I don't know I feel safe with you riding my shell.
You've a less-than-ideal reputation preceding.
There's talk of your victims, all poisoned and
     bleeding,
That fact by itself should be reason sufficient.
I mean, what do you take me for, mentally deficient?'
'I hear what you're saying, but what would that prove?
We'd both drown so tell me, how would that
     behoove
Me, to basically die at my very own hand
When all I desire is to be on dry land?'

The tortoise considered the scorpion's defense.
When he gave it some thought, it made perfect sense.

The niggling voice in his mind he ignored
And he swam to the bank and called out 'Climb
    aboard.'

The tortoise was wrong to ignore all his doubts
Because in the end, friends, our true selves will out.
For, just a few moments from when they set sail
The scorpion lashed out with his venomous tail.
The tortoise, too late, understood that he'd blundered
When he felt his flesh stabbed and his carapace
    sundered.
As he fought for his life, he said, 'Please tell me why
You have done this, for now we will surely both die!'

'I don't know,' cried the scorpion. 'You never should
    trust
A creature like me, because poison I must.
I'd claim some remorse or at least some compunction
But I just can't help it. My form is my function.
You thought I'd behave like my cousin the crab
But unlike him, it is but my *nature* to stab.'

The tortoise expired with one final quiver
And then both of them sank, swallowed up by the
    river."
Nathan paused, cleared his throat, took a sip of his
    drink.
He needed these extra few seconds to think.
The room had grown frosty, the tension was growing,
Folks wondered precisely where Nathan was going.
The prospects of skirting fiasco seemed dim
But what he said next surprised even him.

"So what can we learn from their watery ends?
Is there some lesson on how to be friends?
I think what it means is that central to living
A life that is good is a life that's forgiving.
We're creatures of contact, regardless of whether
to kiss or to wound, we still must come together.
Like in *Annie Hall*, we endure twists and torsions
For food we don't like, and in such tiny portions!
But, like hating a food but still asking for more
It beats staying dry but so lonely on shore.
So we make ourselves open, while knowing full well
It's essentially saying, 'Please, come pierce my shell.'
So . . . please, let's all raise up our glasses of wine
And I'll finish this toast with these words that aren't
      mine:
Yet each man kills the thing he loves,
By each let this be heard,
Some do it with a bitter look,
Some with a flattering word,
The coward does it with a kiss,
The brave man with a sword!"
Where first it seemed that Nathan had his old
      resentments cleanly hurdled,
The air now held the mildest scent of something sweet
      gone meanly curdled.
The thorough ambiguity held guests in states of mild
      confusion
No one raised their eyes, lest a met glance be taken for
      collusion.
Silence doesn't paint the depth of quiet in that room
There was no clinking stemware toasting to the bride
      or groom.

You could have heard a petal as it landed on the floor.
And in that quiet Nathan turned and walked right out
    the door.

The urinal's wall was *The King and His Court*,
A work done in porcelain, precisely the sort
Of tableau of gentility at Le Petit Trianon,
A cast of nobility, designed for the peeing on.
Nate turned his gaze as he hosed down the scene,
It seemed an especially brutish and mean
Treatment of all the baroque figures in it
(Such unlucky placement, poor girl at her spinet).
He needed this pit stop before he took off
To go catch his train, when he heard a slight cough.

There, twisting a swan's head in gold for hot water
Was Lou, who had bankrolled this day for his
    daughter.
Lou had scared Nathan for all of the years
He was with Susan, and now the sum of his fears
Was here, now the chickens had come home to land.
"The man of the hour, with his *schvantz* in his hand."
Nathan started to say that he knew how he blew it
And how he was sorry, but Lou beat him to it;
Lou, who was blunt—some said boorish—and rich.
But a mensch deep at heart, said, "My Suzy's a
    bitch.
You'd think that today I'd be proud, that I'd *kvell*,
But I followed you out here just so I could tell
You: she told her friends she would be able to get
You to come give a toast. It's a monstrous bet,
Made all the more awful that her Day of Joy

Was *still* incomplete, and abusing a boy
In a trick was the thing that she wanted above
All else. It's the mark of a girl who can't love.
Ach, Nathan, this day is a stroke of bad luck.
You, cast in this play, and then played for a schmuck.
But think of it this way, she'll wake up tomorrow
And *still* be unhappy. And that is *my* sorrow."

Lou turned off the swan's head, once more checked
      his tie,
Held his arm out and said, "This is goodbye."
He shook Nathan's hand and then made for the door
Where he paused and he turned to say just one thing
      more.
"That toast, if you give it again (but you won't),
Remember, Nate: turtles swim, tortoises don't."

————

A permeable world where each friend is a trick,
Can feel like it's crumbling when just one gets sick.
Add one more for two, and that queasy sensation
Can feel like a threat to one's very foundation.
Three seems like carelessness, a surfeit of strife
Exposing one to comment on the Platform of Life
(Yes, dear Lady Bracknell, invoked with remorse
But humor was Cliff's one remaining recourse);
For if "sick" becomes "die" and then "three," "*every*
      friend,"
It's the hurricane's eye of a world at an end,
A Vale of Tears reached 'cross a sad Bridge of Sighs,
Cliff and his cohort were dropping like flies:

Victor, a handsome star of the ballet
Whose turnout, they said, could turn anyone gay
Coughed once, and then he expired like Camille—
Not quite, but the true facts seemed just as surreal—
And what could one say about poor lovely Marty?
Whose fever spiked high at his own dinner party
Between the clear soup and the rabbit terrine
By eleven that night, he was in quarantine.
Marco was the anchor of *Bay Area News Day*.
Fevered on Friday and dead the next Tuesday.
Gorgeous and baritone, gifted with words
And felled by an illness that struck only birds.
Before all they'd had to look out for was crabs
But now nothing helped, there were no pills, no
      labs
Nothing to slow down, never mind getting rid
Of this crazy-fast killer they'd weakly named GRID.

A grid: Cliff could see it stretched out, made of wire,
And spanning a canyon of brimstone and fire.
Suddenly, all of them caught unawares
Were one by one falling away through its squares
Rampant infections called opportunistic
Worked at a pace both absurd and sadistic.

The plum-colored smudge, a sloe slowly blooming,
Seemed barely worth noticing; small, unassuming,
As if trying to belie all the terrible harm it
Could do, it stayed hidden, just under his armpit.
But soon it branched out, making siblings and cousins
His lesions were legion, from just one to dozens.
Despite all his nursing, the tears and the dramas

Of friends, when he woke up to find his pajamas
As wet through with sweat as if dunked in the sea
He *still* briefly asked, *What is happening to me?*
He'd loved *Touch of Evil*, when la Dietrich tells
The fortune of corpulent, vile Orson Welles:
"Your future's all used up." So funny and grim.
But now that the same could be spoken of him
It was sadness that gripped him, far more than the
    fear
That, if facing the truth, he had maybe a year.
When poetic phrases like "eyes, look your last"
Become true, all you want is to stay, to hold fast.
A new, fierce attachment to all of this world
Now pierced him, it stabbed like a deity-hurled
Lightning bolt lancing him, sent from above,
Left him giddy and tearful. It felt like young love.
He'd thought of himself as uniquely proficient
At seeing, but now that sense felt insufficient.
He wanted to grab, to possess, to devour
To *eat* with his eyes, how he needed that power.

Not much of a joiner, he'd always been leery
Of groups, although now, he was simply too weary
From all of the death, plus his symptoms now
    besting
Him. He so admired those heroes protesting
The drugmakers, government—all who'd forsaken
The thousands—the murderous silence of Reagan,
Or William F. Buckley, that fucker at whose
Suggestion that people with AIDS get tattoos;
(The New Haven lockjaw, the glib erudition,
When truly, the man's craven moral perdition

Made Clifford so angry he thought he might vomit
Or fly east, find Buckley's address, and then bomb it).

But, just like a child whose big gun is a stick,
Cliff was now harmless, he'd gotten too sick
To take any action beyond rudimentary
Routines that had shrunk to the most elementary:
Which pill to take now, and where is your sweater?
Did the Imodium make you feel better?
Study your shit to make sure you'd not bled,
Make sure the Kleenex is next to the bed.
"Make sure," "be prepared," plan out every endeavor
Like a scout on the stupidest camping trip ever.
The facts were now harder, reality colder
His parasol no match for that falling boulder.
And so the concern with the trivial issues:
Slippers nearby and the proximate tissues
He thought of those two things in life that don't
    vary
(Well, thought only glancingly; more was too scary)
Inevitable, why even bother to test it,
He'd paid all his taxes, so that left . . . you guessed it.

———

Suppose one were trying to gently assert
One's position; an East Eighty-Third Street address
    doesn't hurt.
Nor does a cottage on Georgica Pond,
Or three (Jewish . . . *shah!*) kids who are natural
    blonds.
Susan had banished all unsightly elements

Her latest career would brook no such impediment
To being the personal, shining reflection
Of breeding and privilege, class and connection.
Finally, to match Mayflower Realty, Inc.'s tone
Her business cards now showed her first name as
    Sloan.

Josh was a force of the courts—law and squash—
The family was blessed and seemed wholly awash
In the kind of good fortune one doesn't dare dream,
Near-parodically copious, bursting the seams
Of the sky; heaven-sent, like the biblical gift of the
    manna,
Until her thoughts happened to land upon Hannah.
One Hannah Hint seems to be all that it takes
For Sloan's inner Lexus to slam on the brakes.
Her mind gave a lurch, and Hannah's place in it
Was *poof!* purged and cleansed in just under a
    minute.

Instead, she corralled her thoughts only to roam
On things bright and lovely. For instance, her
    home:
Everything perfect, divine, and appealing,
The pearl-gray luster of the silver-leafed ceiling
Tamed what most rooms might not easily handle,
Tassels and chintzes, a screen (coromandel),
Sofas and slipper chairs, two silk fauteuils
(out of bounds to her girl and both the boys),
Framed scenes of hunts on a hunter-green wall,
A pillow: NOUVEAU RICHE BEATS NO RICHE AT ALL,
Traces of Oberlin, NPR, grunge

Gone, and instead was a WASP-y mélange
Of faux Sister Parish, Buatta, and Trump,
A richness of embarrassments, an opulent sump.

Every time Sloan sipped her tea there, *Hosanna*
She thought, *I've arrived* and then . . . Hannah.
(It drove Sloan bananas how seldom, if ever,
The shit of life didn't demolish her reverie.)
She knew it was harsh of her, bordering on churlish—
She tried, in all things, to seem dainty and girlish—
But her mother-in-law made her furious and sick,
Hannah's decline seemed a purposeful trick
Designed to wreak havoc, annoy, to be grating
And, at the worst moments, just plain nauseating.
Once, during a party—this was early on—
Sloan looked around when she noticed her gone.
The very next moment, the elevator attendant
Was at the front door with a Hannah resplendent
Her skirt 'round her shoulders, like the cape of a
    matador,
Nude and soiled from the waist down, and *walking the
    corridor!*

Josh took his mother straight off to the bath,
While Sloan tried her best to conceal the white wrath
That shot through her with such force she thought she
    might faint,
Especially when friends whispered, "Josh is a saint."
"Yes," she joked, "just the kind I'd like to martyr."
Okay, charade over! It was time now to cart her
Away. She was no longer fit even to visit.
(*That's not the mark of a bad person, is it?*)

She felt for Josh, truly. He'd grown up with no father,
But Hannah was now such an unruly bother
That Sloan was quite worried that she'd grow to hate
    him,
Or soon might resort to some harsh ultimatum
Like "It's her or me!" or the wholesale preempting
Of contact, although it grew ever more tempting
(Her feelings for Hannah, alas, were too late;
That vaginal vernissage had sealed her fate).
Each time she even attempted to air
The topic with Josh, his face was despair
Writ so large, deep, and painful she'd had to leave off
(She'd not known she'd married a man quite so soft).
And then, the true kicker: *Could this be prophetic?*
I've read that dementia like this is genetic.

She thought of the joke she and Josh used to tell,
Although it fit present conditions too well:
"If all of the money was gone from my life,
Would you still love me?" a man asks his wife.
"Of course," she replies. "Come here, let me kiss you.
I'll love you forever, but *boy* would I miss you!"

Enough! There was work to do, one saving grace;
She felt the old thrill of a three-agent race
For the exclusive on an absolute jewel:
Four-bedroom penthouse, two fireplaces, *pool*!
And three thousand square feet of wraparound terrace.
Now that's *what we need*, she thought, feeling
    embarrassed.
She had windows aplenty, but why shut themselves
Up like corpses on one of those mortuary shelves?

Josh might even bid, if she skillfully seeded
The ground, somehow showing that what they both
    needed
Was some sort of shake-up, a change of the scenery,
Somewhere to swim, with salubrious greenery,
A respite of peace from the scourge of Alzheimer's
And no one could ever dismiss them as climbers.
She'd get there, but 'til then, she knew it would
    haunt
Her. *That's good. It means one's alive to still want.*

———

What a difference a day makes.
Now times that by twenty.
Clifford was hollow, a Horn of Un-Plenty.
Tipping the scales at one-fifteen at most
He was more bone than flesh now, and less man than
    ghost.
The CMV daily lay waste to his sight
Now, it was all Renoir smearings of light,
I loathe Renoir, Clifford thought, *chocolate-box hack.*
Chuckling, his hacking cough wrenching his back.
"Renoir is chocolate," he said, the words hazy.
Luis, his health aide, laughed: "Cliffie, you're crazy!"
Luis was bull-strong, endlessly calm and
Had magic hands: always cool, smelling of almonds.
Luis, in place of dead parents, friends, lovers,
Rubbed Clifford's temples and tucked in the covers.

High noon, and yet the light steadily dimming,
Beautiful Schubert's trout beautifully swimming.

Half-thoughts and memories swam through his brain:
Glass-soled shoes, Burbank, a berth on a train;
Sally, who'd taught him to make a martini,
The silk jacquard robe on the Doge by Bellini,
Helen! With mandarins shielding her breasts,
Of all his life's work, this one image was best.
His father, among the most gentle of men,
The powdery scent of geraniums, and then . . .

The inkwell tipped over and spread 'cross his page.
Clifford was gone. Forty-five years of age.

———

"You look like my Josh, only handsome," she'd say.
She said or did one heartbreaking thing every day.
If Tuesday's mere hygiene was markedly worse,
By Wednesday she'd Homerically re-named her nurse
"that cunt who is stealing right out of my purse."
Like a time-lapse filmed flower that blooms in reverse,
Each day brought some further cruel deforestation
Of mind, with no hope for one thought's restoration.
He'd thought that her being alive would defray
His sadness, but all this goodbye without going away
This brutal, unsightly, and cold disappearing
Was so beyond what he'd conceived ever fearing;
A stupid, but no less dispiriting coda
To be slapped by his mother, who wanted his soda.
This someone he'd loved and so viscerally known . . .
It left Josh abandoned and feeling alone.
More than his mother uncensored, unkempt,
Was the non-recognition. Her blanket contempt

Made him feel like they'd never met, wholly a
    foreigner,
Meriting no more regard than the plant in the corner.
This being a stranger was like being dead,
And brought to mind how, in a book he had read
That most folks misunderstood one common state:
The flip side of love is indifference, not hate.
Since Shulamit left with the kids, he had mused
On all of the ways he had sinned and abused
Those people and things in his vacuous life
He'd thought that the money he'd made for his wife
Was all that she wanted. Turns out he was wrong,
But his Augustine moment had taken too long.
It had all come as such a bright bolt from the blue,
He had no choice but to assume it was true.
"You're empty," she'd said. "A money-drunk fool.
Neglected your soul for the sake of a *pool*!"
To add to this gumbo of guilt, there was Nathan;
Remorse was a river so deep he could bathe in.
SusanSloanShulamit told him as much:
He was venal and shallow and used as a crutch
All the trappings and nonsense, the things he had
    bought her.
She wanted the children and he hadn't fought her.
He missed them so much, his sweet girl and boys,
But he *had* to allow it, since he was the poison.

For himself, like some ex-con or monastic novice
He'd found a small studio right near his office.
It struck him as fitting, a concrete admission
Of guilt: one's apartment as form of punition.
In such a bare space, he might do some soul-healing,

With room for the boxes, stacked from floor to ceiling.
He now had the unwanted stuff of two houses,
The one of his boyhood, and all of his spouse's
Possessions. He'd store them and keep a close eye on
The boxes, in case she might ever return home from
    Zion.

Now here he was, fifty, and starting anew
On a path he'd attempt to keep virtuous and true.
He'd found among Sloan's many things she'd acquired
A delicate necklace of sterling barbed wire
Whose points had been rounded with small silver
    bearings
Though it still gave some punishing hurt in the wearing,
And wearing it daily, he was, 'round his waist,
A constant reminder to keep him abased
And not tempted by temporal glorification.
He found that he needed such mortifications.
A bed, chair, and table were all that he had
Along with the knowledge (hard-won): He was bad.
Friends understood the pained cast to his eyes,
He'd won the annus horribilis prize;
Losing his wife and bereft of his Mommy
2006 was a perfect tsunami
Of all that the Lord seemed to have in His toolkit
Of sadism, suffering, spite, pain, and bullshit.

Unpack a box, then an act of contrition.
Draw one bead of blood, could the Bowery Mission
Make use of some never-worn cashmere sweaters?
(Another knife prick: *All on earth are my betters!*)
He'd come to depend on these tiny surrenders.

How does one family end up with three blenders?
Forty more sit-ups, a stone in his shoe,
Keep two suits for work, one gray and one blue.
After eight weeks, he'd grown saintly and lean
And addicted to his ascetic routine.
Until late one night he was mindlessly sorting
Sloan's shoes when a box he found brought him up
　　short.
Just two words in marker, but two were enough
To accordion time. It was labeled, TED'S STUFF.

———

Maybe, she thought, even this rocky tor
Was no random pile, but concealed something more
Than mere sandstone and lichen, wind-smoothed, sun-
　　bleached;
Perhaps it was here where He might have once
　　preached,
Since everywhere seemed to have some place in
　　history,
All was laid bare and yet shrouded in mystery.
She'd heard it on late-night *shmirah*, on guard duty
Where, taking in all of the harsh desert beauty,
Starlit and bleak in the hematite dark,
The words "Son of God," followed by "Joan of Arc."

The news filled her spirit, she felt she might burst
And for a split second thought, *Who to tell first?*
'Til reason returned and she realized they'd hate
　　her,
Label her crazy, a perjuring traitor.

Shulamit knew what they likely would say,
But naturally saw things a different way:

She'd needed to be here. No con game, no trick.
Her life was a cancer, her spirit was sick.
Her impulse in coming was out of pure love,
And a spiritual yearning to cleanse herself of
The secular world that had previously taught her
To name their girl Dylan, like Ralph Lauren's
    daughter.
(As redress, in part, for her *goyische* folly
Chip was now Duvid, and Schuyler, Naftali.)
The searchlights and razor wire, satellite phones
The high keening wail of the Haganah drones,
She'd loved it all, all the belief that it rested on
But knew in her heart that she had to be moving on.

Shulamit knew that she'd tell them all how
Each moment was whole; Then was Then, Now is
    Now.
Moving here, loyally calling this place her new home
    meant
No more and no less than it did in that moment.
The settlement would, she knew, find this appalling
But Shulamit now knew to answer each calling,
The way that a rocket ship's solid-fuel stages—
Sloughed off and discarded—she'd passed through
    such ages
And people to one day reach idealization;
After all, it's the journey, not the destination.

———

TED'S STUFF. Nine letters, the moment was fixed,
A man he'd last seen alive in '66.
An integral part of existence and then
He dropped dead of a heart attack when Josh was ten.
There was no deep nerve touched, no significant
    metaphors
Just a few potent, outstanding sensory semaphores:
Orange juice poured from a cut-glass carafe,
Corn Flakes he drowned in some chilled half-and-half.
And swimming! It seemed he swam a million-and-two
    laps,
"Let all you others have spare tires and dewlaps!
You can be thought of as kindly and honest,
And I'll gladly be the local Adonis!"
Scandalized cries of "You schmuck" and "Oh, Ted."
A pitcher of something grown-up and deep red,
Laughter and drinks on a dark summer lawn,
A green shirt, a candle . . . the moment was gone.

———

Forty years later, the tape simply shattered
To bits. Well, the contents could hardly have mattered.
And yet, Josh's response, he'd have never dared posit
Such a strong recollection of the old front-hall closet.
He was *there* through some magical olfactory feat!
Josh's eyes briefly fluttered, his heart skipped a beat.
He would hide in there, nightly, crouched down on the
    ground,
Until Ted threw the door wide and yelled, "Ha, I have
    found you!"
And here it all was, through the strongest of spells,
That closet brought forth by the myriad smells:

The forest of coats, an old rolled-up rug
Gave off a comforting, camphorous fug.
It almost seemed noisy, the darkness so full
With the various scents wicking out of the wool.
Dust that had burned on the coils of a heater,
Cigarettes, perfume, and nights at the theater
Mothballs, pressed powder forgotten in lockets.
A half roll of Life Savers fused to the pockets,
And in yet another, a lone unwrapped mint
Had bundled itself in a stole of gray lint.
Nightly, in pj's, the smells would surround
Him 'til that thrilling moment of "Ha, I have found
    you!"

And here, some black oxfords, irretrievably scuffed,
Some moth-eaten jackets, the pockets all stuffed
With envelopes—he counted at least thirty-two—
All scrawled with the message, "Josh, these are for you."
Inside each were handfuls of old foreign stamps.
Some of the packets addressed to the camps
He'd been sent to the summers of age seven–eight.
But what were they from? It was now far too late
For questions: Why keep them? Why weren't they just
    tossed?
From "Ha! Being found" to irrevocably lost.

He sifted his fingers through the colorful squares.
They'd been cut and assembled with obvious care.
To do this then keep them seemed such needless
    bother,
Unless the stamps hadn't been gifts from his father.
He was getting a headache, he hadn't intended
In joining a game that was forty years ended.

One last scan of the coats to see what else was there
When his fingers caught hold of a small, rigid square.

Manila and crisp, with a trace of old grime
At one corner, but otherwise, sealed all this time.
And written upon it, a supplicant "T."
Just one timid letter, from which Josh could see
That the script was undoubtedly feminine, tender
And clearly the stamps and this had the same sender.

He eased his small finger just under the flap.
The old glue gave way with a crisp but weak snap.
Inside, an old photo with old scalloped edges,
A girl standing, topless, by flowering hedges.
On the back, a faded almost illegible rune:
He made out, "Helen, L.A., 1954. June."
There was something so present and vivid, alive. It
Was not classic "cheesecake." More artwork, more
    private.
She was holding two oranges, as though she was
    proffering
The fruit to the viewer. Or making some offering
To . . . Josh figured some boy,
But offering not sex, at all, but simply pure joy.
It was *so* pure, in fact, without smut, without guile,
That even Josh in his monkhood could not help but
    smile.

There was just so much Now that the picture
    encapsed
In the shot, this despite more than six decades
    elapsed.

Both the oranges' skin and the girl's sun-stroked flesh
Seemed similarly taut and impossibly fresh.
She's standing and squinting, eyes half-closed from the
    sun
And laughing, delighted at what's still to come.

[Doubleday 2013]

Letter to N.Y.

by Elizabeth Bishop

For Louise Crane

In your next letter I wish you'd say
where you are going and what you are doing;
how are the plays, and after the plays
what other pleasures you're pursuing:

taking cabs in the middle of the night,
driving as if to save your soul
where the road goes round and round the park
and the meter glares like a moral owl,

and the trees look so queer and green
standing alone in big black caves
and suddenly you're in a different place
where everything seems to happen in waves,

and most of the jokes you just can't catch,
like dirty words rubbed off a slate,
and the songs are loud but somehow dim
and it gets so terribly late,

and coming out of the brownstone house
to the gray sidewalk, the watered street,

one side of the buildings rises with the sun
like a glistening field of wheat.

—Wheat, not oats, dear. I'm afraid
if it's wheat it's none of your sowing,
nevertheless I'd like to know
what you are doing and where you are going.

[From The Complete Poems, 1927–1979 *by Elizabeth Bishop*
(New York: Farrar, Straus and Giroux, 1983)]

About the Contributors

Timothy G. Young is a curator and a frequent contributor to *The Yale Review* and *Design Observer*. He has published works on a range of subjects, from children's literature to financial history.

Paul Rudnick is an award-winning novelist, playwright, essayist, and screenwriter, whom *The New York Times* has called "one of our pre-eminent humorists." He contributes regularly to *The New Yorker*, and his work has also appeared in *The New York Times*, *Esquire*, *Vogue*, and *Vanity Fair*.